TAKING SUFFERING SERIOUSLY

SUNY Series in Global Conflict and Peace Education
Betty Reardon, editor

TAKING
SUFFERING
SERIOUSLY

The Importance of
Collective Human Rights

William F. Felice

Foreword by
Richard Falk

State University of New York Press

Published by
State University of New York Press, Albany

©1996 State University of New York

For information, address the State University of New York Press,
State University Plaza, Albany, NY 12246

Production by Christine Lynch
Marketing by Nancy Farrell

Library of Congress Cataloging-in-Publication Data

Felice, William, 1950–
    Taking suffering seriously : the importance of collective human
rights / William F. Felice.
        p.   cm. — (SUNY series in global conflict and peace
education)
    Includes bibliographical references and index.
    ISBN 0-7914-3061-8 (alk. paper). — ISBN 0-7914-3062-6 (pbk. :
alk. paper)
    1. Human rights.   2. Basic needs.   3. International relations.
I. Title.   II. Series: SUNY series, global conflict and peace
education.
JC571.F425   1996
323—dc20   95-41670
                                                                CIP

10   9   8   7   6   5   4   3   2   1

Let us suppose that certain individuals resolve that they will consistently oppose to power the force of example; to authority, exhortation; to insult, friendly reasoning; to trickery, simple honor. Let us suppose they refuse all the advantages of present-day society and accept only the duties and obligations which bind them to other[s]. . . . Then I say that such [individuals] would be acting not as Utopians but as honest realists. They would be preparing the future and at the same time knocking down a few of the walls which imprison us today. If realism be the art of taking into account both the present and the future, of gaining the most while sacrificing the least, then who can fail to see the positively dazzling realism of such behavior?

Albert Camus
Neither Victims nor Executioners

CONTENTS

APPENDICES

ACKNOWLEDGMENTS

It is impossible to acknowledge all those who lived through this book with me and helped me make it what it is. There are a number of individuals, however, who have directly influenced the direction of the manuscript and it is a genuine pleasure to publicly thank them for their impact on my thinking and my life.

Richard Falk was instrumental in exposing me to the normative dimensions of international relations and introducing me to the transnational human rights movement. Richard inspired me to explore the role of values, norms, and rights in international politics. His search for avenues of humane governance has been a source of direction and strength for me over the years.

Bertell Ollman is not only a brilliant scholar and eminent political philosopher, but also a committed teacher. I was truly the beneficiary of his original scholarship into dialectics, internal relations, and alienation.

Nancy Stein read each chapter with enormous care and intelligence. The book benefitted from her insights, political astuteness, and thoughtfulness.

Nancy Mitchell was a continual fountain of encouragement, friendship, and help. She taught me through her example what it means to exercise personal and intellectual integrity. Her interest in my research and willingness to discuss ideas of rights was a source of inspiration.

Michael J. Smith has been selfless in his willingness to review chapters and give me comments and guidance. My work has benefitted enormously from his energy, support, and ideas.

Saul Mendlovitz also reviewed the entire manuscript and gave me a clear direction at a critical time. Saul continues to provide leadership to the World Order Models Project, which endures as a bright light and beacon of hope in a field of study dominated by dark "realist" Hobbesian pessimism and futility.

I am indebted to Betty Reardon for including this book as a volume of the State University of New York (SUNY) Press series on Global Conflict and Peace Education. SUNY press editors Clay Morgan and Christine Lynch were also of great assistance in final preparation of the manuscript.

While at New York University (NYU), Jim Crown showed me the path through the academic maze for which I am most grateful. Also extremely helpful at NYU were: Bruce Cronin, Pat Moynagh, Ken Rodman, and Mark Roelofs.

Over the years many individuals have contributed to the emergence of this work, including: Jerry Atkin, Barry Chersky, Nancy Cook, Ellen Eidem, Jon Frappier, Beth Harding, Susanne Jonas, Janis Lewin, Betita Martinez, Ed McCaughan, Dave McReynolds, Richard Schauffler, and Joseph Starr.

The critical comments of the three anonymous reviewers of the manuscript were particularly useful. I would also like to thank Rhoda Howard, Jack Odell, and George Shepherd, Jr. for their comments and criticisms on chapter 4, "The Morality of the Depths: The Right to Development as an Emerging Principle of International Law."

The Carnegie Council on Ethics and International Affairs invited me to present my theory of collective human rights at their summer faculty seminar at the Monterey Institute of International Studies. The feedback I received there was extremely valuable and I thank them for the invitation.

Publishing a first book is, of course, a difficult and often frustrating process. I have weathered this entire ordeal due to the love and support of Dale Lappe. I can't imagine a more encouraging, understanding, and devoted partner.

FOREWORD

It is at least arguable that if the collective human rights of the Serb minorities in Croatia and Bosnia had been credibly protected, the horrifying Balkans ordeal of the past five years could have been avoided. Yet the prevailing mood at the end of the Cold War was to celebrate the victory of the West in the ideological format provided by philosophical liberalism, namely a market-oriented constitutionalism that prided itself on guarding favored individuals against abuses by the state. At most, such a mood affirmed a new, more radical form of self-determination that endowed territorial units *within* states with the rights to secede and to be treated as an independent sovereign entity. In the case of the former Yugoslavia, such thinking has produced a genocidal disaster, an experience of extreme group wrongs in the shape of multi-dimensional "ethnic cleansing" filling the vacuum created by the refusal to protect group rights.

The collective dimensions of the disintegration of Yugoslavia are being, and have been for centuries, replicated in dozens of other settings. These other settings range from oppressive rule directed at ethnic minorities, to a systemic neglect of the poor in a rush to achieve rapid economic growth with high returns on capital, to a refusal to uphold the dignity of those whose sexuality depends on identifying openly as gay or lesbian. It is against such a background of disregard that this pathbreaking book by William Felice needs to be read, the first truly comprehensive effort to be responsive to the group dimensions of human suffering within the framework of thought and action associated with human rights.

There are several aspects of Felice's approach that seem worth highlighting. First of all, he convincingly grounds the protection of human rights in the deliberate societal effort to alleviate human suffering, and more significantly, demonstrates that the most acute and pervasive forms of distress are a consequence of economic, social, and political *structural* circumstances that impact upon *groups*, as well as upon *individuals*. Given this condition, which makes categories of race, class, gender, and sexual orientation so relevant for creating truly meaningful human rights regimes, Felice criticizes prevailing approaches to human rights, with their insistence of limiting the scope of protection to individuals, as disastrously incomplete. Felice should not be understood in any sense as advocating the replacement of an individual ethos of human rights with a collective ethos. His argument is simply that a collective ethos is essential from the perspective on human rights that he adopts—the alleviation of suffering.

Furthermore, Felice demonstrates that for many important sets of circumstances, the individual cannot be protected adequately without altering the conditions afflicting the relevant group as a whole. As Cornel West so vividly argues in *Race Matters*, a black American, no matter how privileged in economic and social terms, cannot escape the indignities of everyday life so long as racist attitudes persist in American society. This same sort of reality impacts upon formal efforts by the state to lift restrictions on individual members of scheduled castes of India. In a different vein, the safeguarding of indigenous peoples is an inherently collective undertaking, protecting the coherence and integrity of a way of life, generally associated with traditional rights to exist autonomously on land endowed with sacred meaning. It is revealing that only a few decades ago even the idealistic drafters of the main human rights instruments in international law (the Universal Declaration and the two covenants) failed altogether to comprehend the significance of the circumstances threatening the survival of indigenous peoples around the world, and hence, left their specific needs completely out of account while purporting to set forth a universal framework for the realization of human rights.

Perhaps the strongest and most original part of Felice's overall presentation is his critique of neo-liberalism from the perspective of the collective rights of the poor. On the one side, Felice posits the reality that most countries are rich enough to provide easily for the basic needs of their entire population; yet the rigors of the market, which is increasingly globalized, make it more and more difficult for governments, even of social democratic persuasion, to protect the poor, or more accurately, to end the indignity of poverty and joblessness. Indeed, the endorsement by neo-liberalism of a capital-driven conception of resource allocation, with a diminishing role for social intervention by the state, implies an acceptance of the denial of basic economic and social rights to those hundreds of millions of people around the world trapped in permanent conditions of poverty at the margins of modern and modernizing economies. What Felice, in effect, establishes, is that despite the pretensions of promoting democracy neo-liberalism—as an operational ideology—is radically inconsistent with the protection of human rights, if rights are conceived in relation to suffering rather than as abstract ground rules governing the relations of individuals to the state.

There is no doubt that humanizing state/society relations by way of protecting the individual, including dissenters and opponents, has been a great achievement of the Western constitutional tradition, an achievement that was given heroic underpinnings in the course of the American and French revolutions with their strong sense of the rights of citizens. Such achievements need to be guarded as precious ingredients of human dignity, but attaining them was never more than a beginning. As with so much else, the American reality was paradigmatic: the revolutionary process that established independence and a republican polity was combined with a political structure that incorporated slavery, that legitimized violent dispossession and ethnocide against the Indian nations occupying much of the territory that was to become the United States of America, that disenfranchised women, and that imposed a procrustean straightjacket on the choice of sexual orientation. In other words, for all of its alleged commitment to liberty and rights, the American experience encoded into legal, political, and social behavior a high tolerance for cruelty toward groups, made more pernicious by being obscured beneath a rhetoric of commitment that misleadingly appears to be universalistic in its scope and application. Felice's fine book can be read as a belated, yet indispensable, exercise in decoding this ideological cover-up that is carried out in our time under the equally deceptive formulations of neo-liberalism.

The struggle to realize collective rights, precisely because it challenges the structural attributes of the established order, is currently the most formidable task confronting humanity. It will require the diverse energies and imagination of peoples differently situated throughout the planet, with the clear recognition that the relief of suffering is a very concrete and specific matter as well as a condition of generality. William Felice has provided us with the clearest presentation, to date, of the landscape of human suffering. He has also sharpened the normative tools useful for achieving collective human rights. This conceptual recasting of the human rights discourse is a coherent and hopeful way to make the difficult civilizational passage from modernity to a type of postmodernity that is reconstructive, not deconstructive.

Richard Falk, September 1995
Princeton, NJ

INTRODUCTION

As the Representative to the United Nations (UN) for the International League for the Rights of Peoples,[1] I experienced first hand the dilemmas that confront global human rights activists. It is difficult to be dedicated to values of human dignity in a world of sovereign states functioning according to the norms of Realpolitik, that is, power politics. Throughout the 1980s, my admiration and respect grew for those committed individuals and organizations willing to challenge the brutal status quo. These world citizens are global pilgrims engaged in a pioneering effort to build the foundations of a new transnational order based on human values and global justice.

However, I also discovered severe limitations in the language of rights articulating this new vision of transnational civil society. By the 1980s, rights language was used by protagonists of nearly every ideological stripe and political agenda—from Ronald Reagan to Daniel Ortega to Mikhail Gorbachev. Human rights were embraced by businessmen and trade unionists, conservatives and liberals, socialists and capitalists. The idea that all individuals could make claims simply due to their humanness clearly struck a positive chord throughout the global community. Yet there was no consensus as to which claims all individuals could assert. Different people meant different things when they called for adherence to human rights. The very fact that antagonistic forces embraced the notion of human rights was a clear indication that the concept was poorly understood and inadequately defined.

My work at the United Nations focused on "peoples' rights," particularly the right of indigenous groups to protect their cultural heritage. Around the world, different peoples are threatened by forces over which they have very little control. Many of these peoples petition the UN and other global intergovernmental organizations (IGOs) and nongovernmental organizations (NGOs) to take actions to assure their very survival. The International League, a transnational grassroots organization affiliated with the Economic and Social Council, and other human rights organizations publicize these issues of group protection and attempt to articulate new standards by which to judge state behavior.

While individual rights are nearly universally accepted, "peoples' rights" and "group rights" remain extremely controversial. This is partially the result of history. The use of abstract concepts like "peoples' rights" by nation-states has had horrendous consequences for humanity. In the name of the rights of the German people, Adolf Hitler brought genocide and torture to millions. The "rights of the Aryan race" formed the core of Nazi ideology and served as effective propaganda for mobilizing tens of thousands to support racist, supremacist, and imperialist actions. The ideological justification of the apartheid system in South Africa from the 1940s into the 1990s was based on the rights of Afrikaners as a people. In the nation-state of South Africa, such an ideology led to massive forced movements of populations, preemptory uprooting, constant police investigations and harassment, the separation of families, as well as the arrest, torture, and death of black activists attempting to change this system. In Bosnia in the 1990s, "ethnic cleansing" and rape camps sear into our consciousness the reality that racialist doctrines still inflict shocking devastation, horror, and suffering to peoples considered "other." Clearly, concepts like peoples' rights can be twisted by ambitious nation-states to justify policies of aggrandizement at the expense of other peoples.

Yet group protection is critical for many of the world's peoples. The statistics on the startling disappearance of many of the world's indigenous peoples is testament to the importance of group protection. Experts note, for example, that there have been more extinctions of tribal peoples in this century than in any other in history (Durning 1993, 83). Rights based on race and ethnicity are necessary because of the often genocidal policies of majority groups. The challenge is to articulate these demands without repeating the tragic historical lessons when "peoples' rights" were used to deny individual liberty and freedom. Group protection does not mean group superiority.

A further problem with the term "peoples' rights" is that "people" is traditionally used within international relations to define a specific ethnic "nationality." "Peoples' rights" thus often serve to reinforce nationalism and present a conservative framework for thinking about the future. For example, most of the international relations literature on human rights and peoples' rights stays in the nation-state framework, documenting the efforts of elites of different nations to institutionalize and/or legalize rights within the canons of international and/or national jurisprudence. The established literature pays little attention to political theory. The point, according to these writers, is to document "what is" rather than to get lost in the world of "what should be." One such political scientist formulated this position as follows: "Rather than rely on abstract moral theory as found in nongovernmental argument, one should look at what states indicate, by their consent to treaties and resolutions adopted by international organizations, as the primary values of international relations. . . . I am using empiricism to arrive at norms" (Forsythe 1991, 7).[2] This approach, however, is not the only way to look at human rights. In fact, such an elite bias in the formulation of human rights may limit the usefulness of these concepts to confront human suffering.

The sources of human suffering are multifaceted. The continuous repression of and discrimination toward certain groups throughout the world is clearly one source of suffering. Due to this group oppression, the liberal promise of individual rights and individual equality is little more than a mirage for millions. If our understanding of human rights ignores this reality, we artificially obstruct our ability to describe a vision of a world that respects human dignity. To take suffering seriously means addressing both individual and group oppression.

How do we overcome these problems in rights language and principles? On the one hand, individual rights seem inadequate to protect the rights of the world's cultural groups; yet, on the other hand, group rights have served supremacist ideologies with disastrous historical consequences. Is it possible to put together a new paradigm that can address existing human suffering as the global community enters the twenty-first century?

This book attempts to address these dilemmas through an articulation of a concept of collective human rights. With its focus on the group ("collective") and the individual ("human"), the term itself contains within it the dialectical relationship between them. There is a constant tension between the rights of the individual member of society and the collective rights of certain groups. It is imperative for a global conception of rights to encompass both aspects of this dialectic. There is an individual and a social component to every human being. The concept of collective human rights presented here embraces this totality of the human experience.

The collective human rights formulated in this book are based upon an identification of the "groups" in which the human species naturally congregates as a result of its social nature, which include not only ethnicity/race, but also gender, class, and sexuality. Further, this expanded notion of collective human rights challenges the deference to elites and nation-state rulers in the establishment of universal rights. Within civil society, groups themselves have the right to define and defend necessary protections.

The hypothesis here is that a radical conception of rights which focuses on the "collective" and "social" dimension of the individual human being will provide a language to articulate the human dilemma in this era, characterized by Louis Henkin as the "Age of Rights" (Henkin 1990). The argument of this book is that it is vital for a rights analysis to integrate group rights based on class, race/ethnicity, gender, and sexuality, because these group rights address major spheres of human suffering in today's world. Expanding collective human rights to include group rights in all these key areas greatly enhances the vitality and usefulness of the concept. To limit our understanding of collective human rights to only one of these areas not only diminishes the effectiveness of the idea, but, as noted, is potentially dangerous. The linking of ethnicity/race, class, gender, and sexuality mutes supremacist tendencies by denying the right of any one group to assert supremacy over a different group. Such a framework revokes the license of any group to justify rights claims based on the subservience or subordination of other individuals and groups.

Citizens of Western liberal democracies are most familiar with individual human rights claims which attempt to articulate a broad spectrum of rights deemed necessary for a person to live a life of dignity. Individual human rights reflect a range of protections for the person from the right to vote to the abolition of torture. As a supplement to these individual claims, collective human rights articulate the broad spectrum of group rights that are also necessary to overcome suffering. Collective human rights are designed to reflect a range of protections to groups from the rights of ethnicity/race to rights of gender and class. The protection of the dignity of the individual and the group requires nothing less. This broader approach to the concept of rights opens up previously unexplored vistas and avenues. This collective formulation of rights attempts to reinforce human sociability and break down the forced separation of human from human which is present in modern society. Those who pursue collective human rights seek to empower each individual *within* his or her own community.

This book examines the evolution and development of collective human rights in international relations both theoretically and practically. Controversy surrounds this endeavor because, as already noted, some ideas of peoples' rights have been used to rationalize supremacist notions and aggressive actions by nation-states. However (as documented below), when utilized by peoples striving to articulate and overcome conditions of suffering, the ideas have often successfully provided a useful political language to clarify issues of social justice. The ideas of collective human rights themselves (as developed throughout this book) reject nation-state hegemony over the norms and structures that determine individual and/or group existence. Collective human rights are based on the concept that there are certain rights for all peoples that stand above nation-states and intergovernmental bodies.

Further, they are premised on the idea that peoples cannot only independently assert and claim these rights, but that nation-states and intergovernmental bodies should be held accountable to these standards. Transnational grassroots organizations have been able to use these norms with some success to call attention to violations of claimed rights by particular nation-states and intergovernmental organizations. When not in the hands of the organized state, these ideas have proven to be effective tools in challenging existing structures of domination.

This book explores the following questions: Do formulations of collective human rights help define justifiable claims of individuals and groups denied basic rights? Do they help conceptualize a vision of a future society free of human suffering? Do they help determine the necessary preconditions or steps to be implemented today for such a vision to be achieved tomorrow? What is the relationship between conceptions of collective human rights and the major theoretical paradigms of the twentieth century, Marxism and liberalism? Do the new theoretical approaches of postmodernism, poststructuralism, and post-Marxism address these issues? Does the establishment of international norms like collective human rights challenge the primacy of nation-state "sovereignty" in the international system?

THE STRUGGLE FOR HUMAN DIGNITY

Some U.S. academics oppose the ideas of collective human rights and argue that the conception of individual human rights is sufficient to articulate basic norms of human dignity.[3] Why labor over a whole new formulation of rights when so much work and effort has already gone into defining individual human rights? Is it not a meaningless academic exercise?

Individual human rights have proven to be of enormous value in identifying individual rights that are to be respected by all governments, independent of ideology. They have had an effect on outcomes. Torture and genocide, for example, are now considered illegal in international law. There is a worldwide movement toward democratic reforms, based on an understanding of individual civil and political rights. Vaclav Havel put it well when he wrote: "Freedom of the individual, equality, the universality of civil rights (including the right to private ownership), the rule of law, a democratic political system, local self-government, the separation of legislative, executive, and judiciary powers, the revival of civil society—all of these flow from the idea of human rights, and all of them are the fulfillment of that idea" (1992, 98).

From the vantage point of many groups, however, individual human rights alone are not enough. Societies are torn apart by the denial of all sorts of group rights by powerful elites. Social disorder and decay are directly associated with the violation of collective human rights by the state and global structures. There is thus a moral imperative to move toward the articulation of collective human rights. To protect human dignity, we must expand our understanding of rights. Individual human rights theory often gives rhetorical attention to the economic, social, and cultural rights of individuals, but does not adequately recognize the structural obstacles blocking implementation of these norms. It is fraudulent to guarantee people a right that in fact they are unable to exercise (Shue 1980, 27). Liberal human rights theory often does not recognize that equality of opportunity is an illusion in a society based upon competitive individualism, where not only is individual pitted against individual, but group is pitted against group. In such an atmosphere the rights of those groups on the lower end of the spectrum of opportunity must be protected, or all individual and group rights are diminished.

The conception of collective human rights presented here addresses the lack of a "level playing field" within most nation-states of the world today, due largely to race, class, and gender discrimination. Certain groups, such as ruling elites and majority ethnic groups, are given more opportunities, which they use to consolidate positions of power. The human rights dialogue, when it focuses solely on the rights of the individual, does not address these issues of power.

For example, as a group, African-Americans do not enjoy the same rights as whites in the United States. The statistics are well known. Despite advances in civil rights legislation, the proportionate ratio of blacks to whites below the poverty line is still what it was in 1959, approximately three to one. In the last thirty years, the numbers of white poor have declined by four million, while the absolute number of poor blacks have increased by 686,000. In 1992, 42.7 percent of all African-American households earned less than $15,000, as compared to 21.6 percent of whites (Hochschild 1996, 39–51). Medical researchers estimate that over 60,000 preventable deaths occur each year among blacks in the United States—60,000 people who would not have died had they received the same standard of preventative treatment, medical care, and access to health insurance that the majority of whites have. The unemployment rate in America for black males is more than twice that of white males (Marable 1992b, 46–48).

Individual rights focus almost solely on the right of the individual African-American to be upwardly mobile in a class-based society. Collective human rights focus on the rights of the entire group of African-Americans to have basic needs met, including health care, employment, and housing. Until these group rights are met, individual rights for African-Americans too often remain empty promises.

Globally, issues of class, race, gender, and sexuality have dramatically influenced the human rights debate. For example, issues of gender played a primary role at the 1993 World Conference on Human Rights held in Vienna, Austria. To many conference observers, the strongest and most effective lobby was the 950 women's organizations from around the world organized into the Global Campaign for Women's Human Rights. These women focused less on the struggle to end discrimination than on the need to put an end to a series of acute human rights abuses suffered by women because they are women. The United Nations was asked to clarify the relationship between collective women's rights and individual human rights. In the midst of broad global diversity and difference, the women present were able to find unity on the necessity for the rights framework to address the nearly universal epidemic of violence against women. The conference was a demonstration that women from sharply different backgrounds could unite around a common set of objectives.

As part of the Vienna conference, these women organized a Global Tribunal on Violations of Women's Human Rights. The tribunal heard testimony from women from around the world on a vast range of abuses—from war crimes against women in Japan during World War II and in Peru today, to violence in the home. For example, Rana Nashashibi spoke not only of oppression from Israeli occupation, but also of Palestinian women and children as victims of violence in the home. "We have become aware that Palestinian statehood will not necessarily bring freedom for women from a patriarchal society," she said (*New York Times*, 15 June 1993). For these Palestinian women, a people's right to self-determination means more than solely political rights to self-governance. For self-determination to have real meaning in these women's lives, rights of gender must also be addressed.

Conceptually, collective human rights can be divided into two categories. First, those rights specific to particular groups which are designed to respond to the unique claims of that particular group. For example, womens' rights articulated to meet womens' needs (beyond equality with men), such as rights that flow from the raising and suckling of children. These are unique rights for women as women (see chapter 2 below). And second, those collective human rights necessary so that members of all groups can benefit from the promise of equal opportunity, such as the right to self-determination and the right to development. These rights depend upon global solidarity among all peoples (see chapters 3 and 4 below). There is an interdependence between individual rights and group rights. For individual rights to be real for many oppressed groups in the world, group claims to justice must at the same time be addressed.

The international system appears to be experiencing a number of contradictory trends since the end of the Cold War. On the one hand, there are trends toward integration and globalization, with the world being brought closer together by international trade, investment, travel, civic action, and communications. On the other hand, there are trends toward fragmentation and separation, with the rise of nationalism, xenophobia, and the reassertion of localist identities.[4]

Both globalization and fragmentation work to erode the sovereign state—either by pulling it apart from within or by transcending it from without. The world is faced with a range of new issues that also surpass state power. From environmental pollution to the drug trade to population movements to diseases such as AIDS, state boundaries are porous. On their own, nation-states cannot solve these problems, and a new, radical level of cooperation is necessary to avoid devastating consequences for humanity. Despite this, however, the state remains the fundamental organizing unit in international affairs.

The conception of collective human rights developed here attempts to address both the fragmentation and globalization by presenting a normative framework of values which link the concerns of individuals and groups around the world. Collective human rights are not contingent on nation-state elite approval or sanction. These rights are designed to pressure existing nation-states to change their practice toward certain groups, in the same way that individual human rights have served to moderate state behavior toward the person. Furthermore, such a framework is designed to put forward a vision of the future as to how society might be organized to overcome suffering.

Why is such a vision important? Life today for many means coping with meaninglessness, hopelessness, and nihilism. Within this loss of meaning, we witness a disregard for human life itself (see West 1993, 11–20). A sense of personal worthlessness and despair is widespread. The economy, culture, and politics of a competitive, market-driven world system reinforces this situation by providing only norms of individualism. For someone to win, someone else must lose. Those who lose are personally at fault, whereas those who win are showered with rewards. It is not clear to many groups and individuals that their rights are protected within the current world system. A new framework is thus needed to make rights relevant as tools to help equalize conditions of opportunity.

THE UTILITY OF COLLECTIVE HUMAN RIGHTS

The academic disciplines of political theory and international relations have neither systematically nor theoretically attempted to develop a full conception of collective human rights. The literature on peoples rights, for example, focuses almost solely on ethnicity and does not adequately analyze these rights in relation to political theory, a weakness common to much of the international relations literature on rights. Nor does the peoples' rights literature sufficiently discuss the relevance of the relationship between class and gender to ethnicity and race. This book attempts to draw these connections and broaden the discussion of rights into new domains. Collective human rights are approached both empirically (that is, which of these rights have been adopted and/or acted upon by international IGOs and NGOs), and theoretically (in relation to liberalism, Marxism, and the trio of poststructuralism, postmodernism, and post-Marxism).

The first chapter clarifies the conception of collective human rights and reveals the evolution of these ideas from the efforts to establish global human rights in the post–World War II period. Emphasis is placed first on the interdependent nature of group and individual rights and, second, on the importance of overcoming the structural obstacles blocking their implementation. Nation-states today are besieged with group claims based on ethnicity, class conflict, and social justice and seem unable to address these demands. Collective human rights can begin to provide us with a new normative framework designed to alleviate individual human suffering caused by group oppression.

Chapter 2 explores the intersection of rights of ethnicity/race, gender, and sexuality. The specific rights of these three areas are examined as well as their interrelationship with each other. The argument is presented that a formulation of collective human rights must take all of these aspects into account if it is going to provide a relevant vehicle to not only understand the global community, but to articulate a normative framework useful for confronting human suffering in the world today. Highlighting only one aspect of an individual's character (that is, ethnicity *or* gender *or* sexuality) is not only limiting, but dangerous. The result of such a singular politics can be to pit one oppressed group against another oppressed group, thus serving to divide, rather than unite, forces who in fact have a common interest.

The third chapter looks at the universally accepted collective human right to self-determination and explores the contradictions inherent in realizing this right. Since the time of Vladimir Ilich Lenin and Woodrow Wilson, politicians and academics of just about every political stripe have expressed support for "the self-determination of peoples." What does this collective human right really mean? First, a distinction is made between "external self-determination" and "internal self-determination," with the former referring to the right of a people to be free from "external" interference (colonialism, imperialism, and so on) and the latter referring to the right of a people to form their own government and to be free from dictatorial rule. Within this context, nationalism and sovereignty are viewed through the theoretical lenses of realism, Marxism, and liberalism. For advocates of self-determination to adequately take into account collective human rights, the following considerations are key:

1. A nationalist approach to human freedom must be rejected, because one's objective is the self-determination of peoples and not of nations, that is, sovereignty remains with the people.

2. Class analysis must be incorporated into one's understanding of self-determination in order to give the concept meaning for the majority of the world's peoples, that is, a rejection of the self-determination of nationalist elites.

3. An account must be taken of our multicultural world, which necessitates the full protection and development of cultural and ethnic rights within the definition of the self-determination of peoples.

Adequately addressing these concerns may result in a radical reconceptualization of the sociopolitical units in which the human community is organized and governed.

Chapter 4, entitled "The Morality of the Depths," examines the right to development as a collective human right. In 1993, at the Vienna World Conference on Human Rights, the United States accepted the validity of the idea of the right to development. This chapter explores the content of the right to development through an analysis of the different approaches to this new right taken by academics and activists from the North and the South. The attempt is made to determine the legal basis to the right to development and the legal duties that flow from this right. The argument is presented that the right to development can be understood as an emerging principle of international law from which flow certain legal obligations, including duties to respect, duties to protect from deprivation, and duties to aid the deprived. A legal and moral case in favor of this emerging collective human right is advanced.

Chapter 5 explores in more detail the cross-cutting interest groups that serve as countervailing forces against the sovereign state. With the collapse of the Soviet empire, nationalism appears to dominate the international arena. Yet in this chapter, I contend that to focus on nationalism limits our understanding of complex social factors at work in international politics. Agreeing with Hobsbawm, I argue that the basic political, social, environmental, and economic conflicts confronting the world today have little to do with the nation-state (Hobsbawm 1990). We have entered what Rosenau refers to as a "postinternational" era, in that the current world system can no longer be categorized solely or primarily as consisting of relations between nations (Rosenau 1990).

The ideas of collective human rights help us to define a new framework for understanding justice in this complicated new era. Norms and values can help create a countervailing force to other components of power, including military and economic components. While the norms of individual human rights stake out a realm of limited individual sovereignty which serves as a countervailing force to intolerable state action against the individual, the hope is to develop a comparable conception of collective human rights that would create a new normative order. The chapter ends by exploring the actual movement to incorporate these new norms into the existing international legal framework.

The relationship between liberal theory and collective human rights is reviewed in the sixth chapter, which also documents the evolution of human rights from liberal theory itself. The ideas of collective human rights address structural and economic factors that are ignored for the most part in liberal theories of rights. Particularly problematic for the conception of collective human rights formulated here is the supremacy of individualism and competition found in liberal theory. The *social* conditions of liberal capitalism, in particular its class structure, must be taken into account in any formulation of rights; since (in the current world system) some people always end up more "equal" than others, such liberal rights often serve the role of institutionalizing inequality. The idea of collective human rights presented here begins with the right of all peoples to have their basic human needs met (as demonstrated in chapter 4 on the right to development). Implementation of any claimed right depends upon the political and economic power of those seeking their rights. Oppressed groups hope that by addressing their concerns through the formulation of collective human rights, norms will be established which will help create a political language that articulates their plight and thereby defines a way to move forward. Unfortunately, liberal theory frequently displays a hostility toward collective human rights and is often openly antagonistic toward efforts to pursue this promising path.

However, this attempt to address group suffering, by calling for the protection of certain collective rights, does not mean a denial of individual human rights. In fact, a group is only worth defending if it promotes the moral development of each of its members and tolerates the development of individuals outside that group. Therefore, claims of a racist, skinhead community for autonomy would not be considered as in any way comparable to the claims of an oppressed ethnic or national minority for emancipation. Individual and group rights are symbiotic—both are indispensable and essential. Some liberal/social democratic pluralist scholars state that one can find a place for group rights within liberalism. Kymlicka, for example, asserts in a discussion of liberalism and cultural membership that if the request of the group for special rights or resources is grounded in "unequal circumstances," then the claim would be legitimate. Yet I argue that Kymlicka's formulation does not go far enough. What is suggested here is a radical reformulation of liberalism to fundamentally incorporate group rights to accompany (not replace) individual rights. The liberal demand of equal opportunity requires nothing less.

The seventh chapter explores the compatibility and/or incompatibility of Marxist theory with the ideas of collective human rights. Given the collapse of "existing socialism" is this chapter needed? Is Marxist theory still relevant? Around the world, scholars and activists are engaged in a reappraisal of the utility of Marxism, given the monumental damage done to individuals and groups by the totalitarian regimes in the former USSR and in Eastern Europe. The brutalities of these former (so-called) "socialist" dictatorships can neither be excused nor rationalized. However, we cannot ignore the important criticisms of liberal theory present in Marxist philosophy just because of the brutal governing practices of elites in Eastern Europe. For those of us concerned with human dignity, there are significant gaps in liberal theory that limit our ability as a global society to achieve equality, democracy, and freedom.

The argument in chapter 7 is that Marxist theory adds the following components to a formulation of collective human rights: class analysis, the methodology of dialectics, and a future vision of rich individuality and freedom. A democratic socialist conception of collective human rights could potentially correct some of the weaknesses in liberal rights theories reviewed in chapter 6. Such a conception recognizes the reality of class society at the same time that it confronts the sexual, ethnic, and racial divisions within that society. A democratic socialist view is thus informed by the desire to develop an analysis and political program that addresses the entire social fabric of life (family, nation, sex, and so on) while understanding that class is a central fact of social life. The works of Antonio Gramsci, in particular, share a common framework with collective human rights. He, too, was primarily concerned with the multifaceted reality of life—culture, social relations, the family, as well as work. The Gramscian concept of ideological "hegemony" is of particular relevance in this regard. Gramsci explored the mediations in society—popular ideas, habits, myths, attitudes, and so forth—that played a role in determining social consciousness. He called for the elaboration of a system of "moral principles" that could inform the process of change by establishing a program counter to the prevailing hegemonic ideology, which is precisely what this conception of collective human rights is all about. As noted in this chapter, democratic socialist advocates of collective human rights assert that a strategy for change must take into account the ideological and cultural "mediations" that Gramsci articulated, including values, beliefs, and cultural norms.

Also picking up on Gramsci's challenge to define a new ideological hegemony have been certain "poststructuralist," "postmodernist," and "post-Marxist" writers, who have recently generated a great deal of controversy within the academy. The compatibility of these "post" approaches with a democratic socialist conception of collective human rights is explored in chapter 8. To a certain degree, all three of these approaches attempt to give voice to the "other" in society, including people of color, women, and gay men and lesbians, providing some overlap between the concerns of these writers and the conception of collective human rights presented here. The poststructuralist approach is particularly helpful in breaking out of old ways of thinking about power and about the future, while the postmodernist critique usefully questions the linear assumptions of "progress" found in modern society. The destruction of group values and norms is very much a focus of the postmodern analysis.

However, these new approaches often fail to incorporate issues of political economy and class, thus exacerbating fragmentation rather than building a new ideological hegemony. Particularly useful in exploring the strengths and weaknesses of these new "post" paradigms is the philosophical prism of "internal relations," a dialectical approach toward knowledge. The concept of internal relations is more fully explained below, but in essence it emphasizes the necessary *relationships* between entities, in the sense that entities depend upon the relationship for their very identity (examples include parent/child, boss/worker, and so on). Such an understanding helps us formulate the ways in which capital accumulation and the commodification of labor *condition* social and cultural practices, *and vice versa.* Thus, on the one hand, it is true that many of the concerns of the postmodern, poststructural, and post-Marxist writers, such as racism, gender oppression, homophobia, and ecological destruction, have not been adequately understood through class analysis or by socialist/Marxist approaches in the past. However, on the other hand, it is also true that such phenomena cannot be fully understood without analyzing the processes and interactions between these complex phenomena and the workings of the dominant political and economic system.

Therefore, collective human rights should be understood within the philosophical framework of internal relations. In spite of the fact that much of social science separates parts of reality into isolated components, collective human rights cannot be understood in isolation, nor are they very useful standing on their own. Rather they must be put in the context of the totality of the existing world system. In modern society there is a huge discrepancy between the values of equality and freedom promoted by liberal democracy and actual social relations. The language and norms of collective human rights provide tools to articulate this discrepancy and to project an alternative vision of the future for humanity.

The concluding chapter of this book argues for a "third way," between liberalism and Marxism, toward a world in which decision-making is based on norms of meeting basic human needs, true equality and real freedom. What part could collective human rights play in a transition from a society dominated by destructive competitive individualism to a society that embodies the values of egalitarianism and full democracy?

The chapter reviews the attempts to implement collective economic, social, and cultural rights internationally, by the United Nations and the International Labor Organization, and locally, by the United States. Although a degree of progress has been made in addressing some group protections, unfortunately the results have not been nearly adequate. The necessity to build on these reforms and develop new mechanisms for combining individual and group rights into a whole may be the beginning of a formulation of a new vision for the new century. Such an attempt affirms both the particularist and the universalist components to the human identity.

This vision of a "third way" aims to articulate and construct a true egalitarian ethos necessary to surmount accepted ideological beliefs. Liberal theory in practice accepts values of vicious competition and supreme individualism. "Socialist" experiments, and Marxist theory itself, inadequately incorporate individual and collective human rights, including the need to combat racism, ethnic and nationalist rivalry, and patriarchal hierarchy. The formulation of collective human rights presented in this book may begin to provide us with a language to articulate these concerns and to demonstrate the connections between what are too often seen as separate struggles.

A full elaboration of collective human rights draws together the connections that exist between the world's peoples. The vision presented here includes rights of gender, sexuality, ethnicity, and race within a dialectical framework of class analysis, to create a society based upon ideals of freedom, justice, and equality. Such a formulation speaks for the vast majority of the world's peoples and not to so-called "special interests." Our claim is not for "special rights," but for the inclusion of those individuals and groups who experience suffering into truly democratic structures. Such an articulation should contribute to the creation of a new normative world order of humane governance.

I

THE POLITICS OF COLLECTIVE HUMAN RIGHTS

1

Conceptualizing Collective Human Rights

A right can be defined as a claim on others to a certain kind of treatment. Civil Rights activist and former U.S. Representative Barbara Jordan defines a right as "that which is due to anyone by tradition, law or nature" (1992). Rights are the product of specific historical circumstances with political and economic trends directly influencing how rights are created, defended, and implemented. Rights thus arise from social relations.

To a significant extent, human rights are based on the liberal tradition of the protection of the individual. Internationally, human rights emerged as a result of the failure of the Westphalian[1] system to protect human beings from genocide and abuse. In fact, World War II demonstrated the inability of the nation-state system to prevent governments from carrying out the most extreme, abusive practices toward its citizens.

In the twentieth century, human rights assume a degree of importance similar to that which natural rights claimed in the eighteenth century. Human rights have been defined as "a special class of rights, the rights that one has simply because one is a human being. They are thus moral rights of the highest order" (Donnelly 1989, 12). The source of human rights is often said to arise from a socially shared moral conception of both the nature of the human person and the conditions necessary for a life of dignity. Human rights are thus claims and demands essential to protect human life and enhance human dignity, and should therefore enjoy full social and political approval.[2]

Advocates of human rights for the most part accept the prima facie priority of rights over other justifying principles (such as law and order), accepting Dworkin's concept of "trumping." Human rights "trump" other claims[3] (Dworkin 1977, 364).

As Pollis, Falk, and other human rights scholars point out, any claimed international human right inherently challenges the foundations of the state system itself. International human rights present a higher law, a higher authority to which states are subject.[4] Advocates hope that human rights will help restrain the present-day all-powerful state[5] (Pollis 1982, 1-2; Falk 1983, 246).

Human rights are value-based. Within nation-states, the values embodied in claimed rights, for the most part, reflect the economic and social development of a society. For example, in the United States, rights generally represent freedom *from* governmental interference in our lives. The historical circumstances that led to claiming such rights as inalienable were the preoccupation with limiting capricious governmental interference in the economic and political social order. However, other important human values were not considered inalienable, such as the basic values necessary for human beings to keep on living—food, shelter, and clothing. Survival values were not addressed in the Lockean and Hobbesian experiment that was embraced by the American Revolution. Thus, a very *limited* conception of human rights developed in the United States.[6]

The historical circumstances and economic and social development in other countries have brought about alternative conceptions of human rights. Socialist ideology and social-democratic governments prioritize values which revolve around securing the basic needs of all members of society. This usually requires a great degree of governmental intervention in society, particularly in the economy. The value bias of distributive justice thus dominates human rights priorities in many less developed countries. To some of these countries, Western political rights are often seen as part of the ruling ideas of the day that disguise the viciousness of class rule, with its subsequent exploitation, degradation, and alienation of the majority classes. At the Vienna human rights conference in 1993, this debate once again to a large degree divided along North-South lines, with the underdeveloped countries emphasizing that their economic needs were as pressing as their thirst for democracy. In a switch in American policy, the Clinton administration decided to recognize the "right to development" as a universal human right (see chapter 4 below). And most Western countries paid lip service to the "indivisibility" of human rights, which means, as Pierre Sane, the head of Amnesty International, put it, that "you can't choose between torture and starvation." Yet the West's focus at the Vienna conference remained on civil and political rights (*New York Times*, 20 June 1993).

Collective human rights differ from individual rights. Human rights theory traditionally has focused on the rights of the individual, independent of social groupings, and advocates for individual human rights mainly seek redress through the nation-state system or through intergovernmental structures, such as the United Nations. The focus of collective human rights, on the other hand, is on the rights of social groups, and proponents seek to create a normative framework independent of nation-states to enhance and protect these rights.

There is, however, an interdependent relationship between group and individual rights, in that certain individual rights cannot be exercised outside of the group context. In many instances, individual rights can only be fully realized through an understanding and protection of group rights. For example, trade union rights must be protected to give the individual the freedom to join a union. Or the protection of minority culture must be guaranteed if individuals are to enjoy their culture. Certain rights are collective in nature, even though the individual is the ultimate beneficiary (Triggs 1988, 156).

Although a dialectical and interdependent relationship exists between the two, the human rights tradition has clearly emphasized the individual's rights in these collective situations. In contrast, advocates for collective human rights emphasize the rights of the collective as a whole. For example, a focus on collective human rights implies attention to the ethnic rights of Native Americans as a whole social group, rather than on the status of individual Native Americans. A focus on individual rights, however, implies seeking the protection of the ethnic rights of individual Native Americans, with group protection seen as occurring in the distant future. This often means not seeing the forest for the trees. Equal opportunity, for example, remains a myth for the majority of Native Americans today, while, at the same time, on an individual basis a small minority of middle-class Native Americans may enjoy this right. A framework of collective human rights keeps the problem in focus. It comes down to a question of the vantage point in the relationship between the individual and the group.

In contrast to the liberal premise of the isolated human being, the ideas of collective human rights begin with a view of humans as they really are, that is, as social beings.[7] The concept of collective human rights presented here is based on understanding the human race as primarily a social species—composed of social beings who congregate, associate, and exist within groups. Groups can be based on race, ethnicity, class, gender, and sexuality. This conception of the human species is the opposite of the one which is the basis of Lockean liberal theory: the isolated, lone individual, afraid of other humans. Human here means fundamental relationships, processes, and interactions with others in society.

Collective human rights are subversive to nation-state sovereignty in that they present the people (in the Rousseauean sense) as being the ultimate repository of sovereign rights. As Rousseau wrote: "Sovereignty, being nothing less than the exercise of the general will, can never be alienated. . . . [P]ower indeed may be transmitted, but not the will" (Rousseau [1762] 1973, 182). Our conception of collective human rights rests on this assertion of the sovereignty of peoples over any government and/or nation-state.

ECONOMIC, SOCIAL, AND CULTURAL RIGHTS

There is not an absolute distinction, however, between some rights as formulated by IGOs and NGOs and this conception of collective human rights. For example, economic, social, and cultural rights adopted in various United Nations human rights documents, primarily are concerned with group rights. Less developed countries, in particular, have called on the world community to include these group rights within the human rights dialogue. The conception of collective human rights presented here builds on this foundation and extends it.

Economic, social, and cultural rights are collective rights based upon the rights of human beings in their various group and social roles. Meeting these rights often depends upon positive action on the part of the state. These rights call for the fulfillment of basic human needs and social equality. They are substantive in nature, calling for state intervention in the allocation of resources to address collective, rather than individual, problems (Kim 1984, 202).

Economic, social, and cultural rights were formulated in the Mexican Constitution in 1917, the Declaration of Rights of the Working and Exploited Peoples of 1918 (which was incorporated into the Soviet Constitution), the Weimar Constitution of Germany in 1919, the Constitution of the Spanish Republic of 1931, and the Constitution of Ireland of 1937.

With the growing influence in the 1970s of the Third World on the United Nations (along with strong support from what was formerly called the Socialist or Second World), collective rights took on an added importance within UN institutions. Not only self-determination, but the rights of minorities, the rights of the underprivileged peoples to an equitable share in the world's resources, women's rights, the right to development, and the right to peace were put on the world agenda as collective human rights. Collective human rights demand recognition of the rights of groups and can *only* be exercised with the cooperation of a group. The evolution of human life in modern society has made it increasingly necessary for individuals to collaborate with fellow human beings in order to survive. The Covenant on Economic, Social and Cultural Rights established a minimum level of social protection and welfare whose attainment should be sought by all states, whatever their politics.

Fundamentally, collective human rights posit that the foundation of all citizen/individual rights depends upon the material conditions of each society. Some scholars and activists formulate a hierarchical relationship putting these rights ahead of civil and political rights. Some liberal theorists deny that economic, social, and cultural categories should be considered human rights at all, and do not see how these rights flow from natural law.

Most United Nations scholars and human rights advocates, however, approach these questions by promoting an *interdependence* between the two sets of rights and criticize those who make too sharp a distinction between them. These writers point to article 29, paragraph 1 of the Universal Declaration, which states: "Everyone has duties to the community in which alone the free and full development of his personality is possible" (Brownlie 1981, 26).

The United States has had particular difficulty accepting the legitimacy of economic, social, and cultural rights. Following the great depression of the 1930s, on 25 January 1941, President Franklin D. Roosevelt announced his "four freedoms": freedom of opinion and expression, freedom of worship, freedom from material want, and freedom to live without fear. This marked a step forward in including economic and social rights within the American experience. President Truman also expressed verbal support for economic rights when he stated: "we must declare in a new Magna Carta, in a new Declaration of Independence, that henceforth economic well-being and security, that health and education and decent living standards, are among our inalienable rights" (McCullough 1992, 957). But these collective rights have not come easily to America, and in fact, confront an ideology of supreme individualism which has successfully blocked their implementation. As a result, the 1990s were ushered in with mass beggary on the streets of American cities on a scale not seen since the 1930s, with the differential between rich and poor at an ever-widening level. The right to be free from material want is not a protected right in the United States. In fact, scholars assert that the real reason for a separate UN Covenant on Economic, Social and Cultural Rights, rather than combining it with the Covenant on Civil and Political Rights, was so that "the Western states could avoid economic rights for the most part" by not signing this convention (Renteln 1990, 33).

There has been a great deal of debate about the relationship between human rights and meeting human needs. Galtung locates human needs inside individual human beings, whereas human rights are located between them. His value bias is that of justifying human rights by their relationship to human needs. One method of identifying human needs is by asking people questions such as "What is it you cannot do without?" Human needs thus may serve as a guide to identify victims. A human needs approach may place the human rights debate more firmly among the suffering, where the nonsatisfaction of minimal subsistence needs has drastic consequences (Galtung 1994, 54–58). Christian Bay uses the analogy of any reputable hospital which would serve the most severely injured and in need first. His argument is that the claims of the oppressed, those in global poverty, deserve preferred treatment (quoted in Kim 1984, 211).

Such an approach involves moving beyond "standard-setting" and "norm-making," to examine the *structures* of the existing social order responsible for such things as unemployment and poverty. The causes of human suffering can most often be traced to economic structures that produce as much failure as success. Examining structures means acknowledging that violence and deprivation may, in part, be structural, and often not intended, nor even recognized, by individuals who uphold and even benefit from a particular political system. For millions living in poverty such an approach is fundamental to any discussion of human rights.[8]

A number of scholars believe that the human rights conundrum cannot be overcome to any significant degree without transforming the existing world order system. As Falk has written, "a denial of human needs of the masses is not inevitable, but results from the contingent structures of inequality existing between and within states" (1983, 244). "Our concern rests with the more organic attainment of a development process that encompasses everyone, providing work as well as sustenance, dignity as well as material wherewithal, participation as well as benefits" (1983, 249).[9]

Liberal thinkers continually make a distinction between individual and group rights, and endorse the primacy of individual claims for protection. The Universal Declaration of Human Rights and the UN Human Rights Covenants, however, include both kinds of rights, individual and collective, as human rights. In basing rights on the needs of individuals *and* groups, the international community has actually defined global human rights in a manner that goes far beyond liberal theory.

WHICH GROUP RIGHTS ARE COLLECTIVE HUMAN RIGHTS?

The international community has struggled with various definitions of group rights and peoples' rights. One scholar, for example, defines peoples' rights as: "rights of communities . . . ranging from the family unit to the entire human community (and including national, religious, linguistic and cultural communities, taking special account of minorities, indigenous populations, etc.)" (Marie 1986, 202). Another scholar put it, "the right *to be* and *to live in community with other members of one's own group*" (Hannum 1989, 19). Others contend that what comprises a people is contingent on both objective and subjective elements; the former being the existence of "an ethnic group linked by common history," and the latter "a present ethos or state of mind," that is, that a people is "entitled and required to identify itself as such" (Dinstein 1989, 161). And the former director of the UN Division of Human Rights Theo van Boven defined the issue as follows "for the sake of the distinction between individual rights and group rights, a group should be taken as a collectivity of persons which has special and distinct characteristics and/or which finds itself in specific situations or conditions. Those special and distinct characteristics, may be of a racial, ethnological, national linguistic or religious nature. The specific situations or conditions could be determined by political, economic, social or cultural factors" (1982, 55).

In appraising (1) the contemporary ways in which people objectively and subjectively identify themselves, and (2) the new forms of group suffering in the modern era, the necessity to expand group rights beyond solely rights of ethnicity and race is starkly apparent. Groups based on gender, sexuality, and class also have a common history which has been systematically denied them. Thus self-awareness and group identity for many of these sectors is only now being born. The recognition by these groups of a common identity, a common history, and common sources of suffering, has led to the growth of strong social movements, whose demands include the protection of their rights as social groups.

The significance of this development should not be underestimated. Women's liberation, for example, is not just a cause. It is also a means whereby women bring fresh insights to their understanding of their collective identity as women, the culture of domination which oppresses key aspects of women's existence, and political concepts (such as self-determination). To ascribe theoretical and political importance only to ethnicity in formulating group rights, and *not* address other self-defining characteristics, is a fundamentally *conservative* worldview and orientation toward change. In fact, to stress ethnicity *over* other defining characteristics of peoples can easily lead to racist ideologies and supremacist notions. This is not to argue that all groupings of human beings are of equal importance. For example, the impact of social groups, such as sports clubs, on an individual's self-definition is for the most part minor. However, certain groups have emerged in modern society which, due to their nature and importance, call for a reexamination of collective human rights as well as the corresponding duties. Therefore, formulations of collective human rights must be expanded beyond ethnicity and race to include other group rights based on class, gender, and sexuality.

This expanded conception of collective human rights allows vital connections to be made. A comprehensive understanding of collective human rights would include: the indigenous peoples of the world, such as Native Americans; specific ethnic groups and minorities within a nation-state, such as African-Americans; oppressed segments of a population, such as gays within a homophobic society and women within a sexist society; and trade union and other class-based claims.[10]

Many advocates of collective human rights also accept the autogeneration of law by nonstate actors (see discussion of the "Algiers Declaration" below) which challenges the nature of law itself. Autogeneration refers to the principle of self-creation, namely that norms, values, rules (and thereby "law" itself) can be generated by individuals and groups working with nonstate structures (NGOs and other associations).

THE POST–WORLD WAR II EVOLUTION OF COLLECTIVE HUMAN RIGHTS

Between the two world wars, the concept of collective human rights was utilized in international relations primarily with regard to self-determination. At this time, ethnic groups and minority populations *within* existing states were said to have the right to self-determination.[11]

After World War II, the international community focused on the rights of peoples subjected to colonialism. In fact, it appeared that *only* peoples under colonial rule were entitled to the collective right of self-determination. For people struggling against overt colonialism, this was an important source of support to achieve national liberation. As soon as independent statehood was reached, however, the territorial integrity of the country became sacrosanct. The struggle of oppressed peoples *within* existing and newly created nation-states was not recognized by the international system (Partsch 1982, 63–65).

Recognizing the rights of peoples and minorities within the borders of nation-states threatens those in power for a number of reasons. Rulers (and many intellectuals) fear that such recognition leads to fragmentation and undermines national unity—sentiments expressed, for example, in debates regarding the dissolution of the former Soviet Union and the former Yugoslavia. "Ethnic cleansing" and other inhuman acts in Bosnia against racial and ethnic minorities reinforces this fear. In addition, many ruling elites express their own racism and intolerance toward all minorities.

The debate over expanding collective human rights gained focus and clarity during the anti-imperialist and decolonization movements of the 1960s. This debate took place not only within the United Nations and among nation-states, but also within NGOs, which in certain cases have been influential in shaping both public and official positions. The evolution of the ideas of collective human rights, in the post–World War II period, can be broken down into three relatively distinct periods:

- 1945–1975—Initial formulation of specific collective human rights.

- 1976–1981—Substantial elaboration of collective human rights.

- 1982–1996—Conflicting interpretations of collective human rights.

1945–1975: INITIAL FORMULATION

The world wars of the twentieth century produced a level of terrorism and violence unprecedented in human history. On a worldwide scale, the atrocities committed during World War II shocked all of humanity, aroused universal indignation, and led to the development and acceptance by nation-states of international human rights standards and norms. The frustrations evident in the trials at Nuremberg and Tokyo, due to the lack of international law in the field of human rights, pointed to the importance of developing treaty commitments defining world community standards for the rights of all humanity.

Such was the atmosphere in which the United Nations was launched, and as a result, much of its attention has been focused on the international protection of various human rights. This has not been an easy task. Numerous scholars point to two basic reasons why international human rights organizations often appear weak: (1) International standards directly challenge the statist perspective of the inviolable sovereignty of the nation-state. Human rights places the individual above the interests of any particular nation-state. (2) The development of such standards requires agreement on the perceived values necessary to advance human well-being. In a world of competing ideologies and politics, such unity has been difficult to achieve.

Creating norms to internationalize the legal obligations of states toward their citizens began in the late 1940s. Article 55 of the UN Charter calls for universal respect for human rights and fundamental freedoms without distinction as to race, sex, language, or religion (Brownlie 1981, 5). One hoped-for result of these efforts is that the eradication of human rights abuses can create the conditions for peaceful and friendly relations between states. Before World War II, total *indifference* toward human rights was often seen as necessary for a tolerably peaceful international order. At that time, the international community in general felt that attempts to interfere in the affairs of other nations, even if these nations committed abuses against their own citizens, were counterproductive and could lead to further misery and potentially war. Hitler's actions forced the international community to change their approach, and the United Nations began the process of creating international norms.

While article 56 of the UN Charter called for both joint and separate action to insure adherence to these international norms, the call for enforcement was left ambiguous, and was *not* a direct challenge to nation-state sovereignty. In fact, article 2, section 7 of the UN Charter, denies the right of the UN to intervene in the internal affairs of sovereign states[12] (Brownlie 1981, 4–6; McKean 1983, 56–57).

In 1946, the UN General Assembly established a Human Rights Commission to study human rights and recommend actions on the part of the UN and member states to enforce them (Brownlie 1981, 15–20).

On 10 December 1948, the General Assembly passed the "Universal Declaration of Human Rights" (48-0:8; pursuant to art. 13(1)(b) & 55(c) of the UN Charter). The Universal Declaration, which is like a global Bill of Rights, begins by stating that all human beings are born free and equal in dignity and rights (Brownlie 1981, 22). The Universal Declaration is considered more than just a recommendation, as was stressed by René Cassin, the person most responsible for the draft and a Nobel Peace Prize winner, because the states pledge to work in cooperation to achieve respect for human rights.[13] The Universal Declaration represents a compromise resolution embodying civil and political rights as well as economic and social rights.

The declaration is not a treaty and does not have binding authority, but it puts forward a common standard to which states should aspire. In fact, the Universal Declaration represented a shift from the establishment of recommendations to the establishment of norms embodied in customary international law.

The "Universal Declaration of Human Rights" strongly emphasizes individual rights but also contains broader provisions. Article 28 contains the right to a "social and economic order" in which basic human rights can be achieved. In addition, the "Convention on the Prevention and Punishment of the Crime of Genocide," adopted on 9 December 1948, defines genocide as "a crime under international law," in terms of certain acts "committed with intent to destroy, in whole or in part, a national, ethnical, racial or religious group, as such." This multinational treaty went into force in December 1951, and over one hundred states are now parties. Both documents thus implicitly refer to peoples' rights (Brownlie 1981, 26, 31).

The most important collective human right to gain official acceptance in this period was the right to self-determination. The "Declaration on the Granting of Independence to Colonial Countries and Peoples," approved 14 December 1960 by the United Nations General Assembly (resolution 1514[XV]), addressed this issue (Brownlie 1981, 28–30). Control over natural resources was included in the discussion of self-determination. This was expressed in the "Resolution on Permanent Sovereignty over Natural Resources," passed on 14 December 1962. This UN General Assembly resolution (1803[XVII]) declared "the right of peoples and nations to permanent sovereignty over their natural wealth and resources," as "a basic constituent of the right to self-determination" (Weston, Falk, & D'Amato 1990a, 537–38). Later, in December 1966, the International Covenants on Economic, Social and Cultural Rights and on Civil and Political Rights, were approved, both referring to the rights of peoples to self-determination and to freely dispose of their natural resources. Group rights are also implicit in references to rights to food, health, education, science, and culture. In addition, article 27 of the Covenant on Civil and Political Rights, extends individual rights based on membership in a group (ethnic, religious, or linguistic) (Brownlie 1981, 137). If read in connection with article 1(1) on self-determination of peoples, it could be argued to imply, at least, an endorsement of collective human rights.

The International Covenants on Civil and Political Rights and on Economic, Social and Cultural Rights, both of which entered into force in 1976, provide legally binding obligations embodying the standards of the Universal Declaration (Brownlie 1981, 118–46). As with the declaration, the covenants are of general character and in principle cover all fundamental human rights. As such, they include both individual rights and collective rights. The subjects of civil and political rights are individuals; for economic, social, and cultural rights, the subjects are individuals and groups.

More than 125 nation-states have signed these two covenants, representing to some a potential normative leap for the world community. For example, according to Lynn Miller, "a genuine worldwide *consensus* may have emerged in recent decades on explicit and wide-ranging standards for the acceptable treatment of human beings. If that is so, its implications for the future growth of a global sense of community should be very great indeed" (1985, 160).

However, the issue of sovereignty remains a contradictory one for the international protection of individual and collective human rights. As noted, nothing contained in the UN Charter shall authorize any nations belonging to the UN to intervene on matters "which are essentially within the domestic jurisdiction of any state" (Brownlie 1981, 4). The recognition of human rights questions the primacy of sovereignty, but in the fifty-year history of the United Nations, and despite the various declarations on human rights, states have been generally unwilling to voluntarily limit their sovereignty or delegate their rights to any international organization.

Also during this initial period, documents were approved by the General Assembly and UNESCO regarding the elimination of racial discrimination, the protection of cultural rights, and the suppression of apartheid.

1976–1981: SUBSTANTIAL ELABORATION

Three documents, the "Universal Declaration of the Rights of Peoples," the "African Charter on Human and Peoples' Rights," and the "Convention on the Elimination of All Forms of Discrimination Against Women," drafted during the period 1976–1981, provide the most complete elaboration of collective human rights to date (see the appendices below for the text of all three documents). It is noteworthy that the first document was written by an NGO in conjunction with individuals and movements dedicated to combatting exploitation and protecting peoples' rights. In contrast, the latter two documents were drafted by nation-states themselves.

The "Universal Declaration of the Rights of Peoples" is also known as the Algiers Declaration, as it was proclaimed there on 4 July 1976. This document is divided into the following seven sections: Right to Existence; Right to Political Self-Determination; Economic Rights of Peoples; Right to Culture; Right to Environment and Common Resources; Rights of Minorities; and Guarantees and Sanctions. Each section contains specific articles outlining relevant claims. The document has been used with some success to legitimate struggles against oppressive regimes. The declaration was drafted by a group of nongovernmental scholars and jurists, and has provided a framework for examining grievances which have not been sufficiently addressed by established institutions.

The Algiers Declaration has guided the work of the Permanent Peoples Tribunal (PPT), an organization which evolved out of the Bertrand Russell War Crimes Tribunal on Vietnam a decade earlier. The PPT established rules and decision-making procedures through which peoples can appeal for the protection of their rights. It is a tribunal of opinion whose authority is not based on any state power. The tribunal comprises sixty members, representing thirty-one nationalities, of whom twenty-three are legal experts and five are Nobel Prize winners.

Since 1979, the PPT has held sessions on the Western Sahara (1979), Argentina (1980), Eritrea (1980), the Philippines (1980), El Salvador (1981), Afghanistan (1981 and 1982), East Timor (1981), Zaire (1982), Guatemala (1983), Armenian genocide (1984), Nicaragua (1984), Puerto Rico (1989), and Tibet (1992). In addition, the tribunal extended the subject of its concerns to deal with: the question of the external debt during the 1988 Berlin session on the International Monetary Fund and the World Bank, the Brazilian Amazon (1990), impunity in Latin America (1991), the conquest of America (1992), the environment and industrial hazards (1991 and 1992). In most of these cases, the results of the tribunals have been effectively utilized by the victimized people in their quest to alter the status quo.

One advantage of this NGO tribunal is that it can address the structural factors associated with the imperatives of capital accumulation by market-oriented economic systems, which many believe pose the principle threat to collective human rights today. International bodies composed only of nation-states (like the United Nations) have proven incapable of drawing the links between the economic and political structures of domination and the denial of peoples' rights. The PPT provides mechanisms to make these links and assert claims in international arenas, thus potentially influencing public opinion on a world scale. A clear disadvantage of the PPT, however, is its lack of enforcement ability; it cannot force nation-states to change policies which violate the rights of peoples.

The second document that provides a significant elaboration of collective human rights is the "African Charter on Human and Peoples' Rights," approved by the thirty-seventh ordinary session of the Council of Ministers of the Organization of African Unity (OAU) and the OAU Assembly of Heads of States and Government, meeting in Nairobi, Kenya in June 1981.[14]

Certain events took place on the African continent in the late 1970s which compelled such an action on the part of the OAU. The most important of these were the large-scale killings of political opponents and others by Idi Amin in Uganda (1971–79), Macias Nguema in Equatorial Guinea (1968–79), and the killings of high school students in the Central African Empire in the last year of the regime of Jean-Bedel Bokassa (1966–79). The worldwide condemnation of these regimes led the OAU to draft and later adopt the charter on human and peoples' rights.[15]

The charter entered into force on 21 October 1986, at which time thirty African states were parties. It is the *only* human rights treaty (universal or regional) to deal specifically with peoples' rights in general. Articles 19 through 24, in particular, assert the rights of peoples in the following areas: existence, self-determination, political status, economic, social, and cultural development, disposal of wealth and natural resources, and the elimination of foreign economic exploitation. Notably, the charter asserts the right to development, the right to national and international peace and security, and the right to a general satisfactory environment as collective rights of peoples. The charter establishes an African Commission on Human and Peoples' Rights to "promote human and peoples' rights and ensure their protection in Africa."

By explicitly endorsing the concept of peoples' rights, the document attempts to be responsive to African traditions and needs. "All peoples shall have the right to their economic, social, and cultural development with due regard to their freedom and identity. . . . States shall have the duty, individually or collectively, to ensure the exercise of the right to development."[16]

Theo van Boven argues persuasively that the African charter presents a dialectical relationship between the human rights of the individual and the collective rights of peoples. He contends that the highly innovative element of the charter is that it imparts "to peoples a set of existing or emerging rights" which were already identified in connection with States. "That makes the African Charter a peoples oriented document." And later he writes, "It is the notion of peoples' rights that is not destructive of individual human rights but places peoples' rights and human rights in a mutual relationship as complementary concepts" (van Boven 1986, 190, 193).

The third document, the "Convention on the Elimination of All Forms of Discrimination against Women," was drafted in New York in 1979 and entered into force on 3 September 1981. This important convention affirms numerous collective human rights of women in political, economic, social, cultural, and civil arenas. For example, state parties to the convention agree in article 5 to take all appropriate measures: "To modify the social and cultural patterns of conduct of men and women, with a view to achieving the elimination of prejudices and customary and all other practices which are based on the idea of the inferiority or the superiority of either of the sexes or on stereotyped roles for men and women."

Collective human rights are affirmed throughout this convention including article 11, in which state parties agree to take all appropriate measures to eliminate discrimination in the field of employment to ensure, (a) "The right to work as an inalienable right of all human beings; . . . (e) The right to social security." Other rights upheld include the prohibition of sanctions or dismissal on the grounds of pregnancy or maternity leave; the introduction of maternity leave with pay or with comparable social benefits without loss of former employment, seniority, or social allowances; the right to family benefits; and the right of rural women to have access to adequate health care facilities, including information, counseling, and services in family planning.

One hundred thirty-one states have ratified the women's convention, while seven states signed the convention but have yet to ratify it (including the United States) (Cook 1994, 585).

1982–1996: CONFLICTING INTERPRETATIONS

Since the 1979 women's convention and the 1981 African charter, various organizations have tried to develop specific rights as collective human rights of peoples. For example, in September 1984, the World Conference of Indigenous Peoples (WCIP), a confederation of indigenous organizations from around the world, proclaimed a Declaration of Principles of Indigenous Rights. The declaration represents the common views of its member associations, and presents a clear statement of indigenous rights.[17]

On 4 December 1986, the UN General Assembly approved the Declaration on the Right to Development (UNGA resolution 41/128—see chapter 4 below). This declaration asserts the right to development as "an inalienable human right by virtue of which every human person and all peoples are entitled to participate in, contribute to and enjoy economic, social, cultural and political development. . . . The human right to development also implies the full realization of the right of peoples to self-determination" (Weston, Falk, & D'Amato 1990a, 486).

Among scholars, there continues to be a great deal of controversy about the conception of peoples' rights and collective human rights. International law professor James Crawford outlines three clear categories of such rights: (1) The right to self-determination, a right vested in people and not governments; (2) the right of peoples to existence; and (3) the right of people to permanent sovereignty over natural resources (Crawford 1988, 159–75).

Other scholars outline a broad range of individual and collective human rights, conceptualizing "three generations" of rights (see Rich 1988, 41; and Weston 1992, 18–20). Karl Vasak, formerly UNESCO's legal adviser, popularized the concept of three generations of human rights as follows:

The first generation of rights emerged from the American and French revolutions and were aimed at securing the citizen's freedom from arbitrary action by the state. Articles 2–21 of the Universal Declaration of Human Rights are often included in this first generation, embracing: freedom from racial and equivalent forms of discrimination; the right to life, liberty, and the security of the person; freedom from slavery or involuntary servitude; freedom from torture and from cruel, inhuman, or degrading treatment or punishment; freedom from arbitrary arrest, detention, or exile; the right to a fair and public trial; freedom from interference in privacy and correspondence; freedom of movement and residence; the right to asylum from persecution; freedom of thought, conscious, and religion; freedom of opinion and expression; freedom of peaceful assembly and association; and the right to participate in government, directly or through free elections. The core value in this first generation conception of human rights is freedom and the notion of liberty, that is, to shield the individual from abusive political authority.[18]

The second generation of rights emerged from the Russian Revolution and were echoed in welfare-state concepts which developed in the West. They correspond largely to economic, social, and cultural rights, and are found in articles 22–27 of the Universal Declaration of Human Rights, including the right to social security; the right to work and to protection against unemployment; the right to rest and leisure; the right to a standard of living adequate for the health and well-being of self and family; the right to education; and the right to the protection of one's scientific, literary, and artistic production. The core value of second-generation rights are claims to equality.

The third generation of rights are a response to the phenomenon of global interdependence, and correspond to the core value of fraternity. Individual states acting alone can no longer satisfy their human rights obligations. International cooperation is required to solve contemporary problems, leading to the classification of this third generation as "solidarity rights." Such claims include: the right to peace; the right to a healthy and balanced environment; the right to humanitarian disaster relief; the right to political, economic, social, and cultural self-determination; the right to economic and social development; and the right to participate in and benefit from "the common heritage of mankind" (including earth-space resources). These third-generation rights are collective human rights which benefit individuals and groups.

Different lists of collective human rights and peoples' rights were discussed by scholars in the 1980s and 1990s.[19] Academics documented how the existing world system did not display much hospitality toward defining and implementing a program of collective human rights. In fact, the dominate categories at the UN (and in international relations in general) remained the individual and the state. Others noted a certain "ideological fatigue" over the "unceasing elaboration and reformulation of new human rights at a time when the existing norms are systematically ignored and violated" (Kim 1984, 207).

In the mid-1990s, the most successful group internationally to articulate rights claims was women. The 1993 "Vienna Declaration and Programme of Action," adopted at the World Conference on Human Rights, emphasized eliminating violence against women as a human rights obligation. Governments recognized gender-based violence as a human rights violation, rather than dismissing it as incidental to the horrors of war or as private conduct solely within the realm of domestic law (Sullivan 1994, 155). The conference also endorsed the draft "Declaration on the Elimination of Violence against Women" by calling for its adoption by the General Assembly. This draft declaration is significant because it is a clear expression of an international commitment to address violence against women in private life by explicitly addressing gender-based violence in the family and violence by nongovernmental actors in public life (Sullivan 1994, 157). The denial of women's economic, social, and cultural rights, and the impact of development on all their human rights, however, did not receive similar attention at the conference.

In June 1994, the Organization of American States, meeting in Belem do Para, Brazil, adopted the "Inter-American Convention on the Prevention, Punishment and Eradication of Violence Against Women." This convention also recognizes that violence against women constitutes a violation of human rights and defines violence in both the public and private spheres.

The United Nations Fourth World Conference on Women meeting in Beijing adopted a final declaration on 15 September 1995 embracing the collective human rights of women. The broad declaration called on world governments to raise the economic circumstances of women and protect them from increasing levels of violence. Key collective human rights of women agreed to by the nation states include [see *New York Times*, 15 September 1995].

- Women have the right to decide freely all matters related to their sexuality and childbearing.

- The systematic rape of women in wartime is a crime. Perpetrators should be tried as war criminals.

- Domestic violence is a worldwide problem that demands governmental intervention.

- Critical to the empowerment of women is access to credit. Therefore, governments and international lending institutions should support banking services for low-income women.

THE GROWING IMPORTANCE OF TRANSNATIONAL NORMS

Although the nation-state is still the most viable actor in the international arena as we approach the end of the twentieth century, its authority and supremacy is currently challenged on several fundamental levels. First, ethnic groups within existing borders of many nation-states are contesting the legitimacy of the states' control over their lives, with demands ranging from the protection of social and cultural rights to the establishment of independent nations.[20] Second, in most nation-states, because class conflict remains intense, the state is functioning to diffuse unrest and prevent the explosion of class contradictions. In addition, in many countries, people increasingly expect that an "interventionist" state will guarantee basic human needs, including health care, a job, and housing. In the vast majority of countries in the world today, the state has not come close to meeting these demands. At some point, the legitimacy of the state is called into question by those whose basic needs are ignored.[21] Finally, issues of social justice challenge basic social relations and structures of political power that exist in most nation-states. Women and gays, for example, confront cultural norms and the patriarchal hierarchy in governing structures with demands that, for the most part, go unheeded by ruling states and classes. The environmental and peace movements raise critical problems affecting the future survival of all forms of life on the planet. Yet the nation-state system appears limited in its ability to seriously incorporate or resolve the basic issues of social justice raised by these movements.[22]

Conceptions of collective human rights attempt to address many of these failures in the current statist world system. Advocates of these ideas argue that a fundamental restructuring of the international system based on transnational collective human rights is necessary for the survival and development of the human species. These proponents actively utilize the ideas of collective human rights to confront the authority of the nation-state. The review of three critical arenas of collective human rights, ethnic rights, women's rights, and lesbian/gay rights, in the next chapter makes this point fundamentally clear.

2

Ethnicity/Race, Gender, and Sexuality

In 1993, after agonizing over it for four years, the New York City Human Rights Commissioner, Dennis deLeon, revealed his HIV status. There were many factors causing his agony: fear of employment discrimination, fear of being shunned by colleagues and employers, fear of becoming a pariah. But in addition, because of his activist role, as a Latino, a gay man, and a person with HIV, revealing his status would put him in a delicate position with many of his constituents. In a moving editorial in the *New York Times*, deLeon wrote that New York's Puerto Rican and Latino political agenda never recognized the needs of the thousands of gay and lesbian Latinos. Conversely, gay and lesbian leaders rarely speak to the needs of racial and ethnic minorities. Most gay organizations have only token recognition of the city's Latino homosexual presence. "The unspoken rule is that you can exist only as one thing at a time—a Latino or a gay man—with no recognition of reality's complexity" (*New York Times*, 15 May 1993).

Reality's complexity involves issues of class, ethnicity/race, gender, and sexuality. To highlight one area without incorporating all of these dimensions into one's understanding of each individual, creates a worldview that is artificial and limited. Politically, such an approach can have the affect of pitting group against group, identity against identity, and thus destroying any hope for unity among individuals who in reality share common oppressions. A full elaboration of collective human rights, encompassing all these dimensions of the human experience, serves to combat this artificial fragmentation.

The traditional conception of peoples' rights strongly embraces the centrality of ethnicity and race, affirming the right of each individual culture to develop fully, free from degradation by more powerful groups. This chapter will begin by emphasizing the importance of these rights, stressing that the abolition of discrimination based on race depends upon universal respect for the uniqueness of each ethnic group in our multicultural world. Individual enjoyment of one's cultural heritage depends upon the protection of the cultural rights of the entire group. Individualist-oriented human rights alone often neglect the importance of group rights of ethnicity and culture.

Following this affirmation of ethnic rights, the specific rights being defined by women and by lesbians and gays are discussed. These social groups are demanding certain protections due to the profound levels of sexism and homophobia plaguing most societies in today's world. Our framework of collective human rights addresses all these components of an individual's self-definition.

ETHNIC RIGHTS

We have always lived here: we have the right to go on living where we are happy and where we want to die. Only here can we feel whole; nowhere else would we ever feel complete and our pain would be eternal.

—*Popol Vuh: Antiguas leyendas del Quiche*

What hurts Indians most is that our costumes are considered beautiful, but it's as if the person wearing it didn't exist.

—Rigoberta Menchu, Quiche Indian leader,
winner of the 1992 Nobel Peace Prize

Conceptions of collective human rights and peoples' rights address the multicultural reality of our world. Formulations of individual human rights have been criticized harshly by many Third World scholars and activists who believe that they reflect a strong Western bias. This bias is demonstrated in the obsession with protecting individual freedom and private property, while ignoring the socialized reality of life. As a result, the Universal Declaration of Human Rights may not be as "universal" as is commonly asserted. In an important study on "universalism versus relativism" in international human rights, Renteln asserts that "to date, negligible progress has been made in the direction of establishing that human rights are universal or even that certain moral principles are widely shared" (1990, 95). This debate resurfaced at the Vienna Human Rights Conference in 1993, where Western nations were strongly urged to expand their understanding of rights to include certain group rights, as well as individual political freedoms.

How can the varied norms of the numerous cultures of the world be taken seriously by the global community? Are differences among groups in their moral norms, values, and worldviews so great that a formulation of global rights is doomed? There is no question that the content and character of a group's moral norms and values is derived from the specific culture and survival needs of the group. Such moral diversity has led observers to take positions ranging from "skeptical relativism," on the one hand, to "prescriptive relativism," on the other. Advocates of skeptical relativism see no rational method for choosing or justifying universal moral norms and values, and are therefore critical of the West for imposing one set of values on other cultures. Proponents of prescriptive relativism not only respect differences in moral attitudes and practices, but also see value in trying to incorporate different beliefs into universal norms (Nickel 1987, 69).

By adhering to the skeptical relativist position, some Third World scholars assert that the Western concept of individual human rights does not apply to them. For example, Panikkar points to interrelated dangers that the poorer countries of the South face in accepting universal human rights. He believes that modern culture, which usually accompanies the ideology of human rights, demonstrates little respect for indigenous cultures. Cultural traditions become restricted by the "universalistic" nature of human rights, which thereby limits the society's ability to form its *own* views of human rights. Instead of a dialogue among cultures as to the content of human rights, an external ideology is imposed on peoples everywhere, minimizing their input (see Moderne 1990, 317).[1]

As previously noted, Western political theory often emphasizes a contentious relationship between the individual and the state, assuming a universal egoistic and aggressive "human nature." This assumption is alien to many traditional societies in other regions, where such a separation between the individual and his/her society does not exist. Advocates of African socialism, for example, draw a connection between Marxism and traditional African society in that both emphasize the human being in their social context. In traditional African society, the individual and the group are complementary. In this context some scholars argue that rights are not part of each person just because they are human, but are contingent upon each individual's fulfillment of their obligations to the group.

Ifeani Menkiti explains this point as follows:

> Personhood is the sort of thing which has to be attained and is attained in direct proportion as one participates in communal life through the discharge of various obligations defined by one's situations. . . . [I]t is the community which defines the person. . . . [P]ersons become persons only after a process of incorporation. (quoted in Moderne 1990, 320)

Adamantia Pollis points to the importance of group consciousness in cultures outside of the West.[2] Professor Collomb notes that living in Africa "means abandoning the right to be an individual, particular, competitive, selfish, aggressive, conquering being . . . in order to be with others, in peace and harmony with the living and the dead, with the natural environment and the spirits that people it or give life to it" (quoted in M'Baye and Ndiaye 1982, 589).

Pollis also describes how the colonial experience reinforced notions of group identity, while shattering preexisting concepts of human dignity. Colonialism brought social disorganization and anomie. "Respect for the individual, liberty, democratic values, and freedom of dissent were hardly the values the colonialists transmitted to the peoples they ruled" (1982, 17). The disruption of traditional society and the dramatically changed social relations caused by the slave trade and forced labor, fundamentally denied Africans the right to enjoy human rights and freedoms.

Today, in most of the Southern Hemisphere, poverty and the lack of economic and social development are the main impediments to individual and collective human rights. The "liberal constitutions" bestowed on African nations by the departing European colonialists, remain to many "artificial instruments" (Moderne 1990, 339).[3]

It is, therefore, not accidental that Africa is the only region which has included the concept of peoples' rights in one of its major documents, the "African Charter on Human and People's Rights" (see p. 29 above). The concept of people's rights, as elaborated in the African charter, attempts to incorporate some of these traditional African interests. Africans remain concerned with economic issues, protecting their fragile independence, and shaking off all forms of colonialism. In this document, traditional civil, political, economic, social, and cultural rights are validated, while strong emphasis is placed on collective human rights.

Some Third World scholars make the point that political systems are, in the final analysis, carried and informed by substructural cultural forces. Western leaders too often ignore this political truth and maintain the illusion that "their own vocabulary and values in the sphere of politically significant behavior and organization are still meaningful in the rest of the world" (Bozeman 1971, 28–29). For centuries in Africa, real government was carried out by local kinship and tribal organizations. Africa's system of social organization stresses the group, and human relations are dominated by tribal and kinship considerations above the individual. The primary function of law is the conservation of the community and the maintenance of public order, not the development and protection of individual rights. As a result, many believe that the task of nation-building has yet to be accomplished in Africa.

In Asia, Africa, and Latin America, there has been continued confidence in "small organizations": extended families, clans, villages, tribes, guilds, crafts, and so on. People find security and satisfaction in these formations. In many cases, the organization of the nation-state has *not* provided the spirit or momentum that cultural consciousness provides (Migdal 1988).

In sum, the concept of collective human rights (including ethnic and economic rights) has an historical basis that runs far deeper in some of these cultures than does the Western concept of individual rights. Thus, if rights are to become universal, the concept of collective human rights must be as protected as individual human rights. For many, the lack of recognition of these concerns casts a Western bias over the rights debate, reflecting, in numerous cases, cultural arrogance. The collective human rights framework presented here attempts to incorporate both individual and group rights, thus hopefully overcoming the Western prejudice often found in the traditional human rights approach.

We must not underestimate the challenge of cultural relativism to the universality of human rights, nor concede too much to its claims. Abdullahi A. An-Na ͨim proposes an approach that "seeks to explore the possibilities of cultural reinterpretation and reconstruction through *internal cultural discourse and cross-cultural dialogue*, as a means to enhancing the universal legitimacy of human rights" (1992, 3). He describes a process through which existing international standards of human rights would be maintained since they provide a useful framework to begin the process of articulating standards of genuinely universal human rights, but changes would come through cross-cultural dialogue. On the one hand, some protection can be drawn from existing standards and we may never "regain the ground gained by the international human rights movement thus far if these standards are repudiated today" (1992, 5). But, on the other hand, there exists a need to verify and substantiate the genuine universality of the existing standards through a process of retroactive legitimation of the existing international human rights standards. This would involve the possibility that revisions and/or reformulations may be necessary (1992, 6).

> [T]his process must be both mutual between cultures and sensitive to the needs to internal authenticity and legitimacy. Those of one cultural tradition who wish to induce a change in attitudes within another culture must be open to a corresponding inducement in relation to their own attitudes and must also be respectful of the integrity of the other culture. They must never even appear to be imposing external values in support of the human rights standards they seek to legitimize within the framework of the other culture. (An-Na ͨim 1992, 5)

While the protection and development of cultural and ethnic rights are paramount in considering collective human rights, there is also a focus on the individual. The world is composed of culturally diverse peoples, who have the right to internal and external self-determination.[4] History has shown that all people will fight to protect their way of life. From the perspective of collective human rights, each individual ethnic group (from the Tamils to the

Quebecois to the Basques, and so on) have the right to secede from the dominant state. However, having this right does not mean having the duty to carry it out. In fact, many writers on self-determination believe that the very recognition of the right to secede along with the democratic treatment of all nations and nationalities within a particular state, would lead to the voluntary union of nations rather than secession.[5]

University of Cambridge professor John Dunn believes that the search for a more intuitively plausible scale of community lies behind the worldwide pressures for decentralization and localization of political choice and control. The problem is that the species has not yet conceived of a practical form in which to transcend the nation-state (1979, 63–64). Perhaps this is our task as we enter the twenty-first century.

WOMEN'S RIGHTS

> Representation of the world, like the world itself, is the work of men; they describe it from their own point of view, which they confuse with absolute truth.
>
> —Simone de Beauvoir

> The servant role of women is critical for the expansion of consumption in the modern economy.
>
> —J. K. Galbraith

The human rights dialogue has not adequately addressed the concerns that affect the majority of the world's women on a daily basis. Rather, women's rights in the international context are primarily concerned with placing women in the same situation as men. These rights are therefore not specific to women, but rather rights thought to be held by all people. Noreen Burrows clearly states the affect of such an approach:

> A definition of rights which omits to take on board the needs and aspirations of half the human race cannot thereby lay claim to universality nor can it be seen to have an overriding moral authority. For most women, what it is to be human is to work long hours in agriculture or in the home, to receive little or no remuneration, and to be faced with political and legal processes which ignore their contribution to society and accord no recognition of their particular needs. (1986, 82)

According to Burrows, the differences between men and women can be broken down into those largely defined by the structure of society, and those based on the biological distinction between the sexes. "The former relate to the fact that typically certain functions are performed by women, such as child-care, housework, subsistence farming. The latter relates to the exclusive performance by women of bearing and suckling children" (Burrows 1986, 82).

A longstanding feminist argument holds that true sexual equality can emerge only if women are defined in their own right and not with reference to men. If women's rights are to be truly recognized, they must have their own identity and should not be equated with rights for men. Men should stop being the referent for all human beings.

Adrienne Rich wrote the following on how a woman's search for individuality is different from a man's:

> All she said was that her needs consisted of more than meeting the needs of others. She observed that her potential to be creative, to see in new ways, to use her energy, extended far beyond, and was different in kind, from the ways men had seen her "potential." She was met with resistance. In expressing herself, as she really was, rather than how others saw her, she presented a threat to the ways others understood the world. In a more urgent voice, she questioned the right of her rapist to violate her, her husband to beat her, male dominated systems (legal, educational, religious, etc.) to define her being, ascribe to her a role, and to pass judgment on her. She was met with rage. In revealing herself as something other than the "woman" in a male-constructed vision of reality, she became a traitor. She was "disloyal to civilization." (1979, 108)

Jus cogens in international law refers to a peremptory norm, recognized by the international community as a whole and from which no derogation is permitted. Certain norms of human rights have assumed this level of acceptance within international society, but unfortunately they often reflect a gender bias. The human rights that are frequently asserted to constitute *jus cogens* do not in fact operate equally upon men and women. The choices made reflect male concerns, often bearing no relevance to women's lives. As Christine Chinkin notes, the violations that women most need guarantees against do not receive this same protection or symbolic labeling. (1991, 350).

A number of scholars have pointed out that the development of international human rights has been almost totally from a male perspective. Mainstream human rights law, represented by the Covenants on Human Rights, do not present female concerns, which are instead marginalized into separate documents (International Labor Organization conventions and the Convention on the Elimination of All Forms of Discrimination against Women).

The right to life in article 6 of the Civil and Political Rights covenant is a recognized norm of *jus cogens*. What is protected is arbitrary deprivation of life through public actions, which does not address the many ways in which being a woman is in itself life-threatening and the special ways in which women need legal protection to be able to enjoy their right to life.

> Being a woman is life threatening from before birth through abortion of female fetuses, and immediately after birth through the higher incidence in many societies of female infanticide. The phenomenon of the feminization of poverty causes women to have a lower life expectancy, especially when coupled with government policies with respect to birth rates without adequate medical care and appropriate diet. Violence against women is endemic. Statistics show a similar picture of violence across Western, African and Asian societies; at times it seems the only area where there is genuine consistent and uniform state practice across countries and cultures. In the face of these realities for so many women a guarantee of the right to life appears weak and meaningless. If the right to life is a currently recognized norm of *jus cogens*, it provides little assistance for many of the world's women. Worse, even as an aspiration, this universally acknowledged right does not cover the situations where women's lives or bodily integrity are in jeopardy. International lawyers must ask why not, and why their discipline is apparently inadequate to provide legal guarantees of protection against foreseeable and demonstrated harms to over half the world's population. (Chinkin 1991, 351)

According to Chinkin, the following should be included as *jus cogens* rights to take seriously the needs and interests of women: the right to bodily integrity and reproductive freedom; the right to food; the right to be free from violent attack and to be free from fear of violent attack on the streets and in the home; the right to peace and not to lose one's home and security through conflict, for example, by becoming a refugee; the right to be free from sexual exploitation. The concept of *jus cogens* has a promotional, aspriational character, and these suggested rights are fundamental to the existence and dignity of women (1991, 352).

Women as a group have a relationship to the means of production that differs from that of men. Most household labor, including child care, remains in the pre-market stage, even though it constitutes a huge amount of socially necessary production. However, since it is outside of the market relation, it is usually not adequately compensated or recognized. In most societies, a sharp distinction exists between the public and private spheres. In the private realm of the family, mothering and housework are not considered real work, despite their overall economic importance. This leads Margaret Benston to "tentatively define women, then, as that group of people who are responsible for the production of simple use-values in those activities associated with the home and family. . . . In a society in which money determines value, women are a group who work outside the money economy." Thus we find the material basis for the inferior status of women in the market economy that dominates the current world system. "In structural terms, the closest thing to the condition of women is the condition of others who are or were also outside of commodity production, i.e. serfs and peasants" (Benston 1989, 33–34). The reality for women from countries as diverse as Cuba, Russia, Canada, the United States, or elsewhere is that equal access to jobs outside the home is not sufficient to guarantee equality for women, as long as the home remains a matter of private production.

In the 1980s in the United States, women's participation in the work force increased from 51 to 57 percent, and to more than 70 percent for women between 25 and 34, with the steepest increase among working mothers (Faludi 1991, 84). This increase in women's participation in the market economy has not meant a reduction in women's responsibilities at home. On the one hand, a woman is more dependent on the limited, lower wages she receives from her job, but on the other hand, she is not freed from family responsibilities or the work of the home. Child care, in particular, remains an urgent problem.

As feminists have pointed out, women exist in a realm of "difference," which allows a variety of injustice and oppression to take place. Every day the papers are filled with accounts of rape, sexual abuse, sexual harassment, domestic battering, and other manifestations of direct physical violence. Women are also subjected to abuse due to social policies on divorce, abortion, and birth control. Poor women of color are victims of what has been called "triple jeopardy."

Most of the 43.4 million Americans without medical insurance of any kind are women and children (*New York Times*, 27 August 1995). The consequences include soaring infant mortality rates due to lack of prenatal care and low birth weights, startling increases in drug dependency with no therapeutic relief, and high rates of ovarian cancer due to lack of preventive care. AIDS is now the leading killer of women between the ages of 25 and 44 in the United States, according to the Centers for Disease Control and Prevention (*New York Times*, 5 July 1995).

Women's rights and the feminist movement in the United States, as Susan Faludi so accurately documents, are under attack. As Faludi explains, the backlash against women's rights has two central pressure points. The first is a woman's claim to her own paycheck. As women gain in strength in the work force, "the culture simply redoubles its resistance, if not by returning women to the kitchen, then by making the hours spent away from their stoves as inequitable and intolerable as possible: pushing women into the worst occupations, paying them the lowest wages, laying them off first and promoting them last, refusing to offer child care or family leave, and subjecting them to harassment." The second pressure point is a woman's control over her own fertility. "In periods of backlash, birth control becomes less available, abortion is restricted, and women who avail themselves of it are painted as 'selfish' or 'immoral' " (Faludi 1991, 54–55).

Gender bias is a worldwide phenomenon and a primary cause of poverty. For example, conventional economic theories hold that both men and women will benefit equally from economic growth. Yet, as Third World economies develop, existing gender gaps in the distribution of wealth and in access to resources not only persist, but in many cases grow worse. Even in industrial countries, from the 1950s into the 1990s, UN statistics reveal that women never achieved parity with men. According to the Gender-related Development Index (GDI) published by the United Nations Development Programme in 1995, in no society do women enjoy the same opportunities as men. Some of the evidence of the unequal access to opportunities documented in the 1995 *Human Development Report* include:

- 70% of the 1.3 billion people in poverty are women, a result linked to their unequal situation in the labor market, their treatment under social welfare systems and their status and power in the family.

- All regions record a higher rate of unemployment among women than men.

- Women's labor force participation has risen by only four percentage points in twenty years—from 36% in 1970 to 40% in 1990.

- In fifty-five countries that have comparable data, the average female wage is only three-fourths of the male wage.

- Women occupy only 10% of the parliamentary seats and only 6% of the cabinet positions.

- Women work longer hours than men in nearly every country—53% in developing countries and 51% in industrial countries. (UNDP 1995, 4–6)

Given this skewed access to resources, unless specific steps are taken to redress inequity, women will fall even further behind. For example, among the developing world's 900 million illiterate people, women outnumber men two to one. The UNDP also reports that girls constitute 60% of the 130 million children without access to primary school. As population grows faster than educational opportunities for women, the number of illiterate women continues to increase (UNDP 1995, 4).

Throughout the world, men and boys do much better than women and girls. In India, for example, far more girls than boys die in the critical period between infancy and age five, because sons consistently receive more and better food and health care.[6]

Jodi Jacobson points to similar patterns of discrimination in Bangladesh, Nepal, Pakistan, throughout the Middle East and North Africa, and in parts of sub-Saharan Africa. It has been calculated by Harvard economist Amartya Sen that 100 million women in the developing world are "missing," having died prematurely from the consequences of gender bias (Jacobson 1993, 65; Sen 1990).

For a conception of collective human rights to have meaning to the female population of the world, these concerns must be incorporated into the analysis. A new formulation of collective human rights should demonstrate a commitment to accept the dignity and worth of women (as women and not as men), if it is to be a useful tool in ending oppression for over half the human species. The women attending the 1993 Vienna Human Rights Conference clearly articulated these issues, and to many observers women's human rights were the only area at the conference to define a forward-looking agenda twenty-five years after the last world conference on human rights. The "Vienna Declaration and Programme of Action" identifies particular gender-specific abuses as human rights violations and calls for the integration of women's human rights throughout UN activities. A political consensus emerged that various forms of violence against women should be examined within the context of human right's standards and in conjunction with gender discrimination (Sullivan 1994, 152).

LESBIAN AND GAY RIGHTS

In the evening news I'm told that violent acts against homosexuals are up forty-one percent over last year and to get away from all this I go to a cinema in the neighborhood to see a movie and it's called *Hollywood Shuffle* and it's about the plight of certain minorities in the movie industry and halfway through the movie I have to watch this stereotypic fag with a dick and designer perfume for a brain mince his way through his lines and I want to throw up because we're supposed to quietly and politely make house in this killing machine called America and pay taxes to support our own slow murder and I'm amazed that we're not running amok in the streets, and that we can still be capable of gestures of loving after lifetimes of all this.

—David Wojnarowicz, *Close to the Knives*

The language and politics of rights have been of particular importance to the lesbian and gay community in organizing against homophobia. Lesbians and gays have struggled for the same rights as those held by heterosexuals and for the right to define and create a lesbian and gay culture. Lesbian and gay rights are group rights. Lesbians and gays are not born into a particular class or social group. A person identifies himself or herself as homosexual, and until the last thirty years in most of the world, proceeded to feel a profound sense of isolation. There is no collective existence, as there is with other oppressed groups, such as African-Americans. The gay rights movement helped to forge a sense of collectivity and a strong gay and lesbian subculture has emerged globally.

In the United States in the early 1950s, the gay male Mattachine Society and the lesbian Daughters of Bilitis were founded. Both of these groups sought to promote a better understanding of homosexuals among the public at large and began to challenge the inequalities of the U.S. legal system. However, it wasn't until 28 June 1969, when the New York City Vice Squad raided a bar called Stonewall Inn, that the lesbian and gay movement burst forward. The "Stonewall riots" that followed created the militant homosexual and the public image of lesbians and gays began to go through a profound change (see Bronski 1984, 2–13).

The breakout of the gay movement was clearly a product of its times. The movements of the 1960s, the anti-Vietnam War movement, the Black Power movement, the women's movement, had all challenged the "American way of life," portrayed in the mass media as benefitting white and middle-class people. After Stonewall, lesbians and gays demanded recognition that U.S. society was not only heterosexual. At first, the U.S. press and public did not take the gay rights movement as seriously as other movements, but they could not ignore it. The movement cry of "we are everywhere," not only shocked middle America, but brought attention to the demands that gays were making for legal and civil rights. It also resulted in an increase in open homophobia which had been latent below the surface. Physical and verbal attacks on gays and lesbians rose proportionately. The Right was able to mobilize homophobic fears for its own political ends by pronouncing homosexuality to be un-American and antithetical to traditional religious and sexual values, gender roles, and the family.

In the U.S. legal system and around the world, lesbians and gays fought for civil rights and equal protection under the law. Throughout the cities and states of America there were countless other legal struggles for rights, including anti-discrimination ordinances, custody cases, injunctions against police harassment, fights to get permits for gay pride marches, and so forth.

The politicization of sexuality continues to be the cornerstone of gay liberation. Prior to Stonewall, even most liberals saw homosexuality as a private choice that had nothing to do with social or political identity or politics. Gay liberationists borrowed the slogan of the women's movement: "The personal is political." The slogan reflect the reality that, in fact, the personal and the political are intimately linked (Bronski 1984, 6). For example, the decimation of contemporary family life to a large degree comes from matters decided in the larger political realm (e.g., policy decisions regarding job programs, welfare benefits, child care, and unemployment insurance have a direct bearing on U.S. families). Americans experience social isolation and political alienation, and to repair them both perhaps involves an examination of their linkages. Drawing people out of their private pain, cynicism, and passivity and opening them up to their connections with others creates the possibility for collective action. Gays and lesbians, in particular, have felt the effects of political decisions on their personal lives. Rather than remain isolated, passive, closeted individuals, gay liberationists push the political dimension to the surface and demand that society alter the political basis to their personal oppression. Since Stonewall, gay men and lesbians have consciously created a politically motivated culture that is based upon their own analyses and experiences.

On the floor of the 1984 Democratic convention in the United States, African-American presidential nominee Jessie Jackson embraced lesbians and gay men and called for the protection of their civil rights. As a further indication of how far the movement had come, some forty-six gay and lesbian democratic clubs were present at the convention.

The legal struggle for gay rights intensified throughout the 1980s in response to the backlash against gays that began in the late 1970s and continued during the Reagan years. In July 1986, the United States Supreme Court, in the *Hardwick* decision, ruled that the Constitution does not protect homosexual relations between consenting adults, even in the privacy of their own homes. Writing for the majority, Justice White declined to extend to homosexuals a line of decisions involving heterosexuals, in which the Court recognized constitutional rights to sexual privacy. Justice White stressed the "ancient roots" in English common law of statutes criminalizing homosexual relations, noting that all fifty states outlawed homosexual sodomy until 1961 and that twenty-four states and the District of Columbia still do. Leaders of various gay rights organizations described the decision as the "Dred Scott case" for the gay movement, referring to the 1857 Supreme Court ruling upholding slavery, in which blacks were not held to be citizens.

However, in the presidential election of 1992, a spirited national lesbian and gay activist network mobilized in response to the virulent homophobia and blatant prejudice oozing from the Republican Party. Lesbians and gays were highly visible at the Democratic Convention in New York and throughout the national campaign, contributing significantly to Clinton's victory.

The lesbian and gay movement has experienced a tremendous growth worldwide from the 1970s to the 1990s. The International Gay Association, was founded in Coventry, England in 1979, to provide a forum for gay groups from around the world to share ideas and strategies for organizing. In March 1993, the International Lesbian and Gay Association (ILGA), was granted roster status as an NGO by the United Nations Economic and Social Council. Roster status allowed the ILGA to submit papers to the UN on issues concerning the worldwide lesbian and gay community. The UN later withdrew this official status when the ILGA was unable to convince the UN that ILGA member groups did not condone sex between adults and minors. Although currently in a financial crisis, the ILGA is a worldwide, interactive network of grassroots organizations committed to overcome legal, social, cultural, and economic discrimination on a global level. There are over 300 ILGA member groups in more than eighty countries on all five continents.

The second international gay group is the San Francisco–based International Gay and Lesbian Human Rights Commission (IGLHRC). The IGLHRC documents, monitors, and mobilizes responses to human rights violations against gay men, lesbians, bisexuals, and people with HIV/AIDS worldwide. It is in its second year of operation as the "action secretariat" of the ILGA.

In Europe, the right to legal recourse for people denied employment or shelter because of their homosexuality was affirmed in the mid-1980s by Norway and France, and by the European Parliament itself. In fact, the 1984 European Parliament resolution is perhaps the most comprehensive statement on the civil rights of gay people to date. In Italy and the United Kingdom, lesbian and gay organizations won municipal support for community centers in several cities (Adam 1987, 122–23). In the Netherlands, lesbians and gay men live with considerable state acceptance. In Spain, a gay and lesbian movement sprang forth following the death of Francisco Franco (Adam 1987, 138). In Ireland, in 1993, gays and lesbians were accepted matter-of-factly as part of the main St. Patrick's Day parade in Dublin. Irish President Mary Robinson spoke at the Dublin event, encouraging tolerance and inclusion of all groups (*Advocate*, 20 April 1993). The Irish government followed through on its campaign pledge, and, in May 1993, agreed to decriminalize homosexual acts between consenting partners, with the age of consent set at 17 (*New York Times*, 16 June 1993).

In the Southern Hemisphere, the gay movement has also made progress. In Mexico in the 1980s, the Frente Homosexual de Accion Revolucionaria revived in response to numerous anti-gay assaults and murders and police harassment. In Colombia, the first public gay pride parade occurred in Bogota in 1983, and has grown since that time (Adam 1987, 142–43). In March of 1992, a gay and lesbian organization was granted legal recognition by the Argentine government after three years of court battles.

In South Africa in October 1992, over 1,000 people took part in Johannesburg's third annual lesbian and gay pride march. The march concluded a week of gay and lesbian events, including a reading of gay books banned in South Africa and an exhibit of lesbian and gay art. Several organizations, including the South African Communist Party and the Women's League of the African National Congress Party, sent letters of support to the march organizers (*Advocate*, 17 November 1992).

In China, the first official study of homosexuality indicates that attitudes toward homosexuals are easing. A 1992 survey, by China's best-known sexologist, shows that in large cities homosexuals are treated better than they have been in the past but are far from gaining acceptance. Although China has no law against homosexuality and officials have consistently claimed that homosexuality does not exist there, in the past people believed to be homosexual were automatically arrested and often charged with hooliganism. In 1993, the first open group for gay men, Men's World, was organized. Police agreed not to harass the Beijing organization (*Advocate*, 15 December 1992, 23 February 1993).

In Australia, Tasmania remains the only Australian state with a law banning homosexual sex. The laws carry a maximum of twenty-one years in prison for sexual intercourse "against the order of nature." In April 1994, the United Nations Human Rights Committee found that Tasmania's laws against private, consenting, adult homosexual acts breach the International Covenant on Civil and Political Rights. This decision is precedent-setting, in establishing that the United Nation's Covenant on Civil and Political Rights include sexual orientation. The committee made clear that the covenant's right to privacy provisions are breached not only by the possibility of arrests under the challenged laws, but also by the discrimination, harassment, and stigma created by those laws. The committee's rulings are not legally enforceable, but a nation must offer the United Nations an annual explanation if it has ignored one (IGLHRC, May/June 1994).

A gay group in Bermuda petitioned for the repeal of the nation's antisodomy law because it violates the European Convention on Human Rights Treaty. Bermuda is a colony of Britain, which signed that treaty, but Bermuda's criminal code makes male-male sex punishable by up to ten years in prison.

Finally, the gay movement has emerged in the former Soviet Union and Eastern Europe. In Russia, some homosexuals are open for the first time about their sexuality, even though they say they continue to feel mistreated and threatened by hostile public attitudes. Today, gay groups are officially registered and gay newspapers are published under municipal government laws. Article 121 of the Russian Criminal Code, a holdover from the Soviet era, stated "sexual relations between men are punishable by prison terms of up to five years." Lesbian sexual relations were not mentioned and thus legal. The Russian government sentenced ten people to prison for engaging in homosexual relations in the first half of 1992 (*New York Times*, 10 February 1993). In April of 1993, Russia repealed article 21 and Boris Yeltsin signed the code changes into law, eliminating the "crime of homosexuality" (*New York Times*, 29 May 1993). However, old attitudes of prejudice remain. In 1994 23 percent of Russians polled said homosexuals should be killed, 24 percent said they should be isolated, and 29 percent said they ought to be left alone (*New York Times*, 8 July 1995).

The Parliament in the Ukraine, the most populous state outside Russia of the former Soviet Union, decriminalized homosexuality in 1992. Also in 1992, Estonia decriminalized gay and lesbian sex, and the Estonian government committed itself to promote the use of condoms in large cities. Sex between men remains illegal in Lithuania, and at least six men are known to be serving prison sentences for gay sex. By the summer of 1993, Lithuania remained the only one of the three Baltic states that used to belong to the Soviet Union, to retain its sodomy law. The law has been used to deny legal status to the Lithuanian Lesbian and Gay Association, whose founder has been subject to continual harassment and violence (*Advocate*, 17 November 1992). On 20 January 1995, the Albanian parliament legalized homosexual relations, doing away with article 137 of the old penal code, under which "being homosexual" could be punished by up to ten years in prison (IGLHRC, April 1995).

GAY RIGHTS: A "SUSPECT" GROUP ADVOCATING "SPECIAL RIGHTS"?

In 1994 Amnesty International USA released a dramatic report documenting human rights violations based on sexual orientation. From Europe to Africa to the Americas to Asia, case after case of brutality and discrimination against lesbians and gay men was carefully chronicled. For example, the headless body of a local politician in Brazil is found, mutilated and decapitated, in a garbage heap following his public announcement of his bisexuality and a political battle to remove him from office. In the United States, a woman loses custody of her own child because a Virginia judge decides that as a lesbian she is by definition an unfit mother—using the fact that it is a crime in that state to have same-sex relations. In Iran, the authorities reiterate publicly that death is a possible punishment for persons guilty of homosexual acts. And in Colombia, "death squads" routinely target and kill gay men and transvestites as local authorities promote "limpieza social" (social cleansing). The death squads operate without fear of prosecution as the gunmen themselves are often police officers (Amnesty International USA 1994). These are just a small sampling of the thousands of cases of despicable acts against lesbians and gay men and demonstrate the necessity for the protection of this group's rights.

As we enter the mid-1990s, the lesbian and gay movement continues to fight a backlash. The AIDS crisis reinforced homophobic prejudice throughout the world. In the United States, violence against gays is soaring, as "queer-bashing" has become an accepted pastime for many teenagers. According to a report released in December 1994 by twenty-three victims services and anti-violence groups throughout the United States, bias-related slayings of homosexuals are often gratuitously violent and many go unsolved. Almost 60 percent of the underreported list of 151 murders of homosexuals occurring in twenty-nine states and the District of Columbia between 1992 and 1994 involved "overkill": four or more gunshot or stab wounds, the repeated use of blunt objects or the use of more than one killing method. The degree of violence was even more striking when broken down along racial and ethnic lines: 71% of Hispanic victims and 63% of black victims were "overkilled" in contrast to 52% of white victims. Arrests have been reported in only 51% of the cases studied (*New York Times*, 21 December 1994).

Observers note how fag jokes are still commonplace in schools, offices, and the entertainment industry at large, while derogatory jokes against other minorities and groups are no longer acceptable.[7] In a number of decisions, U.S. courts have pitted "family values" against the prerogatives of gay parents (Hunter 1991, 406–7).

In fact, in the United States the justice system has become the ultimate arbiter for determining the definitive legal status of gay rights in this country. For example, voters in the state of Colorado approved an anti-gay rights ordinance, Amendment 2, which overturned existing civil rights protections based on sexual orientation in Denver, Boulder, and Aspen as well as Governor Romer's executive order giving protections for gays, lesbians, and bisexuals. It also makes it unconstitutional for municipalities and government entities to enact future laws that protect gay people from discrimination in jobs and housing. A suit was filed challenging the constitutionality of the law, which may take several years to resolve.

In 1994 the Colorado Supreme Court struck down Amendment 2. The measure was never in force because a lower court had also issued an injunction against it. In its 6 to 1 decision, the State Supreme Court found that Amendment 2 singled out a class of people for denial of basic rights and thereby violated the equal protection clauses of the Colorado and Federal Constitutions (*New York Times*, 12 October 1994). The decision marked the first time that the highest court of any state had found it unconstitutional to deny certain rights to homosexuals. The verdict calls into question ballot initiatives modeled on the Colorado law put forward in at least eight states, including Arizona, Florida, Idaho, Michigan, Missouri, Nevada, Oregon, and Washington.

The battle is far from over, however, as Colorado's attorney general appealed the decision and the U.S. Supreme Court agreed to hear the case. Gay and civil rights groups petitioned the White House to file an amicus brief challenging Amendment 2's constitutionality. In a highly politicized decision, the Clinton Justice Department decided not to file a friend-of-the-court brief in the Colorado case disappointing gay activists.

In Cincinnati, federal district court judge S. Arthur Spiegel voided the Issue 3 Amendment, a successful referendum seeking to overturn the city's gay rights law. The voters of Cincinnati approved the anti-gay measure by a vote of approximately 62% to 38%. The ruling states, "this Court is in no way giving any group any rights above and beyond those enjoyed by all citizens. To the contrary, we are simply, but crucially, preventing one group of citizens from being deprived of the very rights we all share." The ruling makes a number of critical "findings of fact" including: "#8. Sexual orientation is set in at a very early age—3 to 5 years—and is not only involuntary, but is unamenable to change; #13. Homosexuals have suffered a history of pervasive, irrational and invidious discrimination in government and private employment, in political organization and in all facts of society in general, based on their sexual orientation."[8]

In May 1995, however, the U.S. Court of Appeals for the Sixth Circuit overturned Judge Spiegel's decision and upheld the right of Cincinnati voters to deprive homosexuals of specific legal protections (*New York Times*, 14 May 1995). The ruling has national implications since the Court of Appeals is the highest court yet to rule on voter initiatives that overturn existing anti-bias laws, prohibit their enactment, or do both. This decision was thus a serious setback to the gay and lesbian civil rights movement.

Opponents of the amendment are appealing the decision to the Supreme Court. Anticipating a Supreme Court fight, the group that sponsored the Cincinnati referendum received some critical help when rejected Supreme Court nominee Robert Bork joined their legal team. Bork will be co-counsel for Equal Rights, Not Special Rights (ERNSR), who also signed up Reagan administration attorney general Edwin Meese III to fundraise for their effort.

The U. S. courts have also become the forum for determining the status of the U. S. military's new policy on homosexuals. During the 1992 campaign, candidate Bill Clinton promised to end the discrimination and harrassment of gay and lesiban military personnel. However, once he became president this "promise" was tossed aside and President Bill Clinton refused to stand on principle. A new policy was hammered out in negotiations among the White House, Congress, and the Joint Chiefs of Staff in 1993, and took effect on 28 February 1994. The policy, known as "don't ask, don't tell, don't pursue," allows homosexuals to serve in the military, but only if they hide their sexuality. Commanders are still instructed to pursue investigations of homosexual activity if they have compelling evidence that such activity has occurred. The new policy continues the military's longtime ban on homosexual acts and further requires gay and lesbian service members to keep their sexual orientation private. A declaration of one's homosexuality in a public forum is considered evidence of an intent to commit homosexual acts and can be grounds for discharge. As a result, during the first eight months of the new policy, the military discharged 507 people for homosexuality, about the same rate as under the old absolute gay ban.

In March 1995, a federal judge struck down the military's new policy on homosexuals saying it violated the First and Fifth Amendments and catered to the fears and prejudices of heterosexual troops. Judge Eugene H. Nickerson called the government's attempt to distinguish between sexual orientation and a propensity to act on such orientation "nothing less than Orwellian." The issue before Judge Nickerson was whether someone could say they are gay and still serve. Gay rights groups argued that the policy violated homosexuals' First Amendment rights to freedom of speech. Judge Nickerson concurred, and wrote: "To presume from a person's status that he or she will commit undesirable acts is an extreme measure. Hitler taught the world what could happen when the government began to target people not for what they had done but because of their status." Judge Nickerson said the new policy forces homosexuals into a life of secrecy that itself could undermine morale and discipline. "The policy of the act is not only inherently deceptive. It also offers powerful inducements to homosexuals to lie." "Congress may not enact discriminatory legislation because it desires to insulate heterosexual service members from statements that might excite their prejudices." The Justice Department is appealing this decision (*New York Times*, 31 March 1995).

In fact, the repression of gays and lesbians and the backlash against gay rights continues around the world. In Iran, over ninety homosexuals were arrested in August 1992 in a raid of a private party. Under Iranian law, the detainees will likely face the death penalty. It was reported that a doctor in the central Iranian city of Shiraz was executed for homosexuality that same year. Iranian law requires only the testimony of four male witnesses to impose the death sentence for homosexuality (*Advocate*, 20 October 1992).

The Grupo Gay da Bahia, a Brazilian gay organization, has documented the murders of 1,200 gays and lesbians in Brazil over the last decade. In Colombia over 328 anti-gay killings have been reported between 1986 and 1990, though, according to the Bogota-based human rights group Intercongregational Commission for Justice and Peace, most crimes against homosexuals go unreported. In Quito, Ecuador, in December 1991, eight homosexuals were killed on the streets, with the press reporting that the police knew in advance of at least one group of residents who had threatened to "clean up" the tourist sector by ridding it of homosexuals and prostitutes in this manner (Green & Asis 1993, 4–5).

In Nicaragua, President Violeta Chamorro is heading a conservative campaign against homosexuals, by signing into law a new penal code (article 204) which includes mandating sentences of one to three years for anyone who "induces, promotes, or practices in scandalous form sexual relations between persons of the same sex." In March 1994, the Nicaraguan Supreme Court rejected the claim that this tough anti-gay law was unconstitutional. The court labeled sodomy an "attack" on matrimony that threatened the "political, economic and social advancement of the country." Nicaragua is now enforcing the hemisphere's most draconian anti-gay law (IGLHRC, September/October 1994).

ACCEPTANCE AND EQUALITY

The concept of rights provides a language with which lesbians and gays as a group are able to confront such bigotry and prejudice. It is a useful tool for the community to utilize in the struggle for acceptance and equality. It is extremely significant that in the "Bill of Rights for a New South Africa," the African National Congress (ANC) Constitutional Committee includes a section on "Gender Rights," which categorically states that "discrimination on the grounds of gender, single parenthood, legitimacy of birth or sexual orientation shall be unlawful." The introduction to this document also calls attention to the importance of non-discrimination toward gay men and lesbians (ANC Constitutional Committee 1990, xi, 15). And article III of the Constitutional Principles of the new Constitution of the Republic of South Africa states: "The Constitution shall prohibit racial, gender and all other forms of discrimination and shall promote racial and gender equality and national unity" (Constitution of the Republic of South Africa 1994, 210).

TOWARD AN INTEGRATED UNDERSTANDING OF
INDIVIDUAL RIGHTS AND GROUP RIGHTS

The intersection of race/ethnicity, gender, and sexuality inform the outlook on collective human rights presented here. All three areas represent critical components to each individual identity and thus, by human necessity, must be incorporated into a normative framework of collective human rights. Collective human rights cannot be concerned with only one of these self-defining characteristics. An individual cannot just be defined by his or her ethnicity or gender or sexuality. Rather each identity revolves around a combination of all three. To highlight one at the expense of the others often leads to further fragmentation rather than cooperation, when groups assert their particular rights over other group rights. An individual should not have to face the dilemma confronting Dennis deLeon, that is, revelation of his sexuality alienating leaders of his race.

And finally, this unified conception of collective human rights needs to be understood in the context of the structures of class and power within modern society. These issues will be explored throughout this book, beginning in chapter 3, with an examination of a people's right to self-determination.

3

The Right to Self-Determination

The most commonly accepted collective human right is the right to self-determination. Both the Covenant on Civil and Political Rights and the Covenant on Economic, Social and Cultural Rights begin article 1 by declaring the right of peoples to self-determination, to "freely determine their political status and freely pursue their economic, social and cultural development." The next paragraph affirms the right of peoples' sovereignty over their natural resources. "All peoples may, for their own ends, freely dispose of their natural wealth and resources without prejudice to any obligations arising out of international economic co-operation, based upon the principle of mutual benefit, and international law. In no case may a people be deprived of its own means of subsistence" (Brownlie 1981, 118, 128). As Karel Vasak explains: "self-determination is to peoples what freedom is to individuals, that is to say, the very basis of their existence. While self-determination cannot be an individual human right, it is definitely the necessary condition for the very existence of human rights in the sense that, where it does not exist, man cannot be free since he is not allowed to liberate himself" (Vasak 1982, 5).

The concept of self-determination has been vigorously debated for decades, with advocates from opposing political perspectives often using the term to justify contradictory politics. In many respects, the concept taps into the essential questions regarding peoples and states, from which definitions of sovereignty emerge.

Early in the twentieth century, Wilson and Lenin presented competing visions of the right of nations to self-determination as an alternative to colonialism. As opposed to a balance of power operating among unequal states, they suggested a new international order of equal states operating collectively for their common security. For Wilson, the organization to provide this collective security was the League of Nations; for Lenin it was the Comintern. National self-determination was a popular demand of the socialist movement during the late nineteenth century. Lenin and Rosa Luxemburg had debated the phrase before World War I, but it was Wilson who popularized the phrase, in arguing that "all nations have the right to self-determination," and incorporated it into the League of Nations Covenant. In 1918, Wilson stated to Congress, "Self-determination is not a mere phrase. It is an imperative principle of action, which statesmen will henceforth ignore at their peril." As Schaeffer notes, to both Wilson and Lenin, self-determination meant the right of secession. As Lenin put it, "The right of nations to self-determination implies exclusively the right to independence in the political sense, the right to free political separation from the oppressor nation" (quoted in Schaeffer 1990, 50–51). Wilson drafted a secessionist proviso into article III of the League's covenant.[1] Both men saw their respective countries leading others toward this new international system. With Lenin's death and the United States refusing to follow Wilson into the League of Nations, these visions became blurred.

In the recent period, Salvatore Senese, Leo Matarasso, and other scholars have articulated a useful distinction between "internal self-determination" and "external self-determination," which helps clarify the relationship of the concept to peoples' sovereignty and democracy. Briefly, the distinction is as follows:

External self-determination is concerned with the international status of a people. It involves the recognition that a people has the right to constitute itself as a nation-state, or to integrate into, or federate with, an existing state. It embodies the right of all peoples to freedom from foreign, colonial, or racist domination. This principle is found in article 6 of the "Universal Declaration of the Rights of Peoples" (see appendix A), which states: "Every people has the right to break free from any colonial or foreign domination, whether direct or indirect, and from any racist regime." The notion of external self-determination is a critical facet of peoples' sovereignty (Senese 1989, 19; Matarasso 1989, 12).

Internal self-determination is concerned with the right of a people to freely choose its own political, economic and social system. This principle is found in article 7 of the "Universal Declaration of the Rights of Peoples," which states: "Every people has the right to a democratic regime representing all the citizens without distinction as to race, sex, belief or color, and capable of ensuring effective respect for the human rights and fundamental freedoms for all." Democracy is thus encompassed within the concept of internal self-determination (Matarasso 1989, 12).

This conception of external and internal self-determination provides a useful framework to analyze the idea in relation to issues of power, class, and rights.

EXTERNAL SELF-DETERMINATION AND PEOPLES' SOVEREIGNTY

The historic roots of the principle of external self-determination include the American Declaration of Independence and the decree of the French Constituent Assembly of May 1790, which refer both to individual rights and the rights of peoples. In fact, many scholars maintain that self-determination is the fundamental concept elevated by the Enlightenment and the French Revolution, both for individuals and for a people or nation. Self-determination has been credited with giving birth to all the important modern ideologies—liberalism, democracy, socialism, and nationalism (including anti-colonialism) (Kamenka 1988, 130).

In the twentieth century, the world has witnessed the drive for external self-determination on a global scale. The right to be free from unwarranted external interference, from colonial and imperial control as well as less visible international manipulations, is fundamental to the protection of peoples' sovereignty. Article 1, section 2, of the UN Charter states that one purpose of the UN is: "To develop friendly relations among nations based on respect for the principle of equal rights and self-determination of peoples" (Brownlie 1981, 4). The General Assembly has formally recognized self-determination as a fundamental human right and instructed the Economic and Social Council and the Commission of Human Rights to suggest means to ensure the right of peoples and nations to self-determination.

Further declarations from UN bodies regarding self-determination include the "Declaration on the Granting of Independence to Colonial Countries and Peoples," which declares that: "The subjection of peoples to alien subjugation, domination and exploitation constitutes a denial of fundamental human rights, is contrary to the Charter of the United Nations and is an impediment to the promotion of World peace and co-operation." Further, the declaration states: "Any attempt aimed at the partial or total disruption of the national unity and the territorial integrity of a country is incompatible with the purposes and principles of the Charter of the U.N." The document ends with the plea for all governments to respect the principle of "non-interference in the internal affairs of all States" (Brownlie 1981, 29–30).

Nation-states essentially agree on defining the principle of self-determination as freedom from external intervention. This does not mean, however, that they respect the principle; on the contrary, they have often violated it for perceived concerns of Realpolitik. External self-determination is a necessary, but not a sufficient, condition toward addressing the myriad of issues that fall within the scope of peoples' sovereignty.

THE DOMINANT STATIST FRAMEWORK

State sovereignty and self-determination are both upheld by international organizations, even though at times they conflict with each other. On 21 December 1965 in resolution 2131 (XX), the "Declaration on the Inadmissibility of Intervention in the Domestic Affairs of the States and the Protection of Their Independence and Sovereignty," the General Assembly declared state sovereignty to be based on the "inalienable right" of an independent state "to choose its political, economic, social and cultural systems, without interference in any form by another State" (Weston, Falk, & D'Amato 1990a, 195–96). It is a conservative principle—to preserve the structure of the international order. Advocates of self-determination, on the other hand, first promote the right to independent statehood for colonies or other entities under foreign control. In addition, such advocates also believe that ethnic minorities within the boundaries of existing nation-states deserve the right to self-determination, which includes the protection of each individual culture and heritage. And, finally, these advocates look beyond rights based on ethnicity to explore the essential relationships between other collective human rights to the principle of self-determination in order for these rights to have real meaning for the majority of humanity.

Self-determination provided the justification for what has been called the most far-reaching political realignment in recent international history—the collapse of formal imperialism and the post–World War II movement toward colonial independence (Beitz 1979, 93). However, the conflict between state sovereignty and self-determination remains unresolved.

For example, the 1966 International Covenant on Economic, Social, and Cultural Rights and the International Covenant on Civil and Political Rights, both provide the basis for claims of ethnic and indigenous peoples. In particular, article 1 in both covenants affirms the right of self-determination as belonging to "all peoples."[2] The "principle of equal rights and self-determination of peoples" is also embodied in the "Declaration on Principles of International Law Concerning Friendly Relations and Co-operation Among States in Accordance with the Charter of the United Nations" of 24 October 1970 (UNGA res. 2625 [XXV]):

> The establishment of a sovereign and independent State, the free association or integration with an independent State or the emergence into any other political status freely determined by a people constitute modes of implementing the right of self-determination by that people.

But, on the other hand, the territorial status quo is upheld by the following language in the same section:

> Nothing in the foregoing paragraphs shall be construed as authorizing or encouraging any action which would dismember or impair, totally or in part, the territorial integrity or political unity of sovereign and independent States

conducting themselves in compliance with the principle of equal rights and self-determination of peoples as described above and thus possessed of a government representing the whole people belonging to the territory without distinction as to race, creed or colour. (Weston, Falk, & D'Amato 1990a, 111–12)

In fact, upholding the primacy of state sovereignty was essential to the United Nations system from its inception. Charter provision article 2 (7) has been exceptionally controversial with regard to questions of discrimination and human rights:

Nothing contained in the present Charter shall authorize the United Nations to intervene in matters which are essentially within the domestic jurisdiction of any State or shall require the Members to submit such matters to settlement under the present Charter. (Brownlie 1981, 4)

This article provoked bitter comments from participants and activists at the time. For example, one professor noted: "As almost all, if not all, measures violating the fundamental rights of the individual, however defined, are held to be matters of domestic jurisdiction one cannot escape the conclusion that the United Nations have denied themselves the possibility of protecting such rights by international legal action" (McKean 1983, 56–57).

The affirmation of the rights of peoples to external self-determination is thus officially qualified in UN bodies by the centrality of state sovereignty.[3] Hence, peoples are dealt with in a very artificial and contradictory way. In many recognized nation-states, antagonistic nationalities as well as indigenous peoples are excluded from governments. When state power is captured by one people, too often minorities and other peoples are subjected to injustice and a denial of human rights (see, for example, Schaeffer 1990, 153–86).

A statist view of self-determination holds that the concept only applies to those states subject to control and domination by an external foreign power. For many suppressed people, however, self-determination thus becomes empty and meaningless, as they are at the mercy of domestic laws (not foreign aggressors). Examples include Kurds subordinated within the states of Iraq, Iran, and Turkey and indigenous people, who have been overwhelmingly marginalized and placed outside the framework of normal political functioning (see Falk 1988, 26–27).

PEOPLES' SOVEREIGNTY

This statist framework has, nonetheless, been challenged by advocates for peoples' sovereignty. The determination of which people are eligible for self-determination has generated controversy and a challenge to the position that states and peoples are synonymous. Brownlie believes that the principle of self-determination has "a core of reasonable certainty . . . the right of a community which has a distinct character to have this character reflected in the institutions of government under which it lives" (Brownlie 1988, 5).

Makinson points out that peoples cannot simply be identified with states. "A people is a kind of collectivity, or group of human beings; a State is a kind of governing and administering apparatus." Thus, even when a state in theory represents the people, the two are distinct (Makinson 1988, 73).

The UN covenants avoid any clarification of what is to count as a people. Rather, the concept of a people was politically understood to apply only to those within the borders of European colonies in Africa and other regions. The normative grounds for these decisions were said to be based on the protection of distinct peoples. The irony of this action was that the application of the "right of peoples to self-determination" in practice meant *moving single peoples* from the former colonies into different artificially created states. A major task confronting these newly formed states was to forge a sense of national unity.

Some scholars critique modernization theories, Marxist theories, dependency and world system theories, and empiricist descriptions, as being too concerned about power at the top and too state-centered. "For the Third World, a state-centered approach is a bit like looking at a mousetrap without at all understanding the mouse" (Migdal 1988, xvi). Western powers historically seek to accomplish their objectives through established states or by creating new ones. There remains a duality, however, within Third World states. On the one hand, they have demonstrated an unmistakable strength in being able to control aspects of society, such as foreign and military policy. Yet, on the other hand, they have proven to be surprisingly weak in effecting fundamental internal economic or social change.

The weakness of the state stems partly from the reality of strong social relations that exist *independently* of the state's control. Such relations include small families and neighborhoods, clans, clubs, communities, tribes, and so on, which "behave in their interactions according to certain rules or norms, whether those were interactions between father and son, employer and employee, landlord and tenant, priest and parishioner, . . . including what age to marry, what crop to grow, what language to speak" (Migdal 1988, 25). In the Third World, Migdal finds that "legions of strategies" have been at work in areas claimed by single states, and as a result social control is highly fragmented. Society cannot be depicted as part of a dichotomous structure, as assumed by practically all past models of macro-level change (e.g., center-periphery, modern-traditional, etc.) Rather, the distribution of social control is shared among fairly autonomous groups. The struggle is then over whether the state will be able to displace or harness other organizations—family, clan, domestic enterprises, tribes, and so forth—which make rules against the wishes and goals of state leaders (Migdal 1988, 31).

As new concepts regarding the rights of peoples are developing, a statist world order may no longer provide the answers. Within established states, demands of racial and cultural minorities for recognition as independent peoples under the principle of self-determination could be the beginning of a new international realignment. As Senese wrote: "to draw all the consequences implied in the principle of self-determination, would lead to an upheaval in the world order" (Senese 1986, 10). The international order has inadequately addressed humanity's dramatic problems, which has led many to call for a reexamination of the relationship between the individual and the state. For the majority of people in Third World countries, the state form is nothing more than a recent functional implant. Every population should be able to determine its own choices and orientation, according to its own life conditions and its own customs (Chesneaux 1988, 38–41). It is not clear that the state, in terms of a territorial entity, is the most appropriate basis for this kind of autonomous development. For millions of people in the Third World, state sovereignty did not constitute a change for the better in their lives.

INTERNAL SELF-DETERMINATION AND DEMOCRACY

Gaining freedom from colonial, racist, or foreign domination is a necessary condition for the exercise of peoples' sovereignty, but it is not sufficient. Self-determination is also the right of a people to take its destiny into its hands, to be permanently master of its own fate free from authoritarian and repressive regimes. Internal self-determination involves the right of a people to determine their political status freely.

Internal self-determination is the right to choose a government freely, which involves the exercise of all the liberties which make such a choice possible, including freedom of thought, of assembly, of association, and of political choice. Further, it attempts to guard against tyranny, by asserting the collective human right of peoples' sovereignty, that is to say, that a government is always founded on the consensus of the people (Matarasso 1989, 11).

The classical Marxist framework insists that any talk of self-determination must include a discussion of class. Rosa Luxemburg, for example, felt that it was incorrect and non-Marxist to talk in terms of absolute rights, including the right to self-determination. A dialectical analysis does not recognize the existence of rights in general; rather the rights and wrongs of a given situation must be evaluated through an analysis of the given historical circumstances. There is no absolute right to freedom from oppression. Such questions, she maintained, are questions of power, and are settled as such. She said that telling workers that they had the right to self-determination was like telling them that they had the right to eat off gold plates (quoted in Davis 1978, 58).

Robert Cox describes the Marxist dialectic as a "dialogue seeking truth through the explorations of contradictions . . . the knowledge that each assertion concerning reality contains implicitly its opposite and that both assertion and opposite are not mutually exclusive but share some measure of the truth sought, a truth, moreover, that is always in motion, never to be encapsulated in some definitive form" (Cox 1986, 215).

Marx focused on abstractions which incorporate both change and interaction in the particular forms they take in the capitalist era. Such a process of abstraction moves beyond appearance, and searches for systemic and historical connections. This means looking at where something came from and where it seems to be heading as part of what it is today. The Marxist dialectical method of abstraction allows one to analyze contradictions in the concept of collective human rights, and, by adopting the vantage point of the working class, to perceive its strengths and limitations.

According to Marxist theory, in a class society, to speak of self-determination for the people means, in most circumstances, the self-determination of the ruling class, with the workers remaining in a subordinate position. Third World revolutionary leaders have long made this point. Frantz Fanon was extremely critical of the bourgeois nationalism which developed in the colonies and ex-colonial countries. "[They favor nationalism] in order to transfer into native hands those unfair advantages which are the legacy of the colonized period. . . . [They follow] the Western bourgeoisie along its path of negation and decadence." The native bourgeoisie would not build up their respective countries, would not industrialize them or launch them on the road to prosperity and progress. Power will continue to be exercised by the metropolitan countries, operating through the new bourgeoisie and through the army and police forces which they build up and train. Fanon saw alienation arising as much from class oppression, as from national oppression. Class oppression is not de facto ended by national liberation (Fanon 1966, 122, 124).[4]

Julius Nyerere suggested that overemphasis on the slogan of self-determination in the campaign for decolonization may make the eventual attainment of a just and equitable society more difficult.[5]

In the Marxist paradigm, nationalism, national unity, and self-determination are not ends in themselves. Rather they are seen as means to an end, often effective instruments that can permit the working class to concentrate on its true class interests. As Horace Davis posed the question: Why would one take a position for or against self-determination? One does not take a position for or against a hammer, or a can opener. Nationalism and self-determination as a movement against national oppression, has a positive moral content; as a vehicle of aggression, it is morally indefensible. Therefore, according to Marxism, for self-determination to be of importance to the oppressed, it must be anti-capitalist and anti-imperialist (1978, 31).

Marx and Engels wrote, in a letter to Kautsky (with reference to Poland), that a people desiring development must first secure independence, and it is not the job of others to tell them that their national independence is a secondary matter. Some Marxists argue that self-determination is thus part of Marx's vision of the future—not in the sense of national chauvinism, seeking to advance the interests of one's own nation at the expense of others—but nationalism in the Rousseauean sense of seeking the welfare of the collectivity (Davis 1967, 17–18).

Lenin called for the right of self-determination of nations, and argued that the working class should be free of national as well as class oppression. After the worldwide proletariat revolution, national partitions will disappear; *but* the differentiation of humanity, in the sense of "the wealth and variety in spiritual life, ideological trends, tendencies and shades," will increase "a million-fold." Nationalism as a cultural phenomenon will survive and increase.[6]

Marx's frame of reference was the world capitalist system. When he writes of the entire society, he is referring to the world system dominated by the capitalist mode of production. It is from this vantage point that one begins to understand Marx's view on the role of the nation and the state. Divisions of geography, politics, language, culture, and so on were secondary, whereas the real unit of historical analysis was the whole of human society.[7]

Marx saw that the international ruling class had a general, common interest that went beyond national boundaries. He wrote, "the *wolf* as a *wolf* has an identical interest with his fellow wolves, however much it is to the interest of each individual wolf that he and not another should pounce on the prey"[8] (Marx [1971] 1975, 275).

In sum, within Marxism, nationalism is part of the dominant ideology which causes humans to live in isolation from one another. Liberation means freeing people to live as "world-historical" individuals. However, Marx had a very *practical* attitude toward the nationalism of his day. He supported struggles for self-determination in Poland and in Ireland. These struggles were important to take into account while developing revolutionary strategy. Marx would not ascribe *theoretical* significance to nationalist struggles, because ultimately they are based on ruling ideology. He would, however, ascribe *political* significance to such struggles, if they served to weaken bourgeois forces on a national and international level (Szporluk 1988, 51–53).

CONCLUSION

Advocates of collective human rights argue that nationalism, as the sole expression of self-determination, does not satisfy the individual desire for freedom, and leads to fragmentation, as demonstrated by demands of ethnicity/ race, class, sexuality, and gender throughout the nations of the world. As previously noted, however, coinciding with the fragmentation of nation-state power are strong economic forces promoting global integration.

In the context of such upheaval, the nation-state has no special status. The dilemma of resolving the individual's relationship to society may not necessarily be through the nation-state. It may be easier to achieve democracy and individual freedom through smaller organized units. If large-scale economic frameworks could be established that preserve the benefits of extensive cooperation, then the nation-state might be replaced by smaller units.[9]

Rousseau's image is still influential—each individual uniting herself or himself with all and yet remaining as free as before. The nation-state system has not lived up to this image, as more and more groups and individuals are denied their rights. In fact, on two counts, it has failed miserably: First, as Marxists continuously point out, economic inequality and rigid class structures are incompatible with political equality. Second, there is an unresolved tension between the importance of the individual versus the importance of the community. Rousseau's solution was to look in the direction of a small utopia, and perhaps more freedom could be provided today through smaller political units within a world society. World society or world community has been used to refer to an integrated worldwide system possessing common interests, values, rules, and institutions, often distinct from those of states. Collective human rights can be seen as part of these evolving values and norms.

Proponents of collective human rights clearly reject a nationalist approach toward human freedom and emancipation. However, self-determination as a collective human right during this historical time period, as a mechanism to expose suffering and inequities present in the current world system, *is* often strongly advocated. Much depends upon how the concept is used and whether it is seen as an end in itself, or as a step on the way to a larger project of the emancipation of all peoples.

The objective of most advocates of collective human rights is the self-determination of peoples and not of nations. Respect for the culture, language, history, and customs of a people is central to the concept of self-determination.

Each people has the right to develop all of these aspects free from all inter-ference. This approach does not require replacing a class analysis of society. Rather, by incorporating class analysis into one's understanding of self-deter-mination, the value of the concept is enhanced in the following way: Instead of being a conservative doctrine dedicated to upholding the current world system of sovereign nation-states, self-determination potentially becomes a tool useful in exposing not only the workings of imperialist domination and new forms of neo-colonialism (external self-determination) but also the root causes of economic oppression which deny the majority of humanity the ability to determine their own lives (internal self-determination).

4

The Morality of the Depths

The Right to Development as an
Emerging Principle of International Law

> Everyone is entitled to a social and international order in which the rights
> and freedoms set forth in this Declaration can be fully realized.
> —Article 28 of the *Universal Declaration of Human Rights*

For decades philosophers, political scientists, and economists have grappled
with the relationship between morality, justice, rights, and development.[1]
Through various organs of the United Nations (UN), the international community has addressed these concerns in an ongoing debate on the idea of a
collective "right to development." At the 1993 Vienna World Conference on
Human Rights, the United States accepted the validity of development as a
human right. A priority at the UN's 1995 Copenhagen World Summit for
Social Development was to formulate the duties and obligations of states that
flow from this emerging, internationally affirmed right to development. To
many activists and academics in the poorer countries of the Southern Hemisphere, a successful articulation of a state's duties and obligations arising
from the UN's right to development could represent breakthrough progress in
the human rights arena.

The historical evolution of the right to development has been summarized in detail elsewhere.[2] The purpose of this chapter is threefold:

1. To articulate a conception of the right to development as a right to equal
   opportunity and an emerging principle of international law.

2. To discover if the legal and moral basis to the right to development has
   significantly deepened as a result of the work of international governmental organizations (IGOs).

3. To begin to explore the legal and moral duties that arise for states from
   the right to development.

69

It has been almost a decade since the UN approved the Declaration on the Right to Development. During this time, have the legal obligations of states been clarified so that the right to development is more than a rhetorical appeal from the South for justice?

1. THE RIGHT TO DEVELOPMENT AND INTERNATIONAL LAW

The Debate

Controversy continues to swirl around the validity of a right to development, defined by the United Nations in 1986 as the right of "every human person and all peoples . . . to participate in, contribute to and enjoy economic, social, cultural and political development, in which all human rights and fundamental freedoms can be fully realized." The UN declaration continues: "States have the right and duty to formulate appropriate national development policies that aim at the constant improvement of the well-being of the entire population and of all individuals, on the basis of their active, free and meaningful participation in development and in the fair distribution of the benefits resulting therefrom" (Weston, Falk, & D'Amato 1990a, 486).

On one side of the debate are those scholars who believe that this right remains on the level of political rhetoric. Many of these writers see no legal or moral basis for the right, and some advocate that it be abandoned altogether. One characterized the right to development as "mumbo jumbo par excellence." The lack of legal positivist action on the part of the world's elites is pointed to as proof of the lack of grounding for this new right.[3]

Proponents, on the other side, discuss the importance of an "emerging right" to development within international human rights law. They argue that it is a general principle that is in the process of being transformed into positive law. Key to that process is article 28 of the Universal Declaration (quoted above). Respect for human rights involves not only the obligations of states to individuals, but also all economic, social, and political relations. Human rights apply at the local, national, and international levels. In addition, there is a collective, social dimension to what it means to be a human being that must be included in any discussion of "human rights." The emerging right to development, as a collective human right, attempts to take these relations into account (Alston 1985, 515–16).

Critics may be correct that the all-encompassing nature of the UN definition of the right to development makes the task of defining the specific legal duties and obligations of states required by this emerging right more difficult. Critics may also be correct in pointing to the rhetorical manner in which the right has often been used. However, I believe that it would be a mistake to dismiss the political and theoretical importance of the right to development. First, the right to development points to a fundamental truth: for human rights to be taken seriously, conditions of equal opportunity must be developed. Development is multidimensional, and the UN should be applauded for attempting to address the complexity of the issue. Second, the international community has put a great deal of work into conceptualizing this new right. It has been accepted by state and nonstate actors to such an extent that, as I argue below, it can now be considered an emerging principle of international law. For those of us concerned with human dignity and justice, it would be foolish to disregard this, for the right to development gives us a vehicle to vigorously pursue a dynamic human rights agenda for the twenty-first century.

Equal Opportunity

The key to understanding the right to development is to take seriously the importance of equal opportunity. Human rights scholars and activists acknowledge that for human rights to achieve their intended purpose, they must be available to all equally. Otherwise, these rights can become one more tool for the powerful to maintain privilege, often using the very language of rights to justify continuing policies of oppression and exploitation. As a way to avoid this misuse of rights language, many human rights activists assert a "right" to equal opportunity.

In the economic system of global capitalism, a challenge of human rights is to carve out an area of protection that is exempt from the often pernicious and maldistributive effects of this system. For all people to have an opportunity to live a life of dignity demands nothing less. Here lies the solution to the dilemmas found in the "right to development." It is not a call for charity. It is not simply a moral obligation to "help one's fellow man." Rather, it is a call to give everyone an equal chance to participate fully in an economic system that can be unjust and exploitative if protective measures are not taken. The right to development requires that those state and nonstate actors, with power over others, strive to prevent the human suffering often caused from this vigorous economic system. This right declares that these commanding actors have a duty to strive to uphold a minimal economic floor, that is, to meet certain basic subsistence requirements, so that every person is given an equal chance to participate freely and fully in the global economic system.[4] The United Nations Development Programme (UNDP) stated it as follows: "This equity is, however, in *opportunities*—not necessarily in final achievements. Each individual is entitled to a just opportunity to make the best use of his or her potential capabilities. So is each generation. How they actually use these opportunities, and the results they achieve, are a matter of their own choice. But they must have such a choice—now and in the future" (1994, 13).

The right to development can be seen as a collective human right. Earlier chapters have discussed the constant tension between the rights of the individual member of society and the collective rights of certain groups, identifying both an individual and a social component to every human being. We have noted that sociality is an inherent part of the human personality which provides the logic to the formulation of collective human rights, and draws our attention to the relationships and patterns of interactions between the individual and the group. These group rights focus attention on the lack of a "level playing field" between and within most nation-states of the world today, largely because of race, class, and gender discrimination. Certain groups, such as ruling elites and majority ethnic groups, have greater opportunities to consolidate positions of power. By clarifying the right to development as a right to equal opportunity for all, we raise and confront these issues of power. Equal opportunity requires making the structural changes in the global economic system that inform the right to development. In my view, there is a moral imperative that we pursue this direction in our approach to human rights and not limit our framework of analysis to that of an elite worldview.

There is a symbiotic relationship between individual rights and group rights. For individual rights to be available equally to all individuals requires that certain group rights, such as the right to development, also be addressed. They are mutually reinforcing. This dialectical approach toward understanding rights is often missing in individual human rights paradigms.

An Emerging Principle of International Law

To a significant extent the debate on the right to development at the UN has focused on creating conditions of equal opportunity for all. This international process of norm creation within the UN and other international organizations provides a basis for an initial evaluation of how new moral and legal standards are being defined and to assess the degree of acceptance of these new precepts by state and nonstate actors. Through these international fora the world community has taken a strong stand in favor of the right to development. It is thus time to reassess the position of this emerging right within international law.

A state is bound by international law not only through positivist treaty or custom, but also through general principles of law. The norm of equity, for example, is widely accepted as a general principle of international law, even though extensive debate continues as to its specific content. Some international legal scholars note that the phrase "general principles" allows a court to go outside generally accepted rules of international law. Looking to general principles of international law implies, therefore, a break with positivist doctrines that only rules created by a formal treaty process or a reliance on general custom are valid (von Glahn 1992, 12, 21). To most legal scholars, the "sources of international law" are found in article 38 of the Statute of the International Court of Justice (ICJ), which includes a direction to the Court to apply the "general principles of law recognized by civilized nations" in its deliberations.

The phrase "general principles of law" means, of course, different things to different people. Some argue that general principles allow international lawyers to apply natural law. Others contend that such principles can only be drawn from customary international practice. A third group believes that the general principles are found in comparative law, that is, a proposition of law so fundamental that it will be found in virtually every legal system. International tribunals over the years have relied on all three interpretations (Weston, Falk, & D'Amato 1990b, 117–18).

There are principles that are not yet part of customary or conventional international law, but have been consistently affirmed in the international judicial arena and accepted in the practice of states. "General principles of law" has been taken to connote principles so general as to apply within all systems of law that have achieved a comparable state of development. To many international legal scholars, these "principles" are to be looked for in municipal law (Henkin, Pugh, Schachter, & Smit 1987, 89). The ICJ has on several occasions applied principles which are "generally recognized" in municipal law, but which have not acquired the status of customary rules internationally. A study by Judge Mosler of the ICJ found that international tribunals had employed a comparative methodology to establish general principles of law for international rules concerning liability for damages, unjust enrichment, right of passage over territory, administrative law, and the doctrine of *res judicata* (Janis 1993, 58). Oscar Schachter notes that general principles add "a flexible element which enables the Court to give greater completeness to customary law and in some limited degree to extend it" (Henkin, Pugh, Schachter, & Smit 1987, 91–92).

The world's domestic legal systems consistently affirm principles to promote equality and equal opportunity, to provide for the common welfare, and to promote the general happiness. In other words, the core content of the right to development is easily identified in comparative legal systems, which to many legal scholars is the defining element of a general principle of international law. The notion of common consent emerges from this coincidence of municipal rules of law. As a result, although customary law and treaty law may not explicitly affirm these norms, they can nevertheless be considered general principles of international law. To many legal scholars, the right to development is such a norm.

General principles of law are usually "evolved" principles that regularly inform the practice of states and the decisions of international organizations. They have already passed the stage of repeated application. They differ from treaties and customary international law in that customs and treaties are both formulated in what are usually fairly clear rights and obligations with specific subjects bearing these rights and obligations. This is not the case with general principles of law, which are generally formulated as broad axioms (Mestdagh 1981a, 155; 1981b, 38–41).

Clearly this liberal interpretation of general principles is controversial. It is a view of international law as a *process* toward clarifying the moral and ethical standards to evaluate the behavior of global actors, rather than merely as a list of rules. Proponents of this position argue that there is an urgent need within international society to recognize certain rights in principle, even though the obligations pursuant to the rights may not be able to be articulated precisely. This can provide an incentive to work toward an elaboration of their substance, in treaties and in custom. In this way general principles become part of the process of the progressive development of international law.

At this stage in its evolution, the right to development does not clearly demarcate concrete rights and obligations of specified subjects. Treaty obligations and customary practice are missing. However, this does not mean that the right to development is not emerging as a principle of international law with commensurate legal duties and obligations. The Secretary-General of the UN has concluded that there are a large number of principles of law based on the UN Charter and the international texts of human rights laid down in covenants, declarations, and recommendations which demonstrate the existence of the right to development in international law. In addition, other legal scholars argue that over the last two decades, nation-state practice has affirmed the right to development as a general principle of international law. Just as states are bound to respect a people's right to self-determination as a principle of law, even though controversy often surrounds the definition of who has this right, so do all states have the duty to recognize and promote the right to development, even though controversy surrounds the precise nature of this right (Mestdagh 1981a, 156).

Some will undoubtedly argue here that I am engaged in sophistry. The standard way to demonstrate the existence of a right is either a convention or a customary right/duty evidenced by state action connected with *opinio juris*, an indication that states regard the act in question as a matter of duty undertaken to fulfill a right. Obviously no such evidence appears here. Critics could argue that the placement of phone calls to the legal advisers at the U. S. State Department, U. K. Foreign Ministry, French Foreign Ministry as well as the foreign ministries in the People's Republic of China and Russia would quickly disabuse us of the notion that states accept a legal duty to assist the poor of other countries. What is the evidence that a new principle of international law includes a global obligation to assist those in need? Further, critics could argue that while it is true that the right to development is acknowledged in a broad range of international norms, customs, and practices, it is also true that the bulk of nation-state activity serves to sabotage this alleged right. Doesn't the reality of the second premise undermine the authenticity of the first?

Yet, the fact that states violate emerging rights does not in itself negate these new norms. Domestic law is violated all the time. More important to the argument here, however, is how international law is conceptualized. The essence of international law is not the truly neutral application of agreed upon rules codified in treaties. Rather, international law should be viewed as a normative system linked to the achievement of common values. A leader who makes her decisions on the basis of international law is not merely finding the appropriate rule and then applying it. Rather she would be interested in a variety of phenomena—claims and counterclaims, state practice, decisions by a variety of authorized decision-makers, resolutions of international organizations. All of this, according to Rosalyn Higgins, makes up the fabric of international law (1994, 10).

International law has also been described as one vehicle for articulating a universal interest, for example, common threats to human survival. It is a system where norms emerge either through express consent or consensus with reciprocity as a central element. For a variety of reasons, including the advantages of cooperation and self-restraint, states come to regard themselves as bound by international legal norms. As Louis Henkin has demonstrated, it is rarely in the national interest to violate international law, even when there is a short-term advantage to do so (Henkin 1979). Law is thus a process of decision-making—a normative system of decision-making.

International organization, and the United Nations in particular, plays an important role in this normative decision-making process and thus in the progressive development of international law. The requirements of custom—practice, repetition, *opinio juris*—may occur at an accelerated pace in the world of an international organization (Higgins 1994, 23).[5] The International Court of Justice in the *Namibia Advisory Opinion* noted that General Assembly resolutions, while not binding, were not without legal effect. The former legal counsel of the United Nations stated: "The General Assembly, through its solemn declarations, can therefore give an important impetus to the emergence of new rules, despite the fact that the adoption of declarations per se does not give them the quality of binding norms" (Slomanson 1995, 23).

There is thus a strong "soft law"[6] case for the right to development as an emerging principle of international law. The term "soft law" is paradoxical because many of the instruments referred to are not, strictly speaking, law. Many argue, for example, that the wide variety of international instruments pertaining to development—resolutions, declarations, charters of rights and duties, and final acts from international organizations and conferences—present a substantial "soft law" case for this emerging right. These instruments are not "hard law," that is, treaties or customary law, yet their impact on state behavior can be significant. These instruments do create an environment of strong expectation that states will gradually conform their conduct to meet the requirements of the adopted resolution or declaration. Even the ICJ in its judgments and advisory opinions (Namibia case [1971]; Fisheries Jurisdiction case [1974]; Western Sahara case [1975]) has given legal significance to collective resolutions of the General Assembly and of international conferences despite their formally nonbinding character.

This broader approach toward international law challenges legal positivism which limits "law" to state acceptance and adherence to the rules primarily demarcated in treaties and general custom. Legal positivism unfortunately leaves the definition of new norms and rights to the powerful groups that dominate the current nation-state system. Counterposed to this are paradigms presented by such scholars as Philip Alston, Johan Galtung, Rajni Kothari, Keba M'Baye, Ved Nanda, Roland Rich, George Shepherd, Jr., and Theo van Boven, who challenge the status quo and attempt to articulate avenues for the realization of this new right to development.[7] This approach is often called a "structural approach" to human rights, as the concern is with removing the structural obstacles erected by elites that stand in the way of rights becoming actualized (Ramphal 1981, 37–38). These normative approaches often emphasize the fact that rights within inequality are often meaningless for the bottom half of the world's people. These scholars argue that as an approach to human rights, legal positivism represents a pinched and elite-based methodology.

These arguments focus the debate on the right to development on the centrality of the human being in his or her social environment. Instead of examining the development of "things," "systems," "structures," or "productive forces," often the focus of liberal and Marxist development theories, they identify the absolute *needs* of the individual and the group as central to development paradigms, with the idea that such lists constitute a frame of reference to be examined in the development process (Galtung & Wirak 1976, 40, 43). As George Shepherd writes: "The fundamental position of the right to development approach is that development must begin and end with a concern for the human condition and that this is a collective international responsibility" (1990, 9).

A needs-based approach defines an alternative to legal positivism for understanding the right to development. How can individuals who are denied their basic needs make demands on the national and international system to have these needs met? Can they compel a basic reorientation of development priorities? Or, as Charles Dias, president of the International Center for Law in Development, put it, "Can norms be fashioned out of this principle to channel the exercise of discretion in the direction of meeting basic human needs? . . . Can the . . . [right to development] principle be invoked to fashion new obligations/fiduciary relationships for state agencies involved in the production or distribution of basic resources?" (1981, 189). Through the right to development, the poor claim the right to a minimal level of human decency. The rich and powerful, affluent and privileged, are legally obligated to address these demands, not with charity, but with the structural reforms necessary to provide for true equity. The emerging principle of international law established by this new right is that there is a collective international responsibility for the human condition.

2. THE UNITED NATIONS ON DEVELOPMENT

At the United Nations the emphasis on development planning shifted in the 1980s from accelerating economic growth to resolving the problems of income distribution and job creation. The premise that development should be defined solely, or even primarily, in terms of economic growth was fundamentally challenged. In fact, development was seen as equally dependent on the just distribution of goods and services within a society. The lack of attention to distribution meant that after decades of "development," poverty alleviation in many developing countries remained illusory (Vanda 1985b, 432).

During the 1980s the United Nations formulated the right to development in the context of a right of equal opportunity. For example, the UN Commission on Human Rights characterized the right to development as a right to the "realization of the potentialities of the human person in harmony with the community." The right has also been understood as a process designed to *create conditions* in which every person can enjoy and exercise all his or her human rights, including economic, social, cultural, civil, and political rights. In other words, everyone has the right under international law to participate in and benefit from development to improve the quality of his or her life.[8] Just as certain actions must be taken to assure equality of opportunity for all individuals and groups inside the boundaries of nation-states, so must similar actions be taken internationally to guarantee equality of opportunity.

For the poorest peoples of the South this means overcoming the global maldistribution of wealth. Many calls for international distributive justice have thus been made at various UN meetings. A striking theme of these calls is a concern for collectivist, rather than individualist, approaches to human rights. Prime among such collective human rights is the right to development (van Boven 1982b, 20–39, 68–75).

A stark global reality of misery informs the discussion of the right to development at the United Nations. Economic globalization—a single, integrated world economy—has had a profound effect on human existence, *structurally* limiting equality of opportunity. One-fourth of our world is rich, while the vast majority is poor. The most vicious ethnic strife is among the poor. Migration is not permitted. Redistribution of income is not considered.

Two of the structural features within our single integrated world economy that account for the extent of economically generated adversity in the world today are hierarchy and unevenness. Hierarchy refers to the domination of the global economy by North America, Japan, and Europe, augmented by the Asian dragons, while unevenness points to the vastly differing effects of globalization on the economic and social condition of peoples, classes, genders, ethnic groupings, races, and civilizations. Unevenness extends within the North and South itself, as demonstrated by the persistence of homelessness and significant unemployment in the North and an apparently co-opted elite in the South who have more in common with the interests and outlook of the North than with their own peoples (Falk 1992b, 4, 12, 13).

The result of this hierarchy and unevenness in the global economy can be starkly seen in a few statistics from the UNICEF report on *The State of the World's Children 1994* (UNICEF 1994, 16, 20, 46) and the UNDP's *Human Development Report* for 1993 and 1994 (UNDP 1993, 12, 13; 1994, 2):

- Approximately 1.2 billion people in the developing world are today denied access to a bare minimum of safe drinking water. With present patterns of progress continuing, an estimated 770 million people will still be without water by the end of the century, and the number of people without adequate sanitation will have increased to approximately 1.9 billion.

- An estimated 190 million children under age five are chronically malnourished, locked early into a pattern of ill health and poor development.

The problem is most widespread in South Asia, home to half the world's malnourished children.

- While America's economy grew by approximately 20% in the 1980s, some 4 million more American children fell into poverty. In total, one in five youngsters now lives below the poverty line—a rate twice that of any other industrialized country.

- Some 800 million people still do not get enough food. Almost one-third of the total population of developing countries, or 1.3 billion people, are in absolute poverty.

- People in industrial countries make up about one-fifth of world population but consume ten times more commercial energy than people in developing countries, and they account for 71% of the world's carbon monoxide emissions and 68% of the world's industrial waste.

- Global military spending still equals the combined income of one-half of humanity each year. The richest billion people command 60 times the income of the poorest billion.

Advocates for the right to development seek to address these disturbing realities. Without development there are few meaningful rights for the majority of the world's population. This is not rhetoric but reality. If equal opportunity to enjoy human rights and life itself is to be respected, then the *right* to development is a necessity. This approach corresponds to the framework of identifying "needs" for individuals and groups to survive. These needs, in turn, lead to a new definition of human rights—a definition far more compelling than any supplied by legal positivists.

The Global Consultation

The Global Consultation on the Right to Development as a Human Right was convened in Geneva in January 1990. Participants included representatives from more than fifty governments, forty nongovernmental organizations, twenty experts, and a dozen UN programs and agencies. The Global Consultation focused on the ways in which both the structure of international economic relations and the distribution of internal economic power worked as impediments to the achievement of human rights (Barsh 1991, 323, 326).

The report from the Global Consultation links development to democracy and participation, reinforcing the mutually dependent nature of political and economic rights. The report notes that in contrast to the policies of international institutions, "no one model of development is universally applicable to all cultures and peoples." What constitutes "development is largely subjective, and in this respect development strategies must be determined by the people themselves and adapted to their particular conditions and needs." It follows that participation must be "the primary mechanism for identifying appropriate goals and criteria" for the development process (see Barsh 1991, 328).

The conditions for democratic participation include "a fair distribution of economic and political power among all sectors of national society," and "genuine ownership or control of productive resources such as land, financial capital, and technology." Participation is "effective in mobilizing human and natural resources and combatting inequalities, discrimination, poverty and exclusion. . . . States must not only take concrete steps to improve economic, social and cultural conditions and to facilitate the efforts of individuals and groups for that objective, but must do so in a manner that is democratic in its formulation and in its results."[9]

Thus we see the UN continue to embrace a structural approach to the right to development, based on the primacy of meeting basic human needs. The Global Consultation seems to agree with the definition of development given by Keba M'Baye, former president of the UN's Commission on Human Rights, "the recognized prerogative of every individual and every people to enjoy in just measure the goods and services produced thanks to the effort of solidarity of the members of the community" (International Commission of Jurists 1981, 7).

Second, the Global Consultation discussed the direct participation in UN programs on development of "the people and groups directly or indirectly affected through their own representative organizations," including "indigenous peoples, workers' organizations, women's groups," peasants, and other so-called grassroots organizations. The right to development was seen as a process of empowering "individuals and groups within the state by giving them standing to participate in international economic cooperation" (Barsh 1991, 332).

This approach to "participation" was later affirmed in the 1993 UNDP's *Human Development Report*, which focused on "people's participation." The UNDP sought to redefine the concept of security as security for people, not security for land. It attempted "to weave development around people, not people around development," and sought to ensure that "development cooperation focuses directly on people, not just on nation-states." The Report concentrated on participation in development—through markets, government, and community organizations. "Participation means that people are closely involved in the economic, social, cultural and political processes that affect their lives." "The important thing is that people have constant access to decision-making and power. Participation in this sense is an essential element of human development" (UNDP 1993, 21, 29).

The Global Consultation and the UNDP have therefore adopted the understanding of the right to development presented here, that is, that it is a right of equal opportunity. The right to development defines basic protections so that every individual may participate fully in society. Basic protections refers to the basic subsistence requirements necessary for human survival. A claim is made to the state and the international community for continual assistance to facilitate these tasks and provide this protection—everyone's minimum reasonable demands on the rest of humanity. David Makinson writes that the prime external bearers of the obligations to fulfill the right to development are conceived as the wealthy, and more developed countries are understood as bearing a distributive obligation to all of the poorer ones, particularly the poorest (1988, 81). Can we define these obligations more specifically?

3. DUTIES TO RESPECT, PROTECT, AND AID

If we define the right to development as an emerging principle of international law, what are the corresponding duties that flow from this right? The definition of the right to development coming from the United Nations (quoted above) is so broad that defining duties seems almost impossible. However, a key component to *all* conceptions and definitions of this right is the necessity to meet basic human subsistence requirements. This therefore gives us a place to begin defining duties. Other components and aspects to the definition of the right to development depend significantly upon basic subsistence requirements being met.

An analogy can again be made to the right to self-determination, which has both an internal and external component. To achieve self-determination, a people must first free themselves from colonial and imperial exploitation and control. The right to self-determination does not stop there, but then moves to the "internal" phase, that is, a people's right to control their own government and political system. However, we can begin to define the duties that flow from this right by focusing first on the external component—the obligation of states to respect the rights of peoples to be freed from all outside intervention. After those duties are defined we can then outline the other responsibilities and duties that flow from the right to self-determination so that the right can be fully actualized.

This same process of defining the duties of states that flow from a principle of law, like the right to self-determination, can be applied to the right to development. We focus first on the duties that flow from subsistence rights, and after those are met, other duties and obligations can be clarified. For a state to meet this preliminary part of its legal duties under the right to development, what responsibilities to meet subsistence claims must be met? Economic rights are spelled out in the 1966 International Covenant on Economic, Social and Cultural Rights. At a minimum, these rights include adequate food, housing, health care, and the right to work. The collective right to development provides a mechanism for individuals and groups to focus attention on the structural constraints blocking the path toward achievement of these individual economic rights.[10] Only after these economic rights are met can the other parts to the right to development be addressed.

The UN has recognized that subsistence rights alone are not adequate to meet the composite claims articulated in the right to development. A prison, for example, can provide minimal subsistence, yet its inmates obviously live restricted lives. For individuals to benefit from development the full panoply of civil, political, economic, social, and cultural rights must be respected—and thus we have the cumbersome definition of development described above. Therefore, subsistence rights, minimum caloric intake, for example, provide only a first step, a place to begin to specify the obligations and duties from the right to development.

Henry Shue has defined a helpful approach with his notion of "basic rights." Shue eloquently and effectively presents the case for "subsistence" as a basic right. Any developmental program or economic paradigm that does not have a minimal floor of economic security for all people violates this right. All human rights are contingent upon these developmental rights being respected. Everyone is entitled to make minimal reasonable demands upon the rest of humanity to have basic rights met. Shue writes: "Basic Rights are the morality of the depths. They specify the line beneath which no one is to be allowed to sink."[11]

Basic rights are essential because without them other rights cannot be realized. As a principle of international law, the right to development can be placed in this context. The enjoyment of other rights requires that basic development rights be met. For all human beings to be able to compete freely and fully in today's world, their development rights must first be respected. Shue calls this the transitivity principle for rights: "If everyone has a right to y, and the enjoyment of x is necessary for the enjoyment of y, then everyone also has a right to x" (1980, 32).

Just as individuals have a right not to be tortured, they also have a right not to be denied subsistence through the workings of often callous neoliberal economic development doctrines. I draw this conclusion from the Universal Declaration of Human Rights and not from a particular political ideology.

This approach to the right to development places it squarely within a basic rights framework.

Individuals and groups are entitled to assistance and may be entitled to make specific demands and to participate in the decision-making process. Looking at these issues from the perspective of rights takes them *out of the realm of charity and into the realm of entitlement* (Skogly 1993, 769). It is drawing the line beneath which no one is allowed to sink—the morality of the depths. These rights cannot be set aside as economic development doctrines change, or for political or economic considerations. This is a human rights policy designed for those trapped at the bottom—to empower the less privileged.

What are the internal and external responsibilities of all states (wealthy and poor) to meet the obligations of this emerging right? What are the correlative duties under the right to development? One way to approach the process of identifying duties is to apply Shue's basic rights methodology. Shue contends that every basic right has three correlative duties: (1) duties to respect, (2) duties to protect from deprivation, and (3) duties to aid the deprived.[12] To provide something as a right means to provide social guarantees for its enjoyment against standard threats (1980, 76).

The remainder of this chapter will examine each of these three duties in relation to the right to development as an emerging principle of international law. What "social guarantees for its enjoyment against standard threats" must be provided to meet this right?

Duties to Respect

The duty to respect charges those with economic and political power to avoid depriving basic subsistence to those individuals and groups under their control. Given the nature of the global economy, this duty extends to not only the state itself, but also to the international community. For example, local measures of poor states to respect the economic rights of their citizens often will be ineffective unless accompanied by international measures of protection. A state should not be "punished" (through a denial of credit and/or aid) for enacting measures that embrace the duty to respect but do not conform to neoliberal economic principles advocated by international IGOs.

The policies of the International Monetary Fund (IMF), for example, have been criticized for violating the duty to respect. States receiving IMF economic assistance must agree to specific measures the IMF determines are necessary to correct persistent balance of payments deficits. Such measures usually include cutbacks on central government expenditures, limits on credit expansion, interest-rate increases, reduction of personal income taxes, and reduced subsidies on basic goods and services. The pauperization and suffering to the poor and vulnerable caused by these policies have resulted in violent protests against IMF actions in twenty-six of the approximately eighty debtor countries from 1976 to 1991.[13]

The economic "growth policies" that have dominated decision-making since World War II have often worked to undermine the duty to respect, and deprivations of all sorts are consistently inflicted on the poor. In fact, over the last thirty years, the gap between the world's richest and poorest people has doubled. During the 1980s, despite all sorts of foreign aid, the deeply in-debted poor countries were faced with a net transfer of more than $100 billion a year to rich countries (see Rich 1994). The problem is that as poor countries "liberalize" their economies they not only open themselves up to the fluctuations of the world market but find themselves suddenly defenseless and exposed to the actions of powerful economic actors. "National" eco-nomic decision-making moves beyond the control of the nation-state. Market mechanisms of comparative advantage, operating under norms of efficiency, do not adhere to the duty to respect. Without international and national inter-vention in the market, the duty to avoid depriving will go unmet.

To meet this duty, development strategies of states must assure that their policies do not eliminate the means that individuals have to survive. The transformation of the land system in Mexico is illustrative. From 1940 to 1960 the Mexican government maintained a successful policy of self-sufficiency in food production and was able to increase its food production at a rate double that of its very high population growth. This situation changed dramatically by the early 1980s, as Mexico opened itself up to the interna-tional market. Animal feed, sorghum, and other higher-priced grains for the livestock industry earned more on the global market than corn or beans, the staples of the Mexican diet. In the 1980s, Mexico liberalized its trade and investment laws in favor of increased integration into the global economy. The consequences were disastrous. By 1990, 40 percent of the beans, 25 percent of the corn, and 30 percent of the sugar consumed by Mexicans were imported. Imported agricultural products are obviously more expensive than those grown by the side of the house, and per-capita consumption fell dra-matically. "Not surprisingly, large numbers of Mexicans, whose buying power in the 1980s declined almost 60 percent, could not afford what was once the daily bread of Mexican life." The National Chamber of Hospitals reported that almost a half of all children in rural Mexico suffer from malnutrition (Barnet and Cavanagh 1994, 253).

This is not to argue for self-sufficient or autonomous development which, in this era of growing interdependence, may not be a viable direction for Mexico or any other country. Rather, the point is that any development strat-egy, toward global integration or local autonomy, must respect the assertions of the powerless for protection. In Mexico, these claims have been ignored. Between 1982 and 1988 cuts in real Mexican wages amounted to over 41%. This depression of wages reduced labor's share of the national income from 43% in 1980 to 35% in 1987, while unemployment rose to 20% and underemployment to 40% of the work force. Half the population of Mexico was estimated to be living below the poverty line (Grinspun & Cameron 1993, 34, 35).

The national and international actors responsible for the economic policies that are turning Mexico into one of the most seriously malnourished nations in Latin America have clearly not met the duty to respect.

Duties to Protect from Deprivation

Since some actively deprive others of their basic means of subsistence, action is necessary to protect the vulnerable. In addition, sometimes the defenseless need to be protected from "systemic forces," where the deprivations in question may in fact be the unanticipated and unintended result of the joint workings of individual actions and social institutions. In either case, under the right to development national and international actors have the legal duty to protect the vulnerable from deprivation.

For a major power like the United States, this duty can first be met in its foreign policy by withdrawing all support from governments that actively deprive subsistence to their people. At a minimum, the United States could cease all security assistance to those governments engaged in essential and systematic deprivations of subsistence rights. Aid requests would be assessed by the degree to which the nation requesting assistance met this right. Development projects that require the forced removal of indigenous or agrarian populations or place other coercive pressures on individuals could no longer be supported by either foreign aid or assistance from international organizations.

The UNDP proposes a 20:20 compact for human development—whereby all nations pledge to ensure the provision of at least the very basic human development levels for all their people. Most nations can achieve minimal levels of eliminating malnutrition, safe drinking water, primary health care, population stabilization, and provide access to basic education by adjusting existing developmental priorities. Some of the poorer countries, however, will require international assistance, in addition to their own domestic efforts. The UNDP estimates that these additional costs would be $30 to $40 billion a year over the next ten years. How do we meet these expenses? The 20:20 compact for human development is the following: Developing countries devote on average only 13 percent of their national budgets ($57 billion a year) to basic human development concerns. It is proposed that they earmark at least 20 percent of their budgets to human priority concerns ($88 billion).

This money would be diverted from military expenditures, loss-making public enterprises, and wasteful prestige development projects. In 1992, for example, military expenditures in developing countries totaled $125 billion. The restructuring would differ from country to country, but achieving the budgetary goal of 20 percent seems feasible. Developed, donor countries, on the other hand, allocate only 7 percent of their aid to the various human priority concerns (health care, basic education, mass-coverage water supply systems, etc.). It is proposed that donors readjust their aid allocation for human priority goals to 20 percent, this would provide $12 billion a year rather than the current $4 billion. These funds would be shifted from aid already allocated to focus on these priority areas. Thus no new money is required. The proposal is based on restructuring existing budget priorities (UNDP 1994, 7, 50, 77).

Duties to Aid the Deprived

The third duty involves responsibilities to "provide for the subsistence of those unable to provide for their own" (Shue 1980, 53). As is well known, currently there is no international institution to provide adequately for the subsistence rights of persons deprived by either their own national governments or by fluctuations in the global market. A clear example is the abysmal treatment of the world's 23 million refugees (*New York Times,* 9 August 1994), many of whom are children.

Two examples can be cited of when such a duty emerges: (1) where deprivation is the result of the failures to meet the first two duties discussed above, that is, where some people have acted in such a way as to eliminate the last available means of subsistence for other people and the responsible government has failed to protect the victims; and (2) where deprivation is the result of "natural causes" such as hurricanes, earthquakes, and so on.

An interesting proposal from the UNDP is to establish a "global human security fund" to finance international responses to such things as famine, pollution, and ethnic violence—the consequences of which travel the globe. Two different suggestions for financing such a fund come from Nobel Peace Prize winner Oscar Arias and from James Tobin, winner of the Nobel Prize for economics. Arias proposes a "global demilitarization fund" and calls on the nations of the world, both rich and poor, to "commit themselves to at least a 3% a year reduction in their military spending levels over the next five years." The rich would only be asked to earmark one-fifth of these savings toward the demilitarization fund, and the developing countries would contribute perhaps one-tenth. James Tobin, on the other hand, suggests a tax on the international movements of speculative capital. He proposes a tax rate of 0.5 percent on such transactions, but even a tax of 0.05 percent during

1995–2000 could raise $150 billion a year. However the money is raised, the fund could address issues—such as famines, natural disasters, resource depletion—that is, the duties to aid the deprived (UNDP 1994, 9, 59, 70).

The grotesque degree of human suffering existing today graphically demonstrates the failure of traditional international institutions to meet the transnational duty to aid the deprived. But the duty remains and is reasonable. For example, as is by now well documented and established, the food needs of the world's people can be met. According to the UN, even in developing countries, per-capita food production increased by 18 percent on average in the 1980s. There is enough food to offer everyone in the world around 2,500 calories a day—200 calories more than the basic minimum. Hunger cannot be blamed on a shortage of food. Yet the number of hungry people keeps growing and at least 800 million people around the world go hungry. As the UNDP states: "People go hungry not because food is unavailable—but because they cannot afford it" (UNDP 1994, 27). With a reasonable effort, the basic right of subsistence, the need for food, can be met. For country after country with widespread hunger, the World Bank estimates that the transfer of a very small percentage of food could meet the needs of each nation's chronically hungry. For example in India, home to over one-third of the world's hungry people, a mere 5.6 percent of the country's food supply, if eaten by the hungry, would make an active life possible for everyone (Collins 1994, 357–58).

The problem of famine in sub-Saharan Africa supports this analysis. Scholars note how Africa's best lands and most modern productive sectors are directed to the export of low-cost crude agricultural crops and minerals to uncertain world markets. The future will remain bleak, unless there is a fundamental change to aid the deprived. If such changes took place, Ann Seidman concludes, that over "a thirty- to forty-year period the southern African independent states, working together with a liberated South Africa, could achieve self-reliant, balanced agricultural and industrial development" (1991, 159).

The proposed UN "global human security fund" could help in this transition and help states achieve self-sufficiency in food production. But, one could ask, what is the concrete duty of the world's more fortunate in this scenario? How much do the rich have to give to this new global human security fund? And what about the hard cases? What about the barriers to better distribution as illustrated, for instance, last year in Somalia? Does this duty extend to sacrificing lives in an effort to impose an order from without? And even if this succeeded, would this order not violate the principle of democratic participation? If we accept that the rich have some obligation to provide economic aid to the poor, and in this example, to help set up the "global human security fund," how much sacrifice is required to meet the duty to aid the deprived?

There is no firm criterion for the amount of sacrifice required of the wealthy to relieve the distress of the poor. But, as political theorist Brian Barry points out, that does not mean that nothing can be said.[14] A standard answer in moral philosophy—for example, in the case of someone in danger of drowning—is that "the obligation does not extend to risking one's life, though it does require that one suffer a fair amount of inconvenience." Yet how much inconvenience? Well-known ethicist Peter Singer claims that one is obliged to help up to the point at which one is sacrificing something of "comparable moral importance." Barry believes that there is a greater obligation the more severe the distress, the better off the potential helper would still be after helping, and the higher the ratio of benefit to cost (1982, 224–25). Yet, as Marion Smiley notes, such a utilitarian approach often does not help us answer the hard questions. At what point are the affluent expected to sacrifice for the "greater moral good." For example, do they drain their children's college tuition accounts? (1992, 172).

It may be impossible to establish an exact line of obligation for a country like the United States to aid the deprived, but it may be possible to state upper and lower limits. Minimally, this duty can be met through aid that goes directly to the needy, perhaps through the proposed "global human security fund." Barry points out that we could debate whether the level of aid from a country like the United States should be 3 percent of GNP (the level of Marshall aid) or 10 or 25 percent. "But, unless we reject the idea of an obligation to aid those in distress altogether, we can hardly doubt that one quarter of one percent is grotesquely too little" (1982, 225). According to the Organization for Economic Cooperation and Development, current U.S. foreign economic assistance has dropped to a mere 0.15 percent of its GNP (after hovering around approximately 0.20 percent in the early 1990s) (OECD 1994, 160; OECD 1992, 84–85, A-8, A-9, and errata 1 & 2). Once the world's top aid donor, the United States now places last among the twenty-one industrial nations (*New York Times*, 11 June 95). Even the Brandt Commission report of 1980, written by international statesmen and experts in international economics, recommended the goal of 0.70 percent of GNP as a reasonable level of aid from industrialized countries by 1985, and to 1.00 percent before the end of the century (Brandt 1980, 291). Unfortunately, the international community never seriously considered these recommendations.

Siding with the Poor

At the 1995 World Summit for Social Development meeting in Copenhagen, the UNDP presented "A World Social Charter," which included the following:

We propose to build a society where the right to food is as sacrosanct as the right to vote, where the right to a basic education is as deeply enshrined as the right to a free press and where the right to development is considered one of the fundamental human rights. (UNDP 1994, 6)

This notion of the right to development as a collective human right and a principle of international law challenges all of us to side with the poor. It challenges us to move the right to development out of the realm of charity and into the realm of entitlement under international law. It rejects the elite bias found in legal positivism. It begins with the developmental needs of the bottom half of the world's population as a compelling moral framework to locate rights. From these needs it is possible to determine rights and duties for both individuals and governments to meet the right to development. In today's maldeveloped world, it is hard to imagine a more pressing and urgent legal and moral priority.

5

Collective Human Rights in a "World Society": Challenging State Sovereignty

As we enter the twenty-first century, the self-determination of ethnic-based nation-states is a concept which continues to have enormous political impact. However, from an historical perspective, national differences are becoming less significant. The world market permeates just about all national economies; international communications and the international media ideologically impact on all countries; self-sufficient economic development (autarky) is not a viable option for development.

Hobsbawm argues that nationalism is no longer "a major vector of historical development." In contrast to the first half of this century when movements for national liberation and independence were agents of political emancipation, in the late twentieth century he finds nationalist movements to be "essentially negative, or rather divisive . . . most of them are . . . rejections of modern modes of political organization, both national and supranational" (1990, 163–64). The declining significance of nationalism may be concealed by the fact that all states are officially nations. Yet Hobsbawm believes that the basic political conflicts confronting the world today have little to do with the nation-state. Nationalism is obviously prominent in world politics today, from the Balkans to Kuwait, as individuals give their blood for a homeland. Nation-state loyalty remains deep and the main visible identity expressed by most people. Yet "[i]n spite of this evident prominence, nationalism," Hobsbawm argues, "is historically less important." He goes on to speculate that when historians later document this period, it will be written as the history "of a world which can no longer be contained within the limits of (nations) . . . either politically, or economically, or culturally, or even linguistically" (1990, 181–82).

Rosenau asserts that we are now in a "postinternational" relations era, by which he means that the world system can no longer be solely or primarily categorized as consisting of relations between nations. Thus we have moved beyond an international framework. According to Rosenau, the present transformations in the world system are unparalleled since the beginning of the present nation-state system in 1648 (Rosenau 1990, 10). The changes he highlights include technology (particularly the microelectronic revolution in

91

communications) and the emergence of global issues that nations are unable to solve alone. A result of these transformations is that the distribution of power and the authority relations between individuals and collectivities (such as nations) have been called into question. A consequence of the collapse of the old parameters between individuals and collectivities has been the emergence of a multicentric world consisting of thousands of nonstate, nonsovereign global actors. This multicentric world coexists, according to Rosenau, in a nonhierarchical relationship with the nation-state system. Part of the decentralization trend that he identifies, is *the movement of individual loyalties from the nation-state to collectivities closer to them, in which there is more possibility for meaningful participation* (Rosenau 1992b, 11–22; and 1990, 34–37, 96–100). Confining the right of the self-determination of peoples to the existing nation-state framework appears counter to these trends. Yet, at the same time, individuals continue to remain loyal to the nation-state, and in some cases try to turn "subgroups" into states (e.g., the nationalist movements in Slovakia, Croatia, and elsewhere for statehood). Thus, this historical period seems to be characterized by conflicting tendencies producing uncertainty and tension, dialectical forces pushing and straining existing structures, and challenging our limited understanding of the process of global change.

In a vein similar to Hobsbawm, Wallerstein sees the era as signifying the "disintegration of liberal ideology," and the movement of people away from reliance and/or identification with the state:

> We have entered a new era in terms of mentalities. On the one hand, there is the passionate call for democracy. This call is not a fulfillment of liberalism, however, but its rejection. It is a statement that the present world-system is undemocratic because economic well-being is not equally shared, and that is because political power is not in fact equally shared. Not progressive change, but social disintegration is now coming to be seen as normal. Further, when there is social disintegration, people look for protection.
>
> As people turned to the state to secure change, they are now turning to group solidarities (all kinds of groups) to provide protection. (1992, 32)

Again we see the contradictory nature of the present period. Despite the trends that Wallerstein identifies which challenge nation-state hegemony, the nation-state is still turned to most often by individuals to provide protection and continues to obtain the loyalty of millions of citizens. Yet, at the same time, the nation-state continually disappoints and seems inadequate to fundamentally address the material and economic problems confronting an interdependent and fragile world. Thus, individuals look elsewhere, loyalties begin to move in new directions, and strong social movements emerge.

In contrast to the trends toward subgroup identification, doctrines of nationalism, for the most part, include many of the following characteristics: humanity is naturally divided into nations; each nation has its own peculiar character; nations require their own states for fulfillment; all political power is derived from the nation; humans must identify with nations for their freedom; the nation-state has the highest claim to a person's loyalty; and finally the nation-state is the condition of global freedom and harmony. To use Marxist language, nationalism inverts the base-superstructure metaphor, putting culture, history, and language as the base and economics and class as the superstructure (Szporluk 1988, 93–94).

"Realist" theorists in the field of international relations argue that the essence of world politics is the division of the world into sovereign nation-states which seek to improve their position in an anarchic international system with constricted possibilities for cooperation. Each state maintains the right to be free from the scrutiny and intervention of other states in its internal affairs. State sovereignty means that each state is treated as an independent political community free to make its own laws. A state's independence is limited only when necessary to reconcile disputes or enhance cooperative relations with others, especially in economic affairs. State sovereignty thus has little to do with internal self-determination, that is, individual and group liberties. The primary goal of foreign policy-makers, according to the realists, is to serve the national interest defined in terms of power. Ideals do not drive state decision-making, power does.[1]

From the 1960s into the 1990s, different theoretical paradigms in the field of international relations have challenged the realist framework, although it continues to dominate the academic discipline. In particular, critics of realism question the assumption of the unlimited and untouchable predominance of the nation-state in the international arena. Like Hobsbawm, these critics identify cross-cutting currents between states which bind individuals, groups, and societies together *independently* of the wishes and prerogatives of the geographically demarcated nation-state. Significant schools of thought, challenging realist assumptions in the field of international relations, include Keohane and Nye's "complex interdependence" model, Rosenau's framework of "postinternational relations," Wallerstein's World Systems Analysis (WSA), and Falk, Mendlovitz, and Kim's World Order Models Project (WOMP). Aspects of these four paradigms are summarized below.

The framework of collective human rights articulated in this book incorporates both the anti-statist direction of WOMP and the global economic structures and dimensions articulated by WSA. The goal is to identify and define emerging group norms and rights that cut across state boundaries and are part of the growing matrix of forces counterpoised to nation-state power and hegemony in the modern world. The concern for individual human rights from 1945 to today has played such a role in relation to the rights of the individual, attempting to protect the individual from nation-state abuse by positing norms and values above any nation's ideology and practice. The intent of collective human rights is to do the same thing for certain groups.

COMPLEX INTERDEPENDENCE AND THE RISE OF "SUBGROUPISM"

In their seminal work *Power and Interdependence*, Robert Keohane and Joseph Nye put forward a temperate alternative to (or perhaps it is better to say moderation of) realism called "complex interdependence."[2] They argue that interdependence increases the *sensitivity* and *vulnerability* of nation-states to events in the outside world, events over which these states have very little control when acting alone. Critics of realism postulate that as states become more vulnerable to external forces over which they have less and less control, we will witness an increase in the demand for cooperation between states, and the prospects for the development of international institutions that facilitate cooperation will thereby proportionately increase.

Realist approaches often elevate the nation-state as a unitary and rational actor in the international arena. Keohane and Nye effectively argue that this is not the case. Often, in the recent era, domestic interest groups pressure and influence nation-state foreign policy. A government's contradictory responses to these domestic pressures makes it difficult to see the state as a monolith. In fact, the distinction between domestic and international politics can seem at times almost artificial. As a result, the main cleavages in international politics may not be between nation-states, but rather within states. The priorities of a particular domestic interest group may lie in cooperating with a similar group in another country, resulting in efforts to pressure the home state in a certain direction. There are numerous examples: the environmental movement, human rights interest groups, multinational corporate lobbies, and so forth.

Critics of realism contend that the realist framework ignores the impact of other actors operating transnationally, independently of any state. Various transnational actors have emerged, from the multinational corporation to activist groups such as Amnesty International. These organizations act in their own interest, and not the interest of a particular nation-state. They have become pivotal international players. For example, U.S. sanctions against South Africa were far less successful in putting economic pressure on that country than were a series of decisions by private American commercial banks not to roll over South African loans as they came due. These actions by private multinational banks were taken more than a year *before* state-sponsored sanctions even went into affect (Rodman 1994, 314).

Why did the banks act without state approval? Because they had been lobbied by a number of NGOs to pull out of South Africa due to its reprehensible apartheid policies. Further, these NGOs pressured twenty state governments and some prominent institutional investors to divest their pension funds of stocks from companies operating in South Africa. In addition, the adoption by over 140 state and local governments of ordinances conditioning eligibility for city purchases or contracts on various forms of corporate non-involvement in South Africa, had a direct impact on the corporate balance sheet. Many banks and firms, for example, had extensive business dealings with these city governments, which were far more important than their activities in South Africa. When they pulled out, they plunged South Africa into a financial crisis that led to the collapse of the rand, a dramatic loss of new loans and investments, and a withdrawal of most prominent American investors (Rodman 1994, 325–26).

Another aspect of the critique of realism is to question the hierarchy it establishes between "high" politics (i.e., issues of war and peace) and "low" politics (i.e., economic, social, and technical issues). According to many scholars, the most serious threats facing the United States come not from military aggression, but from such issues as energy vulnerability and debt. The most serious conflicts with our allies are not over military security issues, but over trade policies. Because of this, military force is no longer the most useful and effective instrument of statecraft. States, like the United States, with vastly superior military capability have been increasingly unable to translate that military power into positive results in areas of economic and social vulnerability.

Finally, the issues that really threaten national and global security—proliferation of weapons, Third World debt, damage to the eco-system, drugs, poverty, AIDS, famine, and so on—cannot be dealt with through traditional realist mechanisms. Military force is, more often than not, of limited use in solving any of these crisis. Therefore, with increased interdependence there will grow an escalating interest on the part of states for cooperation and a greater demand for institutions that facilitate such cooperation.

Rosenau takes the analysis of interdependence much farther. As the capacity of states to provide satisfactory solutions to the major issues on the political agenda diminishes, there has emerged a corresponding rise in "subgroupism," through which more and more people around the world are ready, able, and willing to act.[3]

Cultural bias can prevent those from the developed world from seeing the importance of these new developments. The state-centric focus is a product of the First World. To break free of this "conceptual jail" it may be necessary to

> conceiv[e] of humanity, not as a collection of countries or relations among states, but as a congeries of authority relationships, some of which are coterminous with countries and states and others of which are either located within or extend beyond state boundaries. Mapped in this way, the globe more nearly approximates present-day experience than does the conventional portrayal of some 160 territorial units. Such a map highlights the many subnational, supranational, and transnational entities that have acquired salience as the complexity and interdependence of global life have become greater. (Rosenau 1990, 39)

An elaboration of collective human rights is an attempt at making such an intellectual leap, to address the demands and rights of these subgroups (subnational, supranational, and transnational) and analyze their importance to the world community. A collective human rights framework can hopefully serve to link together these various forces, uniting seemingly disparate movements into a common political struggle. Advocates of collective human rights believe that there is power to be gained from such a united approach.

Rosenau is critical of using interdependence to refer only to the interconnection among things without discerning their underlying structure and process. The result of this approach is to reinforce the "state-is-still-predominant" litany in the literature of international relations. In contrast, Rosenau posits a *multicentric* world, with a multiplicity of actors on diverse system levels. He stresses the importance of examining the dialectic between the multicentric world of diverse actors and the state-centric world of national actors (1990, 97–99).

Rosenau writes that the "illusion of states as omnicompetent collectivities has been revealed by technological developments that render people ever more interdependent and allow them to transcend national borders ever more easily" (1990, 418). Critical to developing this "bifurcation of world politics" into multicentric and state-centric worlds, has been the emergence of a fundamental shift in values. He believes that the emergence of shared norms is *not* a trivial development. The possibility exists for the creation of a "*global culture*, a set of norms that are shared on a world-wide scale" (1990, 420). "If the underpinnings of a genuine global culture are to evolve, there must be a sharing of basic values pertaining to how the world is perceived and how conflicting loyalties are managed" (1990, 422). "The rise of human rights as a global issue, for example, may well have its roots in a widespread sharing of values as to what constitutes the legitimate sphere of official coercion"

(1990, 430). The legitimacy of political regimes is being judged increasingly by internationally defined human rights standards, even in cases like Bosnia where enforcement implementation is difficult. Indeed, Rosenau and others are struck by the extent to which claims of sovereignty have waned. The peremptory declaration that "this is strictly an internal matter" no longer commands global assent (1990, 436). Routinely, officials of one country openly talk about altering the behavior of another regime, and such language does not provoke complaints about the violation of sovereignty. "Indeed, the emergence of human rights as a central issue of postinternational politics testifies eloquently to the erosion of national sovereignty as an organizing principle" (1990, 437).

WORLD SYSTEMS THEORY AND THE WORLD ORDER MODELS PROJECT

Wallerstein, as does Rosenau, also attempts to depict an increasingly integrated world, in which the state plays an important, though less dominate role. Yet Wallerstein is much more adept and able in explaining the historical international structures and global economic movements that play a determinative role in both enhancing and limiting the power of nation-states. He analyzes the historical growth of an international division of labor and a world market serving to benefit the core states of the North at the expense of the periphery (and semi-periphery) primarily in the South. Through the lens of the global political economy, Wallerstein analyzes the intersection of a capitalist world economic system and the territorial based nation-states (Wallerstein 1974; 1979; 1980).

World Systems Analysis (WSA) thus fundamentally breaks with traditional realist approaches within international relations, which begin with a focus on the nation-state, and instead starts its approach from the vantage point of the international economic system overall.[4] Such a framework attempts to explain the actions of individual states as a result of their interactions with the global structures of the world system. This theory integrates the critical relationships between the state and the expansion of capital and that between the core-periphery division of labor and the world market.

The central focus to world systems analysis is the development of global capitalism. Capitalism is a systemwide phenomenon. Concentrating merely on individual states, or national economies, is an inadequate frame of reference. Capitalism is an integrated system that transcends geographic boundaries. For example, contrary to the liberal economic theories of specialization based on comparative advantage, WSA argues that the global economic division of labor requires and increases inequality between nations and regions.

Therefore, one must first understand capitalism as an integrated system, and only then is it possible to approach the fate of particular countries.

World systems analysis has been criticized for "economic determinism," and thereby subordinating political structures to the machinations global capitalism. Critics also argue that its analysis of a global capitalist system based on exchange relationships as determinative of the structural location of all states into either core, periphery, or semi-periphery too greatly simplifies the global capital accumulation process. Some of these commentators point out, for example, that the class formations between nation-states that world systems theorists accurately document are also found within the state itself.

Thus, while it is true that the concepts of core, periphery, and semi-periphery may apply between states, they may also be applied within states. For example, the conditions within the borders of the United States today, and even within its cities such as New York, reflect vastly uneven socioeconomic development. Similar patterns endure throughout the world, where stark differences in economic and political power exist within most nation-states.

The collective human rights framework presented here attempts to address this reality and articulate the rights of those exploited and oppressed groups found within the "periphery," including, due to the "peripheralisation of the core," those groups within the core left out of economic development. There is a normative unity of purpose now uniting these groups as a result of uneven economic development within and between nation-states. The social movements which attempt to address the rights of these groups, can gain from moving beyond a state-centric focus in their organizing.

The World Order Models Project (WOMP) takes a fundamentally different approach toward critiquing state sovereignty than others within the field of international relations. It posits a set of *values and norms* from which to judge past, present, and future arrangements of power and authority, including peace, economic well-being, social justice, ecological balance, and positive identity. Their intent is to provide a "systems-transforming" alternative to understanding the world.

WOMP sees a world system in crisis with the failure of the statist model. Examine the record: the arms race flourishes despite the end of the Cold War, environmental quality continues to deteriorate, AIDS and other diseases continue to spread, poverty and suffering predominate for the impoverished majority. Constructive negotiations on these issues on a world scale are relatively meager. Why? Because nation-state governments are not well positioned to address these new global concerns. By tradition, a government's emphasis has remained building up national defenses and confronting immediate economic challenges. To a greater degree than other paradigms, this school fundamentally questions the flexibility of the state system to confront these multifaceted problems.

Throughout the 1980s, advocates for the WOMP perspective strongly endorsed developing norms reflecting a global identity designed to challenge national patriotism. They stressed the basic *unity* of the human species as the starting point of analysis. In 1991, Richard Falk summarized several characteristics common to various strands of WOMP thinking:

- a strong sense of the unity of human destiny;

- a belief that security encompasses the basic needs of all peoples to have food, shelter, health facilities, education, meaningful work, human rights, and environmental protection;

- a skepticism about the capacity of the war system to provide security, even in the minimal physical sense of protecting territorial states against military attack and other unwanted forms of penetration; and

- a belief that desirable changes in political life throughout history have been caused largely by popular movements and struggles from below, and that democratization and human rights are necessary, but not sufficient, conditions for global reform. (Falk 1991, 21–22)

WOMP stresses the role of transnational social movements in contributing to the formation of a new reality—a global civil society. Part of this perspective includes the development and protection of collective human rights, which are intrinsic to the normative values at the base of the WOMP perspective.

COLLECTIVE HUMAN RIGHTS: CREATING A COUNTERVAILING FORCE TO STATE SOVEREIGNTY

Foucault viewed governance as the process of "structur(ing) the possible field(s) of action of others" (1982, 221). In this definition, the focus is on the outcome of decisions. Many theorists acknowledge the role of values and ideals in influencing policy-makers, in structuring their fields of action. They recognize the role of normative ideas in the process of governance. Norms and values can create a countervailing force to other components of power, including the military and economic components. Proponents of individual human rights hope to create a countervailing force to intolerable state action. Through exposure and sanction they hope to curtail absolute state sovereignty in order to maintain the dignity of the human being.

Collective human rights advocates hope to put similar constraints on the actions of states and other institutions toward specific groups, and introduce a new normative order into the international arena. Applying the standard of individual human rights has changed the language of modern diplomacy to a significant degree. It has not come close to curbing human rights abuses globally, but it has created a framework through which citizens around the world can question the right of their government to act in particular ways. Advocates of collective human rights hope to extend such a framework around certain group rights, which would require not only constraints against the oppression of these groups, but would also require positive action on the part of societal organizations to meet basic entitlements.

This normative method utilizes the approach clearly articulated by Robert W. Cox: "Our challenge is not to contribute to the construction of a universal and absolute knowledge, but to devise a fresh perspective useful for framing and working on the problems of the present" (1992, 134). Cox's theory as a "set of viable working hypotheses" (1992, 135) postulates the *negation of hegemony* in the emerging future world order (1992, 140–42).[5]

Thus, in addition to the postinternational era that Rosenau formulates, Cox believes we are entering a posthegemonic period as well. This is represented not by the decline in American power, as articulated by some current realists, but rather by *a decline in a coherent ideological framework for understanding the world,* that is, a Gramscian understanding of hegemony (discussed below in chapter 7). During a period of hegemony, the "structures and values and understandings about the nature of order permeate a whole system of states and non-state entities" in a relatively stable, unquestioned manner. They appear to most observers as the natural order, and provide the underpinnings for structures of power.[6]

The importance of the conception of ideological hegemony was clearly expressed by Etienne Balibar:

> The *universalism* of the dominant ideology is therefore rooted at a much deeper level than the world expansion of capital and even than the need to procure common rules of action for all those who manage that expansion. It is rooted in the need to construct, in spite of the antagonism between them, an ideological "world" shared by exploiters and exploited alike . . . formulated in the language of universality. (1992, 4)

Cox doubts that a new hegemony can be constructed to replace the old— ergo, a posthegemonic order. "Previous hegemonic orders have derived their universals from the dominant society, itself the product of a dominant civilization. A posthegemonic order would have to derive its normative content in a search for common ground among constituent traditions of civilization" (Cox 1992, 141). I would argue that the basis for this common ground can be found in the norms and values of *respect for individual and collective human rights.*

Cox believes, and I agree, that the first condition for establishing common ground is "mutual recognition of distinct traditions of civilization (1992, 141)." Meeting this condition involves respecting group rights of ethnicity, race, and gender. Traditions of civilization cannot be found solely by examining the historiography of nation-states, but must also include, as argued throughout this book, those groups in which the human species naturally congregates.

The second condition, according to Cox, involves movement to a kind of "supra-intersubjectivity that would provide a bridge among the distinct and separate subjectivities of the different coexisting traditions of civilization" (1992, 142). Cox outlines three arenas for building these *bridges*: global ecology, restraint on the use of violence, and procedures for coping with conflict. Formulations of collective human rights have incorporated these concerns.

The beginning of any new ideological approach toward this era must begin, however, from the premise of meeting basic human needs (as outlined in the previous chapter on the right to development). Many nations today confront social disintegration, to a large degree the result of the unequal distribution of wealth. The persistent, day-to-day, tragedy of absolute poverty and its consequences is staggering.

The World Bank deduces that one billion people worldwide struggle to survive on less than one dollar a day and therefore live in poverty (World Bank 1995, v, ix). To many NGOs, this statement represents "the big lie." The real figure, according to these NGOs, is that probably over three billion people live in poverty and suffer a life of misery (Chossudovsky 1995, 4–5). NGOs present at the World Summit for Social Development in Copenhagen in March 1995 evaluated how the World Bank arrived at the figure of one billion living in poverty. The World Bank poverty line is set at a per capita income of one dollar a day. Population groups with incomes in excess of one dollar a day are arbitrarily identified as "non-poor." Thus, the World Bank estimate for Latin America and the Caribbean is that only 19 percent of the population is "poor." To many NGOs this is preposterous. For example, the U.S. Census Bureau estimates that 20 percent of Americans live below the poverty line. The World Bank seems to be both discounting the poor in the United States and the developed world and radically underestimating the poor in the underdeveloped world. To many observers, they have thus created a false measure of "poor" which serves to distort the true level of destitution confronting millions. The "poor" in the Third World, according to the NGOs, is not a minority group (as depicted by the WB) but the majority. The true figure of global poverty, according to these NGOs, is truly astounding, probably well over three billion.[7]

The majority of humanity is thus made up of a combination of the poorest and those slightly better off; all of whom, regardless of ethnicity, race, or gender, have a common interest in structural reforms of the global economic system to address questions of equity and justice. The commonality among Cox's "coexisting traditions," the *bridge* that can bring them together, is economic rights on a global scale.[8]

Meeting basic human needs is not a pie-in-the-sky, utopian socialist dream. It is doable. These rights can be met. They are not just dreams. For example, the worldwide right to subsistence is feasible and does not involve staggering costs (see Collins 1994; Foster 1992; Seidman 1991; Reutlinger et al. 1986). It is no more costly than continuing to pay for noninterference rights, which involve considerable expense in law enforcement and defense. As Kai Nielsen has demonstrated, "hunger, malnutrition and famine are fundamentally questions of distribution of income and the entitlements to food."[9] They are not the result of either human nature or the natural order. Thus, the new posthegemonic order that Cox begins to define, can find its bearings in a new era of "moral reciprocity," which does not rest "on . . . schemes of cooperation for mutual advantage," but instead on a conception of "moral equality" (Nielsen 1992, 27). Clearly, such moral reciprocity and moral equality does *not* currently factor into nation-state elite decision-making. It is presented here, rather, as the direction we need to move towards *if* we believe in a conception of human rights that will be most relevant to those at the bottom of the global division of wealth and power.

From a moral point of view, unless we are willing to exclude the poor and weak from protection, such group claims must be addressed. Justice requires that in order to treat each other as equals, we must recognize, and then alter, the mechanisms, including the economic structures, that cause suffering for particular groups. Until such measures to protect group rights are implemented, individual rights unfortunately remain a illusion for the majority of the human species. In addition, ignoring questions of equity often leads to unstable and repressive societies.

Collective human rights operate in what Rosenau calls the "ideational" level of "global order." This is the level at which individuals understand the arrangements through which their affairs are handled. It impacts on the second, "behavioral" level, where people take action to maintain order. And finally, global order is preserved at the "institutional" level, where "rule-oriented institutions and regimes enact and implement the policies inherent in the ideational and behavioral patterns" (Rosenau 1992a, 14).

At the first, ideational level, more and more individuals are realizing that for their specific rights to be protected, certain group rights must first be guarded. (See p. 17–22 on the relationship between group and individual rights.) Unfortunately, nation-state elites do not recognize this relationship and their attention is almost solely on individual rights and state sovereignty. We have seen the limitations of the nation-state, as a vehicle for liberation and freedom.[10] We are also well aware that a world civil society has yet to be born to replace the state system. In such an unstable world, issues of security, have come to encompass more than just military might, and include economic well-being and social justice as well. During this turbulent time of a newly emerging world society, a position is being articulated for collective human rights. The object of such norms is not protection of the state or of the nation. Rather, within this global framework of a world society, the norms call for the protection of the individual, through an appreciation and understanding of the natural groups to which that individual belongs.

A collective human rights approach views norms through a cultural lens encompassing a world society rather than a particular nation-state. Until now, the whole field of international relations has been dominated by the nation-state framework, analyzing the actions of the leading states, which cumulatively represent a small number of world cultural, civilizational traditions. A weakness of the realist theory, in particular, is its lack of focus on indigenous cultures, which impairs its ability to explain and predict. Gellner points out that while there are only about 200 states, there are approximately 800 movements of effective nationalism, plus over 7,000 potential nationalisms, if one accepts the premise that differences in language entail differences in culture (1983, 44–45). A global framework of collective human rights can help define a new politics that is responsive to this localist cultural reality. The collective human rights vision embraces both the particular and the universal dimensions of the human community. Collective human rights thus play a subversive role in relation to state sovereignty, that is, defining a normative framework of principles not only to judge state actions, but also to define a future equitable vision for humankind based upon natural communities and not necessarily the geographic boundaries determined by the world's elites.[11]

In other words, the recent era has seen the global emergence of strong subgroups and social movements which have struggled to define a new normative framework from a global perspective. Given the authority crisis confronting the nation-state system, the importance of these subgroups and social movements will continue to grow. As current economic and political systems weaken, individuals will look not only to nation-states for their identity and support, but also to local and international groups of all sorts. In the past, systemic crises have often been resolved by jingoistic patriotism and imperialist nationalism which has caused great violence and suffering. Yet, in agreement with Rosenau, it seems that "historic patterns may no longer tell the whole story" (1992a, 287). Social movements working through NGOs and IGOs will most likely play a more positive and progressive role in the international arena in the twenty-first century than they ever did in the past. The resolution of the various crisis confronting nation-states may lie in the direction of direct cooperation between peoples in civil society—cooperative actions taken independent of the wishes of the nation-states themselves.

Transnational pressure groups engaging in world civic politics are remarkable demonstrations of global cooperative endeavors. Greenpeace, for example, is now the world's largest environmental group, having grown phenomenally since its founding in 1971. By 1994 it had 3.1 million members and a budget of $145 million. It operates out of forty-three offices in thirty countries, with a full-time staff of 1,200, four vessels, a helicopter, hundreds of dinghies, and the latest communications equipment. Its greatest strength, however, is that it can draw on tens of thousands of volunteers. The power of the organization to challenge a major multinational corporation was seen in their 1995 campaign against Royal/Dutch Shell. To prevent pollution of the seas, Greenpeace sent a team of "Greenpeace commandos" to barricade themselves onto a Shell oil-storage platform as it was being towed toward its ocean grave. Shell wanted to discard the 460 foot tower of steel and concrete in the North Atlantic. The campaign against Shell involved more than just perilous confrontations on the seas, but also a consumer boycott. In two months Greenpeace spent more than $1 million on communications and equipment, including chartered boats and helicopters to take on Shell. By June 1995 public opinion and five European governments adopted the Greenpeace position and Shell was forced to back down. The platform will now be dismantled on land. The Greenpeace Council, an assembly of national and regional directors, has defined the organization's priorities as follows: to oppose all things nuclear, both weapons and energy; to denounce air pollution and threats to the atmosphere; to defend diversity of plant and animal species; and to fight the "chemicalization of the planet"—including a demand to ban chlorine, which they believe is extremely toxic and easy to live without (*New York Times*, 8 July 1995).

The legal protection of the oceans is a clear example of the growing effectiveness of NGOs in international law-making and enforcement. Governments have proven unreliable regarding the protection of the seas from environmental harm, especially when confronted with short-term economic costs. Thus environmental groups have had to engage in a series of lobbying tactics in order to pressure governments toward environmentally sound policies. NGOs also play a research and educational role in crucial areas neglected by governments. There has been mounting evidence of environmental degradation of the seas, some of which are characterized as "at risk" and others as "near death."

A major weakness of international law, is that there is no mechanism for enforcement of established rules or regulatory mechanisms. NGOs have played a significant role in insuring compliance with new standards in international environmental law. For example, to ensure compliance with the London Dumping Convention (LDC), an international treaty relating to ocean dumping, NGOs play the following vital roles: (1) they observe consultative meetings, which would otherwise be closed to the press and would go unreported; (2) they lobby for changes within the political institutions of violating countries; (3) they call for amendments, when necessary, in the convention. The result of their work has been a strengthening of this effort to limit ocean pollution. NGOs also contribute intellectually to the process of lawmaking and regulation. Greenpeace, for example, provided the nations participating in the LDC with the following: detailed critical review of scientific justifications for dumping; linguistic aid to non-English speakers; scientific and technical advice; a willingness to publicize incidents; and the carrying out of primary scientific work. NGO participation has thus improved the quality of decisions and helped correct the often disastrous results when environmental quality is left to self-interested governmental decision-making (Stairs and Taylor 1992, 110–41).

The argument is not that these groups have replaced the nation-state as the primary actors in international relations. Rather, it is our understanding of world politics that is changing. We can no longer limit ourselves to old conceptions of nation-state sovereignty when we try to understand power, relevant political behavior, and changes in human practices. The role of these new transnational NGOs, and the importance of international norms and values like collective human rights, challenges this old framework for interpreting global politics.

Citizenship today, in a "globalizing world," is profoundly different from citizenship in previous centuries. Due to the bountifulness of information, the enhancement of people's analytic skills, and the myriad of ways in which the planet has become smaller to all of us, some assert that national patriotism has lessened, and document how subgroups and social movements move across borders. Nations, in fact, appear to be an inappropriate unit to address the proliferation of global concerns for the emerging century. In many cases, transnational subgroup loyalties have grown stronger as state loyalties have weakened (examples include: on the positive side, the human rights and environmental movements, and on the negative side, Christian and Islamic fundamentalism). If one's concern is individual freedom and justice, these developments may prove beneficial. *If* we can develop a *new normative frame-work* to guide the new global society, perhaps some of the structures causing human suffering can be exposed and changed.

If these tendencies are accurate and we are witnessing a rise in the transfer of loyalties to social movements or subgroups, this new development is not necessarily something to be feared. After all, nationalism, the organizing principle of the current international system, to a large degree has its roots in fear and hatred of the "other," similar to racism. As Benedict Anderson writes, "it [the nation] is an imagined political community and imagined as both inherently limited and sovereign" (1991, 6, 141). Invented (nationalist) traditions are often fabricated to encourage the construction of a past to fit a current political program. If through respect for collective human rights, we can overcome this fear of the "other," than the new emerging global society has the potential to be profoundly more just and less violent.

How important are new norms in the international arena? In this writer's view, in the current era of postinternational relations, the role of norms and values in tangibly affecting the political process is extraordinarily high. Their relevance is demonstrated by the power of ideas and norms to inform a nonviolent movement for social change. Values and norms were critical ingredients behind the political revolutions of 1989. To a large degree, the totalitarian governments were toppled from within, not defeated from without.

This is *not* to argue, of course, that traditional forms of "hard" power, that is, military force, are no longer relevant. Gorbachev decided not to use military force to maintain his position, yet this hard-power resource was there for his utilization. China, on the other hand, a regime widely seen as in violation of numerous human rights accords, maintains power to a large degree by military force.

Yet nonviolent movements from the Philippines to Germany have demonstrated repeatedly throughout the last decades of the twentieth century the impact of norms and values in influencing outcomes. While the role of norms as a basic component to "power" resources appears enhanced, the utility of military force to bring about positive outcomes seems diminished.

INTERNATIONAL LAW:
INCORPORATING COLLECTIVE HUMAN RIGHTS

One possible way to concretize these emerging norms and values is through international law. Traditionally, the law of nations had little to say about the treatment of individuals and groups. We have seen the emergence following World War II of a normatively based program to protect individual rights and "baby steps" toward protecting group rights. A corpus of internationally accepted rules regarding these rights is being developed, and accepted, by state and nonstate actors. Yet questions persist: Is there any point in constantly defining and redefining international norms and rights? Given the sorry record of many governments in the area of human rights, why would we expect any actual progress in the much more controversial area of group rights? What good is customary international law,[12] if national interest can override universally accepted norms? Even if governments accept legally binding obligations, with no effective enforcement body to compel compliance, what effect do these obligations really have?

One can begin to address these questions by exploring the impact of "soft law"[13] on the behavior of international actors. Soft law, as explained in chapter 4, refers to actions by state and nonstate actors which fall between law in the strict sense (for example, international treaties) and a mere political statement with no consequences. The international legal order is evolving into new subject areas. There is a need for the regulation of states' activities and, at the same time, the room to maneuver in the making of claims and counter claims. In the process, hard and soft law both play an important role.

Patricia Birnie, for example, points to the importance of soft law in terms of international regulation of the environment. The development of international environmental law requires that states restrict the customary freedom of their citizens and companies to conduct profitable economic activities that threaten the environment. States have difficulty reaching agreement on this form of regulation, and even when they do so, they are often lax in enforcing the regulation. States are also hesitant to adopt binding regulations and prefer merely to set standards or lay down guidelines, criteria, principles, or recommendations, which they regard as nonbinding.

Binding regulations, most often in the form of treaties, are generally regarded as part of "hard law." They impose mandatory obligations on states which must then implement and enforce such law in their national legal systems. Generally, guidelines and standards set out in resolutions or declarations are not binding. As a result, states can proceed at as slow a pace as they like in working toward implementation, treating the principles as goals only. Birnie believes, therefore, that a more accurate term is "soft settlement" rather than soft law, "since the vague and general terms most often used in such instruments permit states to continue the negotiating process and to develop acceptable interpretations of ambiguous terms or to comply in a variety of ways without exciting complaint." However, soft law is now the commonly used term to refer to this dispute settlement/conflict resolution process and thus has become a key component of international law (Birnie 1992, 52–54).

A further benefit of soft law is that its vagueness in some cases can be an advantage. Allowing a large amount of discretion permits states to assume certain obligations that they might not otherwise accept. States may be hesitant to accept hard forms of regulation, while soft law can eventually harden into binding customary law, or be included in treaties. Examining one area of soft law, the actions of the General Assembly of the United Nations, gives insight into how international law might be utilized to enhance a framework to protect collective human rights. In the General Assembly, the poor and underdeveloped states have pushed for legislative power for this world body in order to exploit their majority position.

Even the International Court of Justice (ICJ), which, due to its composition, is inherently biased in support of state sovereignty, has to a limited degree supported this view of General Assembly actions. For example, in the *Barcelona Traction, Light and Power Co. Ltd. Judgment* (1970) the ICJ referred to outlawing acts of aggression and genocide, and protecting basic human rights, including freedom from slavery and racial discrimination, as obligations of every state *erga omnes, although not every state had ratified the relevant conventions*. In *Legal Consequences for States of the Continued Presence of South Africa in Namibia* (1971, 50), the ICJ held that it would be incorrect to assume that "because the General Assembly is in principle vested with recommendatory powers, it is debarred from adopting, in specific areas within the framework of its competence, resolutions which make determinations or have operative designs" (Levi 1991, 47).

Legal scholars have noted the conversion of aspirations of Third World states from soft law resolutions into binding customary law. In *Filartiga v. Pena-Irala* case (1980), U.S. Court of Appeals Judge Irving R. Kaufman determined that torture was a crime against international law, *upon the various declarations and resolutions passed in international organizations* (Levi 1991, 48).

Soft law in its many forms—recommendations, declarations, clarifications, directives, standards—is important in providing a means for articulating a new normative international program. Such a development makes it harder for governments to ignore these evolving concerns and continue a practice that is being declared immoral or unjust. The realm of soft law provides a mechanism for values to be formulated in the international arena in a manner that impacts on the actions of states and nonstate actors. These international actors find it harder and harder to ignore internationally accepted normative guidelines and normative principles. Soft law can provide us with some generally agreed upon rules as to "what is permissible and impermissible."

In the area of collective human rights, soft law provides the ability to determine violations of entitlements and establish standards of accountability, from which one is able to point an accusing finger. Reliance on hard law alone is clearly inadequate. In fact, one can demonstrate the importance of soft law by applying Dworkin's distinction between rules and legal principles. Legal rules are utilized in an all or nothing fashion, whereas principles are discretionary, and inherently have a dimension of weight or importance to be considered in every case. Rules do not share this characteristic. As Kratochwil notes, this argument "demolish[es] the conception of law as a static system of rules" (1989, 193–94).[14]

TRENDS IN INTERNATIONAL LAW

Why would international actors resort to such agreements, which could then be used against them? Kratochwil demonstrates how human action in general is rule-governed. Rules and norms are "guidance devices which are designed to simplify choices and impart 'rationality' to situations by delineating the factors that a decision-maker has to take into account" (1989, 10). For any self-interested actor having to relate to others, such guidelines often simplify functioning.

Nation-states, in particular, have often seen rights primarily as special devices "for the creation and maintenance of social order." The theoretical father of realist theory, Thomas Hobbes, framed the necessity of establishing public authority as intimately connected with the problem of the enforcement of individual rights (Kratochwil 1989, 162–64). One could summarize that states have been willing to accept a minimal level of interference by a human rights network because it is often in their self-interest to do so.

From the nineteenth through the twentieth century, we have witnessed the progressive humanization of international relations. The nineteenth century saw the humanization of international rules regarding prisoners of war, the taking of booty, military occupation, the treatment of civilian populations, and more dramatically the abolition of the slave trade. In the twentieth century we have seen a new respect for individual rights and human dignity, and distinctions made between those states which respect individual rights and those which do not.

Dorothy Jones believes that international law articulates "a picture of the way that they [nation-states] think the *world* ought to be . . . open[ing] themselves to the possibility that they will be taken seriously enough that there will be attempts to hold them to their word" (1992, 43–44).

Jones goes on to clarify two fundamental principles emerging in international law: (1) the creation of an equitable international economic order; and

(2) the protection of the environment (1992, 50–52). Thus we see international law moving into the realm of social justice, with pressures growing to address the entire international economic system. Obviously, these efforts do not legally bind states, but they do appeal almost always to conscience, if not to courts. They provide standards from which the conduct of states can be judged. This is a dynamic process, a continuous process of change, encompassing the use of principles to guide and judge state behavior (1992, 50–56).

Where is international law headed? According to D'Amato, one can see a transition from the nineteenth century, where international law was characterized by state versus state, to the twentieth century, where international law became the individual versus the state, to the twenty-first century, where we will see international law addressing the claims of individual versus individual. By that he means that we will see transboundary international legal claims involving individuals only, but invoking public international law. We may be moving toward "a universalist concept of international law where individuals and groups within states can assert legal claims against individuals and groups in other states." As the notion of human rights becomes increasingly perfected, "it requires giving standing to individuals and groups to claim entitlements under international law" (1987, 199).[15]

This new direction of international law is reflected in the *Expanded Bill of Rights for the 21st Century*, approved at the 21st Century Convention in 1992, organized by the National Organization of Women (NOW) and other groups. This expanded bill of rights clearly articulates the emerging importance of collective human rights. Asserted rights include:

- The right to freedom from sex discrimination.

- The right to freedom from racial and ethnic discrimination.

- The right of all women to freedom from government interference in abortion, birth control, and prenatal and pregnancy services.

- The right to freedom from discrimination on the basis of sexual orientation.

- The right to freedom from discrimination based on religion, age, size, economic status, health condition, parenthood, marital status, or a person's disability.

- The right to a decent standard of living, including adequate food, housing, health care, education, and jobs.

- The right to clean air, clean water, safe waste disposal, and environmental protection.

- The right to be free from violence, including the threat of war between nations and the threat of violence at home, especially by men against women, by the rich against the poor, by adults against children, by majorities against minorities, by straights against lesbians and gays, and among races and ethnic groups.

- The right of working people to join together in unions, bargain collectively and use economic sanctions, such as strikes and boycotts.

- The right of all to participate in and have representation in our government.

This document represents an effort to move beyond the individualist liberal approach to rights, and grapple with group issues of ethnicity, gender, sexual orientation, and subsistence. This approach thus addresses a major weakness of the human rights dialogue which too often takes place solely within the realm of elite behavior and, subsequently, nation-state preferences. The assertion of collective human rights, independent of elites and nation-states, begins to examine the societal relations within the structures of modern society causing human suffering. These relations and processes result in the denial of many rights to probably the majority of individuals on the planet. There is a moral imperative that we pursue this promising direction and not limit our framework of analysis to that of an privileged worldview. To do otherwise leaves our virtuous rights talk, just that—talk.

II

THE THEORY OF COLLECTIVE HUMAN RIGHTS

6

Liberal Theory and Collective Human Rights

Theories of rights assume a position of critical importance in Western liberal political thought and are associated with leading philosophers, such as Locke and Hobbes, in relation to natural rights, and Rousseau in relation to political rights. The American and French revolutions largely emphasized so-called natural rights. This chapter will review the major contribution that liberal theory brings to our understanding of rights, and the limitations inherent in confining oneself to solely this paradigm.

Fundamental to liberal theory is the belief that the basis of rights is within the individual. McDougal, Lasswell, and Chen clarify this position: "Our postulated, overriding goal of human dignity favors the widest possible freedom of choice and, hence, the fewest possible coerced choices for individuals. This is part of the great liberal tradition which champions the least possible degree of politicization or governmentalization of social interactions compatible with the achievement of other goals" (1980, 465). The authors favorably quote Bell as the tradition on which they build:

> The principle of equality of opportunity derives from a fundamental tenet of classic liberalism: That the individual—and not the family, the community, or the state—is the basic unit of society, and that the purpose of societal arrangements is to allow the individual the freedom to fulfill his own purposes—by his labor to gain property, by exchange to satisfy his wants, by upward mobility to achieve a place commensurate with his talents. (1980, 464)

From this basic belief in the supremacy of individualism, private property, and competition, the authors condemn in strong language "[a]ll blanket assignments of individuals to allegedly different groupings. . . . None of the historical groupings, such as race, color, sex, religion, opinion, and culture, has any invariable and uniform relevance to capability for performing roles in modern society. We condemn such groupings as bases for permissible differentiation" (1980, 464).

A similar framework of analysis is found in Dworkin's concept of trumping: "So a claim of political right is a claim to a trump over the general welfare for the account of a particular individual" (1977, 364). Such rights could include but not necessarily be limited to, an individual's claim to the following: freedom from slavery; freedom from torture and from cruel, inhuman, or degrading treatment or punishment; freedom from arbitrary arrest, detention, or exile; freedom from interference in privacy; freedom of movement; freedom of opinion and expression; freedom of peaceful assembly and association; and the right to life, liberty and security. According to Dworkin and other liberal theorists, these rights "trump" competing claims and should be protected even if the general welfare suffers as a result. Claims that disadvantage the individual are wrong even if they improve overall political and/ or social goals. In these spheres at least, the individual is entitled to protection against the majority even at the cost of the general interest.

Dworkin bases his theory on the concept that there are rights that are natural, that is, "not the product of any legislation, or convention, or hypothetical contract" (1977, 176). A naturalist logic implies that "certain rights inhere in human nature and should be respected by all organized societies" (Falk 1981, 42). Hence, rights do not depend upon sovereign consent, as they rest on moral, normative standards. Yet how these natural rights are determined is not often clear, and further, their vagueness often allows self-serving interpretations by those with power as to what is required. Dworkin, however, does not see such an approach as essentially metaphysical, as some critics state, nor as so vague as to invite constant misinterpretation and misuse. "It requires no more than the hypothesis that the best political program, within the sense of that model, is one that takes the protection of certain individual choices as fundamental, and not properly subordinated to any goal or duty or combination of these" (1977, 177).

Finally, Dworkin states that anyone who professes to take rights seriously, must accept one or both of two important ideas. "The first is the vague but powerful idea of human dignity. . . . The second is the more familiar idea of political equality" (1977, 198). Such an approach involves accepting certain minimum standards of behavior. The abuse of the individual by the state is seen as contrary to nature, and perceived as wrong. The central sense of human decency and fairness, as an active moral force, found within the liberal conception of rights, has achieved popular global support.

The ideas of collective human rights presented here build on the foundation of individual rights in liberal political theory, and continue the search for avenues of human dignity and political equality. However, there are fundamental flaws in the liberal conception which advocates of collective human rights attempt to correct.

To begin with, liberal rights theory largely addresses only political and civil rights, including free expression, religion, due process, equality of opportunity, and especially property. Economic and social rights, even though they exist in UN declarations as human rights, are largely disregarded. In the United States, for example, there are no guarantees of decent housing, food, shelter, work, and living standards. Rights are recognized as long as they support the values of liberal capitalism (see Elias 1986, 200–206).

Liberal rights theory is not conducive to strengthening the rights of peoples and groups and, as a result, defines the individual in an artificial way. Individuals do not naturally exist in a solitary state, but rather within social contexts and natural groups. Further, throughout its history liberal capitalism has produced an extreme polarization of wealth within society. As a result of these social circumstances, individuals have widely divergent capabilities and opportunities. The equality of opportunity so eloquently written about by Dworkin, McDougal, and others, often serves in reality to justify the status quo. Certain classes benefit, generation after generation, from equality of opportunity under liberal capitalism, while others suffer. Legal protections do not prevent some from being more equal than others. All may be legally guaranteed free speech, for example, but access to the media often depends upon material advantage. Thus, individual rights may not only fail to guarantee rights or equality, they may actually institutionalize inequalities by providing the legitimating ideological glue to hold the system together. As a result, inequities and injustices are seen as the result of personal failure and not the product of an unjust system. In the United States, for example, the rags-to-riches modern success stories, according to recent studies, remain the economic exception, not the rule. Being rich or poor is more likely than not to carry over from generation to generation, and certainly from year to year. According to numerous economists, the climb out of poverty has become harder in the United States in the last decade or two. The U.S. economy has become less and less hospitable to the young, the unskilled, and the less educated. This lack of equal opportunity limits the viability of liberal rights. The recent studies cited below indicate a lack of social mobility in the United States and the existence of a fairly rigid class structure, in contrast to conservative views that there is a great deal of mobility:

- The Congressional Budget Office reported that the richest 1 percent of American families reaped most of the gains from the economic "prosperity" of the 1980s. Sixty percent of the growth in the average after-tax income of all American families between 1977 and 1989 (and an even heftier three-fourths of the gain in average pretax income) went to the wealthiest 660,000 families. The slice of total income belonging to the top 1 percent grew by $190 billion, giving them 13 percent of all family income, up from 9 percent. The average pretax income of families in the top percent swelled to $560,000 from $315,000, for a 77 percent gain in a dozen years (*New York Times,* 5 March 1992).

• The Federal Reserve and the Internal Revenue Service reported that the very rich increased their share of the nation's total pool of privately held property during the 1980s. The richest 1 percent of American households accounted for 37 percent of private net worth in 1989, up from 31 percent in 1983. By 1989, the top 1 percent (834,000 households with about $5.7 trillion of net worth) was worth more than the bottom 90 percent of Americans (84 million households, with about $4.8 trillion in net worth) (*New York Times,* 21 April 1992).

• The Census Bureau reported that the percentage of full-time workers who earn less than $12,195 annually grew sharply in the 1980s, despite the economic expansion that brought increased prosperity to the affluent. In 1979, 12.1 percent of all full-time employees earned below the equivalent of $12,195. By 1990, that figure had risen to 18 percent (*New York Times,* 12 May 1992).

• A study by Duncan, Smeeding, and Rogers entitled "Inequality at the Close of the 20th Century" by the Levy Institute, shows that in the 1980s it became harder to climb out of poverty largely because of stagnation and outright decline of real earnings among young, less-educated men. Sheldon Danziger, an economist at the University of Michigan, reported that the proportion of high school graduates likely to earn less than a poverty level income rose by 5% in the 1980s for white men and by 9% for black men (*New York Times,* 18 May 1992).

• The Census Bureau figures reveal that the number of American children living in poverty grew by more than 1 million during the 1980s, with rates rising in 33 states. About 18 percent of children in the U.S. lived in families with incomes below the federal poverty line in 1989, including 39.8 percent of all black children, 38.8 percent of American Indian children, 32.2 percent of Hispanic children, 17.1 percent of Asian-American children, and 12.5 percent of white children (*New York Times,* 8 July 1992).

• The Census Bureau reported in 1992 that the number of Americans living in poverty soared in 1991 by 2.1 million, to a total of 35.7 million, and the poverty rate rose to 14.2 percent (*New York Times,* 4 September 1992).

• The Census Bureau reported in 1993 that the number of poor people in the United States increased in 1992 by 1.2 million to 36.9 million, increasing three times as fast as the overall population. Further, the number of Americans without health insurance rose 2 million in 1992, to 37.4 million (*New York Times*, 5 October 1993). Social scientists at Fordham University released a study linking this decline in the economy to a drastic decline in social health. This study attributes increases in child abuse and child poverty as contributing to the drastic decline in the nation's social well-being which, according to their data, is at its lowest point in two decades (*New York Times*, 18 October 1993).

- The Census Bureau reported in 1994 that the typical American household saw its income decline in 1993, and more than a million Americans fell into poverty. The numbers showed the persistence and quickening of the long-term growth in inequality in the American economy. Labor Secretary Robert Reich declared, "America is in danger of splitting into a two-tiered society. This is not anyone's idea of progress." The poverty rate rose in 1993 to 15.1 percent (*New York Times*, 7 October 1994).

- A 1995 Twentieth Century Fund study by Professor Edward Wolff of New York University revealed that the gap between the haves and the have-nots in the United States is greater now than at any time since 1929. The 1980s were a curse to most Americans. Those at the very top benefitted greatly, while the rest suffered. "Looking at real financial wealth[1] alone—including bank accounts, stocks and bonds but excluding durable goods, housing, and pension wealth—80 percent of households experienced a decline between 1983 and 1989." Further the relative wealth position of most African-American families deteriorated in the 1980s. "In 1983, the median white family had eleven times the wealth of the median nonwhite family. By 1989 this ratio had grown to twenty . . . more than one in three nonwhite households have no positive wealth at all, in contrast to one in eight white households" (1995, 2).

- Federal Reserve figures reveal that the wealthiest 1 percent of American households (with net worth of at least $2.3 million each) own nearly 40 percent of the nation's wealth—twice as much as the figure in Britain, which has the greatest inequality in Western Europe (*New York Times*, 17 April 1995). Focusing more narrowly on financial wealth alone, the richest 1 percent of households owned 48 percent of the total (Wolff 1995, 7).

- Professor Duncan of Northwestern University and Professor Smeeding of Syracuse University released a report in 1995 which documents the lack of social mobility in the United States. They examined surveys of the personal finances of 5,000 households, conducted every year since the late 1960s by the University of Michigan. In a comparison of the 1980s and early 1990s with the late 1960s and the 1970s, they found that the poor were becoming more likely to stay poor and the affluent more likely to stay affluent. Rich and poor children are likely to stay put. The odds of going from poverty to wealth are slim. The best predictor of how well you'll do is still how well your parents did (*New York Times,* 4 June 1995).

Despite these well-documented conditions, the concepts of exploitation and oppression are not taken seriously within American political thought (see, for example, Elias 1986, 200–28). Individuals are on their own to rise or fall as they may. There is a strong belief in personal failure, and little credence given to injustice and suffering as products of class-based corporate and state institutions.

Perhaps the fundamental problem with the language of modern human rights is that the only bearer of rights is the individual within the organized community of the nation-state. Social groupings based on custom or tradition, gender, race, or class, cannot make claims as groups; only the nation-state and the citizen enjoy legitimacy.

The major flaw in this expression of rights is conceptual. The liberal view of rights takes as a philosophical given that social formations are homogeneous: thus the emphasis on individuality. The flaw is that human society today is highly diverse and pluralistic. By ignoring this reality, liberal rights theories are liable to ignore group suffering, and thus are of limited help in the protection of human dignity.

Civil and political rights, in essence, represent the political philosophy of liberal individualism. Civil rights are designed to give the individual her or his personal freedom and autonomy. Political rights allow the individual to organize her or his participation in the public affairs of the community. The core value of both civil and political rights is the focus on the supreme worth of the individual, which liberals believe give these rights a comparative advantage over other rights. The individual in isolation is recognized as an autonomous legal entity. This understanding of the essence of rights has informed the process of norm creation within the human rights community. As Theodoor van Boven has pointed out, it is "undeniable that the general orientation and outlook of the Universal Declaration of Human Rights is towards the individual person." The same holds true for the International Covenants on Human Rights, with the basic idea being that "every human being should have a full and equal chance to develop his personality" (1982, 54). The liberal vision with its strengths and weaknesses has been embraced by the standards adopted within international human rights instruments.

LIBERALISM AND COLLECTIVE RIGHTS

As noted, fundamental to liberal theory is the primacy of individual rights and freedom. The theory should not be distorted into solely a defense of property rights as its lasting strength is found in its commitment to the inherent moral dignity of the individual.[2] Isaiah Berlin's concepts of negative freedom and positive freedom have had a profound intellectual impact. Negative freedom implies the uncoerced opportunity for action, while positive freedom consists of the ability to make one's own choices. The right of movement or the right to travel without fear of coercion or punishment, whether one actually wanted to move or travel, exemplifies negative freedom. While the right of personal decision-making to determine life's choices and act on one's own decisions in all arenas represents positive freedom (see Berlin 1969, 118–34).

John Stuart Mill's contribution, of course, is to stress the importance of variety and tolerance to human freedom itself. He strikes out against social conformity. Great advances in civilization are only achieved by people who are not constrained, but are free to create. A liberal society must not only tolerate the differences among people, but must seek pluralism—seek to increase the variety of choices available to everyone. Communication is the means to make known the freedom of choice that is available, therefore Mill puts great importance on freedom of speech and education. An ignorant person is less free than the person who knows about the options available.

Liberals, therefore, call attention to the rights and freedoms of each individual within a group. Too often when a "people" has emerged either through wars of national liberation, decolonization, or religious movements, the world witnesses a curtailing of political and civil liberties. In addition, certain cultural practices seem to fundamentally violate individual freedom— for example, the French government has banned early adolescent clitorectomys within immigrant African cultures. Liberals would support the right of Muslims in Iran who want to drink whiskey to be able to do so, even if such action is in violation of the cultural norms of the state.

Yet most individuals within Iran or the immigrant African culture in France, probably do not feel that their culture is limiting their freedom. Their individual needs seem to be equal to the needs of the group. Plato called this a movement from Reason controlling the Body to Social Reason controlling the members of society. In a discussion of "higher nature" and "lower nature," Isaiah Berlin makes this point as follows:

> Presently the two selves may be represented as divided by an even larger
> gap: the real self may be conceived as something wider than the individual

(as the term is normally understood), as a social "whole" of which the individual is an element or aspect: a tribe, a race, a church, a state, the great society of the living and the dead and the yet unborn. This entity is then identified as being the "true" self which, by imposing its collective, or "organic," single will upon its recalcitrant "members," achieves its own, and therefore their, "higher" freedom. (1969, 132)

In other words, if the individual agrees with the collective will of the group, then the members may feel that their positive and negative freedoms exist, even if to the outsider it appears that the group controls the actions of all the individual members. And, in fact, these members may feel that this represents a higher freedom, because the will of both the individual and the group is being fulfilled. The question raised by liberal theory is whether group claims to group rights present a costly erosion of individual human liberties. In particular, how does a society protect the rights of those who think or act different from the group culture?

Throughout this book, the argument is presented that groups based on race/ethnicity, class, gender, and sexuality deserve to have certain rights protected. The members of these groups see themselves as normatively bound to each other. The groups exist as a matter of social fact, and are not created by law. These collectivities are not legal fictions. McDonald asserts that "what makes diverse individuals into a group is the existence of a shared understanding." That is to say, each group member sees "himself or herself as part of an *us* rather than just as a separate *me*." Personal identity is formed by group allegiance; with the loss of membership in "an identifying group . . . [a] shattering of personal identity." It is a matter of fact that the most profound sorts of "self-identification are nonvoluntary, that is, not a matter of *choosing* to identify with some group or other" (1992, 135–36).

The group becomes the rights-holder on the basis of this shared understanding between disparate individuals. The group stands as a rights holder vis-à-vis others. It wants its shared understanding recognized and respected as a distinct part of the society of which it is a part. Assimilation and separation are ruled out.

The question is whether there is a place in liberal theory for collective human rights? In classical liberal theory, group rights are respected if each individual within the group, through their "free and informed consent," agrees to pool their individual rights for a specific purpose. The key question often then becomes: Is the group freely and voluntarily formed? For example, individuals voluntarily pooling individual assets to form collective capital to form a business.[3] But this does not help us much in understanding the natural groups based on, for example, race, gender, and sexuality.

As already noted, liberalism attributes rights to individuals and is skeptical of claims to collective rights. But within liberalism it is possible to identify a range of attitudes toward collective rights from the outright hostility we have already examined to moderate skepticism and finally to guarded endorsement.[4]

Some liberal theorists, although not hostile to these collective concerns, remain moderately skeptical about the need for group rights. This skepticism is based on a number of charges against group rights: (*a*) the attribution of group rights to significant groups balkanizes the liberal state; (*b*) group rights are nonjusticiable because they are inherently political; (*c*) group rights are allegedly provincial while individual rights are cosmopolitan; and, (*d*) group rights are redundant and unnecessary.

However, these arguments are perhaps weaker than they may initially appear: (*a*) Rather than create balkanization, the collective human rights argued for in this book address the actual, real differences between groups and individuals that exist in modern society. Human beings have an interest in belonging to and identifying with certain natural groups. The necessity for group rights lies in the fact that such claims are needed to protect these human concerns that otherwise stand vulnerable. (*b*) These claims are designed to protect interests that are inherently collective and social in nature. They are not any more or less political than individual rights. (*c*) In addition, if one examines the global turmoil caused by a denial of group rights of all sorts, from Africa to the former Soviet Union to the Balkans, one can see their cosmopolitan significance.

But what about the skeptics claim (*d*) that collective rights are unnecessary because they are redundant? Do individual rights provide better protection for the good of the community overall? First, it is now generally acknowledged that the protection of certain groups, such as most aboriginal peoples and religious groups like the Amish and the Mennonites, require certain group protections or they would face extinction. Second, the interests of the community are best defined and protected by the community itself. There is then less of an opportunity for individuals to replace the community interest with self-interest.[5]

The final position taken by some liberal scholars is one of a "guarded endorsement" of certain group rights. These "sympathetic liberals" do posit certain additional collective rights. Kymlicka, for example, believes that "the liberal view is sensitive to the way our individual lives and our moral deliberations are related to, and situated in, a shared social context" (1989, 2). He attempts to demonstrate how cultural membership gives rise to legitimate claims, and that "some schemes of minority rights respond to these claims in a way that not only is consistent with the principles of liberal equality, but is indeed required by them" (1989, 4). Kymlicka makes an important and interesting link between responsibility and equality.

He argues that differences that arise in people's circumstances from social environment or natural endowments, are not their own responsibility. "No one chooses to be born into a disadvantaged social group, or with natural disabilities, and so no one should have to pay for the costs imposed by those disadvantageous circumstances." Kymlicka then argues for compensating people who suffer from disadvantages in social environment or natural endowment. The point being that if a request for rights or resources is grounded in differential choices rather than unequal circumstances, it would not be valid. He gives the example of someone who develops a taste for expensive wine having no legitimate claim to special public subsidy, since she is responsible for the costs of her choice. On the other hand, someone who needs expensive medicine due to a natural disability has a legitimate claim to special public subsidy, since she is not responsible for the costs of her disadvantageous circumstances (1989, 186).

It is in this context that Kymlicka, and certain other sympathetic liberals, situate group rights within liberal theory. He can defend aboriginal rights "as a response, not to shared choices, but to unequal circumstances." It is not a question of privileging their choices, but the special measures are demanded by aboriginal people to serve to correct an advantage that nonaboriginal people have before anyone makes their choices (1989, 187). Writing of Canada, Kymlicka states:

> Unlike the dominant French or English cultures, the very existence of aboriginal cultural communities is vulnerable to the decisions of the non-aboriginal majority around them. They could be outbid or outvoted on resources crucial to the survival of their communities, a possibility that members of the majority cultures simply do not face. As a result, they have to spend their resources on securing the cultural membership which makes sense of their lives, something which non-aboriginal people get for free. . . .
>
> A two-year-old Inuit girl . . . [w]ithout special political protection, like the restrictions on the rights of transient workers, by the time she is eighteen the existence of the cultural community in which she grew up is likely to be undermined by the decisions of people outside the community. . . . [A]n English-Canadian boy will not face that problem. (1989, 187, 189)

Everyone cares for the fate of their individual culture. The problem is that members of minority cultures face inequalities which are the product of the circumstances, not the result of their choices. Because of this, Kymlicka, Rawls, and Dworkin call for a place for collective rights within liberal theory. "And since this inequality would remain even if individual members of aboriginal communities no longer suffered from any deprivation of material resources, temporary affirmative action programmes are not sufficient to ensure genuine equality. Collective rights may be needed."[6]

Yet, if we go a bit further in this analysis, its limitations emerge. For example, the point of these collective rights as defined by Kymlicka, Rawls, and Dworkin, is to support the formation of autonomous individuals to be able to compete equally in economic markets and political democracies. This is central to the resource-based view of equality. Key is the role of the market.

> [T]he idea of an economic market . . . must be at the center of any attractive theoretical development of equality of resources (Dworkin 1981, 284). Liberals value the market (or something that replicates the results of the market), not because maximizing wealth or preferences is a good in itself, but because markets provide a way of measuring what is in fact equitable. (Kymlicka 1989, 185)

In other words, in order for the individuals within a given group to be able to compete in a market-driven economic system, certain protective measures, including certain group rights, must be enacted.

The limitations of this approach are numerous. First of all, there are serious problems with a market approach toward equality and justice. These issues are taken up in depth in the next chapter, and so I will not go into detail concerning this objection here. A fair distribution of power and wealth based on individual choice is unfortunately not the historical outcome of such societies. Individualist norms have contributed to the creation of societies of cold isolation, with individuals and groups pitted against each other for their survival. The result has been social anomie, apathy, and despair. Issues of class and power must be integrated into any analysis of rights for these rights to be meaningful to the majority. A brutal competitive, individualist, market-driven society too often respects the rights of the few over the many.

Second, the sympathetic liberal approach seems to extend protection only to those groups whose cultures support the formation of autonomous individuals. Many African cultures, however, are based not in the western models of the rights of the individual, but are more collectively oriented and nonindividualistic in essence. It is difficult to see how these societies would get much support from the sympathetic liberal's approach to group rights.[7]

The whole point of group rights is collective and not individual. It may be true, as Kymlicka argues, that group rights are an effective way of enhancing individual autonomy. But this is not the only, or even the main, value of collective rights. Collective autonomy is valuable in its own right and should not be valued simply as a means to individual autonomy (see Mcdonald 1992, 153).

Kymlicka responds that such group claims are "unfair."

> Why should aboriginal people have more resources to pursue their communal ends than non-aboriginal people have to pursue their less communal ends? Collective rights for aboriginal peoples, if defended on the grounds of different value-systems, seem to amount to unfair privileges, just as it would be unfair to give self-styled aristocrats an unequal share of the resources to pursue their expensive ideals, or to give racists unequal voting rights to pursue their shared ideals. (1989, 243)

Does our conception of collective human rights endorse "unfair privileges" or "special rights" or access to "more resources," for certain groups over others (as asserted by Kymlicka)? I have put the context of collective human rights into that of equal opportunity for specific victimized groups. Therefore, aristocrats would not be able to claim group rights, because they clearly have full access to opportunity. I have also argued that any moral group rights analysis must embrace individual human rights in a dialectical relationship. Therefore, racists, Nazis, and other groups who base their existence on claims of superiority and the denial of the rights of others cannot make legitimate demands for group protections. However, there are certain groups who are victims of continuous abuse in this particular era, who do not advocate "special rights" which deny equal opportunity and freedom to other groups, but merely claim their right as a group to be free from subjugation and to protect their group autonomy. These particular groups deserve to have their group rights met.

These specific groups and communities are fundamental units of value and can be the focus of rights. The liberal grounding of value and rights in the individual is only partially useful. Yes, individual rights and freedoms must be upheld. But so also must certain group rights, in that communities matter in their own right. It is not a question of which should be first. Rather it is a dialectical relationship, a coming and going between the two, each needing and living off of the other. Otherwise, societies are dominated either by individualist competitiveness breeding cynicism and despair *or* groups claiming superior positions breeding hatred and friction. It is a question of how to accommodate both sets of rights. It is a process of determining the often difficult trade-offs between rights that must be made in order to build a just society. There *are* conflicts between rights, and a resolution of such conflicts might involve a concerted effort to accommodate different values. The metaphor of rights as trumps that override all competing considerations is only partially useful. Real life is more complex.

Some argue that "[e]ven in its least satisfactory forms, liberalism has always included some account of our essential dependence on our social context, some account of the forms of human community and culture which provide the context for individual development, and which shape our goals and our capacity to pursue them" (Kymlicka 1989, 253). "Liberal individualism is rather an insistence on respect for each individual's capacity to understand and evaluate her own actions, to make judgements about the value of the communal and cultural circumstances she finds herself in." From this perspective, Kymlicka makes the following claim:

> Liberal individualism of this sort does not conflict with the ideal of community, but rather provides an interpretation of it. The result of this conception of individual responsibility is not to set people against each other, but to tie all citizens in bonds of mutual respect. And the result of this conception of individual self-direction is not to distance people from each other, but to enable various groups of people to freely pursue and advance their shared communal and cultural ends. (1989, 254)

I wish this were true. Unfortunately, the opposite is often the case in most "liberal" societies in the late twentieth century. The reality is that certain individuals and groups are profoundly left out of this liberal community. The "sympathetic liberal's" "guarded endorsement" of certain group rights turns out to be flawed and of limited help. As Virginia Leary put it: "Group rights can be made to fit the liberal ideology, which is fundamentally individualistic, only by stretching the concept of liberalism until it snaps and is no longer recognizable as liberalism" (1992a, 118).

To a degree, the debate comes down to one's vantage point. For those who have their group rights of religion, ethnicity, gender, and so on, met (often majority ethnic groups), the claims of "other" groups for respect and equality often equal "special rights" above society. The *Rocky Mountain News* in Denver published an editorial cartoon by Ed Stein which captured this phenomenon. Two Roman centurions are on a balcony overlooking Christians being fed to the lions. One Roman turns to the other and says: "I'm not a bigot, I just don't think people who choose an openly Christian lifestyle should have special rights." But even this cartoon is misleading, for the group rights endorsed in this book are not a question of "choice." Ethnicity, gender, and sexuality, for example, for most people are not a matter of choice.

CRITICS OF COLLECTIVE HUMAN RIGHTS
AND SOLIDARITY RIGHTS

For some human rights scholars, the very idea of collective human rights is troubling and adds more confusion than clarity to the rights dialogue. Critics question the validity of seeing collective human rights and/or "solidarity rights" as part of a "third generation" of human rights (see Vasak's definition of generations above, pp. 31–32). Generations indicate succession, rendering the previous generation obsolete, and implying the superiority of solidarity rights over political/civil and/or economic, social, and cultural rights.[8] This then allows space for repressive regimes, acting in the name of the people, to neglect internationally accepted human rights.

The major reservation expressed about the conception of collective human rights is that the rights of the individual would become subordinate to so-called higher rights. When a community, a people, believes itself to be on a messianic mission, a very dangerous situation can develop. Nation-states have used these ideas to carry out atrocities against humanity. The real danger of collective human rights is that the concept can be used to let governments of nation-states operate behind a mask, as was the case with Nazi Germany[9] and for decades in South Africa.[10]

Critics also take issue with the source of collective human rights. As outlined above, collective human rights arise from the social nature of the human species. In contrast, Donnelly, ignores humanity's social nature, and asserts that the only acceptable definition of human rights is individual rights. Human rights, he claims, are based "on a view of the individual person as separate from and endowed with inalienable rights held primarily in relation to society. . . . Groups . . . can and do hold a variety of rights. But these are not *human* rights." He further asserts that it is confusing to compare human rights and social needs.

Rhoda Howard, in agreement with Donnelly, writes: "It is dangerous to assume that collective rights are compatible with, or perhaps even superior to, individual human rights. Collective rights can become exclusivist rights. They establish communities and define—on bases other than universalist citizenship—who is or is not a member of them" (1992, 97).

However, Donnelly and Howard seem to apply a very odd logic. How are we "establishing" and "defining" communities by acknowledging certain group rights? Do not these communities exist in and of themselves, making their own rights claims, independent of what academics or politicians say or do? Is it really that helpful to keep proclaiming that the only valid rights claims are those of individuals, when *group* suffering seems fundamental to the late-twentieth-century world community?

In fact, it seems most useful to view group and individual rights as not in contradiction or in hierarchical order. Certain rights may be more individualistic in nature (such as the right to privacy), while other rights are more group-oriented (such as the right to economic security), but both depend upon the other for their actualization.[11]

A strong link exists between advocates of collective human rights and many of their critics in that both see the modern state as often hostile toward group and individual human rights. In fact, a major impetus behind the drive to define collective human rights is to assert the right of certain groups to internationally recognized rights independently of nation-states.[12]

The need for collective human rights is perhaps best seen through an examination of the American experience. As Louis Henkin writes, American constitutional rights are individualistic and deeply democratic in their eighteenth-century conception. "Representative government is freedom," wrote Thomas Paine; but the American view of rights stops right there. For example, to Jefferson the poor had *no right* to be free from want. Feeding the needy is up to charities, not the government, and no individual is morally obliged to give to a charity or help another person. In the Anglo-American legal tradition, there is no general obligation even to save life; no one is punished for failing to do so. "[T]here is no obligation, *a fortiori*, to shelter, cure, educate" (Henkin 1990, 76–77, 101). The right to unlimited accumulation and the free market demand minimal state involvement in the operations of society.

It is impossible for the United States to claim that it does not have the resources to meet basic needs in areas of health, education, welfare, sustenance, housing, employment, the environment, and working and living conditions. Perhaps in some areas of the globe the resources do not exist to meet these needs, but in the United States they do. It is a question of overall priorities and the distribution of wealth and power in society.[13] Instead of evaluating politicians primarily on the basis of their support for a strong military, citizens could demand different priorities. For example, politicians could be voted out of office if homelessness rose during their term or if educational opportunities fell for disadvantaged groups. A government's priorities could focus on relieving human suffering—meeting the basic human needs of food, health, and education for all citizens. To present these basic needs as rights, challenges those who remain oblivious to real social conditions, by revealing the functioning of an unresponsive system.

Through an examination of the needs of oppressed communities, the collective human rights undertaking seeks to establish norms that articulate remedies to these conditions of suffering. These ideas *begin* with the premise of meeting basic human needs, and provide a potential framework for defining a vision based on real equality and social justice. Implementation of any claimed right depends upon the political and economic power of those seeking their rights. The conception of collective human rights hopefully gives those denied fundamental justice and freedom a political language to articulate their current reality and thereby help define a way to move forward.

The problem with liberal political theory is primarily its incompleteness. It fundamentally refuses to acknowledge the importance of humanity's social groups. It does not address structural, primarily economic, factors which contribute to the institutionalization of group suffering. Therefore, in addition to individual human rights, we must add collective human rights in order to make the liberal ideals of freedom, equality, and democracy real for all people, and not just for the percentage who end up on the winning side.

Liberals are rightfully concerned that collective rights can become "a mask for conservative attempts to retain discriminatory communities that deny equal and individual human rights" (Howard 1992, 97). However, it is also true that individual human rights have been distorted by repressive regimes. For example, in *Mein Kampf*, Hitler defined his racist vision within the context of "human rights" (1971, 402). Neither individual nor collective human rights are invalidated because they are abused by elites. Hopefully they provide leverage to expose such misuse.

A framework of rights that incorporates the liberal respect for individual freedom with a desire to end group suffering, perhaps has a better chance of defining and helping to create a world based on human dignity. A conception of human rights, individual and collective, which takes into account questions of class, power, privilege, and vision, addresses many of these concerns (see chapter 9 below).

7

Marxist Theory and Collective Human Rights

The events in Eastern Europe and the former Soviet Union during 1989–90, call upon students of socialist and Marxist theory to reexamine the role of individual and group rights. To a large degree, the movements that brought down the bureaucratic states in the East stated their goals in the form of rights—the civil and political rights objectively denied the general population that were perceived to exist in the West. The pluralist opposition in many of these countries ideologically advocated personal rights and liberties that are at the core of the Western liberal paradigm. For some the new individual rights were to be combined with the collective, social rights already in existence. For others the drive for individual rights was part of a counterrevolution aimed at a total restoration of capitalism, and the destruction of any collectivist, "socialist" rights. Nevertheless, for the broad opposition as a whole, the demand for the protection of individual and group rights was very strong.

From a democratic socialist perspective, perhaps the most significant question concerning collective human rights is: Does the conception of collective human rights assist those who desire a transformation of society toward true equality and freedom? This question will be explored through an examination of Marxist political theory and the concept of collective human rights, evaluating where these theories are supportive and where they are incompatible. The writings of Marx and Engels, as well as current philosophers and academics, will be reviewed throughout this chapter.

According to many socialist and Marxist theorists, there is a basic contradiction in the theory of human rights. On the one hand, human rights, can provide a fairy-tale facade which serves to disguise the often vicious nature of class society. Acting "as if" certain rights are true (equality, freedom, etc.) inhibits people's ability to recognize when they are, in reality, false, and when society does not protect these rights (Ollman 1990, 6).

On the other hand, there are many positive and progressive qualities found within conceptions of human rights. Advocates for collective human rights, for example, are preoccupied with issues of justice and morality as essential principles to inform a process of change. Through identifying with

131

and understanding how people perceive themselves in the world, such proponents see collective human rights as a vehicle for exposing inequality and a direction for organizing.

What are the implications of this fundamental contradiction in the conception of human rights? What is the potential and real impact of these ideas on movements for democratic socialism? In exploring these questions, one finds aspects of Marxist theory useful to individuals and groups who strive for a more equitable and just society. Why? Because Marxist theory adds the following crucial components to a human rights framework:

1. Marxism adds the decisive element of class, without which such rights claims are too often used to perpetuate privileges and inequities in the current world system.

2. Marxism provides a methodology in dialectics, and its accompanying process of abstraction (part of the dialectical method), which allows an examination of the contradictions within claimed rights, so that the mystification and fetishism surrounding them can be confronted.

3. Marxism provides a future vision where such rights could possibly be realized.

Each of these three components will now be explored in detail.

1. CLASS ANALYSIS

In *On the Jewish Question*, Marx clarifies some of his thinking on rights, in which questions of class assume a degree of critical importance. His distinction between political emancipation versus human emancipation explains his attitude toward liberal rights in general.

Marx analyzed the contradictions of the political emancipation that swept the world in the eighteenth and nineteenth centuries. He supported liberal freedoms and political rights and was critical of those "leftists" who sneered at the efforts of liberals to achieve democratic rights. He clearly saw that such efforts were important.[1]

Marx thus did not reject the necessity of rights during the capitalist era. In fact, he supported freedom of speech, dissent, the right for all to vote, and the right to organize.[2] He even thought that it might be possible to achieve a socialist transformation through the vote. In addition, according to Draper, Marx places the "sovereignty of the people" as central to politics. He attacks Hegel for counterpoising the sovereignty of the *state* to the sovereignty of the people.[3] (Draper 1977, 87)

Marcuse writes of a "Marxian insistence" on liberal rights:

The development of consciousness in this (Marxist) sense requires institutionalized civil and political rights—freedom of speech, assembly, organization, freedom of the press, etc. . . . The Marxian insistence on democracy as the preparatory stage of socialism, far from being a cloak or "Aesopian language," pertains to the basic conception. (Marcuse 1958, xxii)

But a political revolution and the establishment of a democratic republic was not enough for Marx. The root of exploitation and servitude inside the present world order was not political but rather emanated from a system of production built upon private ownership, a dehumanized division of labor, and a rigidified class structure.

For Marx the rights that arose out of the French Revolution signified the collapse of feudalism and the beginning of a revolutionary transformation. The French Revolution essentially was a political revolution, marking the transfer of power from the nobility and clergy to the industrial and commercial middle class. Natural rights became the philosophical and political justification for the right to private property and a mode of production based on exploitative social relations.

Capitalist production had been hampered by feudal law and government, which were swept away by the French Revolution. Out of this revolution, the Rights of Man became eternal and self-evident natural truths. For Marx, however, these civil and political liberties were not the rights of man or the working class, but rather the rights of the middle class. According to scholars in political theory, Marx' attitude toward political and civil liberty was dialectical, observing the role of rights in concealing class rule, but at the same time recognizing the need for the protections they could provide.[4]

To become a reality, political freedom was dependent upon the development of economic forces. Marx, in a break with Hegel, stressed the advancement of material forces over ideas. To Marx, the sphere of material activity primarily determined the reality of human life. It therefore followed that human freedom and human fulfillment depended upon material and economic factors. Overcoming alienation and oppression meant focusing on these concrete areas, not only on ideas or the life of the mind. What held back human emancipation was not so much a lack of good ideas, but poverty and exploitation.

Marx believed that political emancipation under capitalism left intact the system of exploitation and rugged competition. His aim was to abolish this system which created such misery and suffering. He distinguished between political rights (which he supported) and so-called natural rights. The latter, referred to as the "imprescriptible rights of liberty, of property, and of security" (à la Hobbes and Locke), are the result of the *separation* of human beings from each other, rather than on relations between people. In the American and French Constitutions, liberty is defined as noninterference and "freedom is the right to do and perform what does not harm others." Man is treated as an "isolated monad."[5] The right to property "leads man to see in other men not the realization but the limitation of his own freedom"[6] (Marx [1844] 1987, 146).

In essence, the modern state declares that real differences between human beings shall not affect their standing as citizens. As a result, relations of domination and conflict remain untouched. Wealth, occupation, race, and so on, become nonpolitical distinctions, with the state standing for the "common interests" of the citizens. What Marx makes strikingly clear is that one cannot say wealth is unpolitical when it provides access to the means of political persuasion; that political opportunities of the single mother of four are not the same as those of the corporate executive; that the uneducated human being is not in the same position as the educated person with respect to policy formulation. These are *real* distinctions, that give some people advantages and privileges over others.

Marx believed that it was critical not to confuse illusory forms of struggle with the final objective of human actualization. Struggles within the state (for the vote, etc.) have some importance, but are also "merely the illusory forms in which the real struggles of the different classes are fought out among one another" (Marx & Engels [1932] 1970, 54). Ruling ideology, often in the form of rights, disguises reality, blurs perception, and creates illusions. Those with the means of material production at their disposal also control the means of mental production. Thus, their ideas become the "ruling ideas of the epoch" (Marx & Engels [1932] 1970, 64–65).

The rights of man become part of these ruling ideas and the right of private property "penetrates the consciousness of the normal man." "In civil law the existing property relationships are declared to be the result of the general will" (Marx and Engels [1932] 1970, 81). Ruling ideas and modern philosophy become accepted as fact.

To stay within the boundaries of the philosophy of the time means to accept limitations which prevent the emancipation of all people. The laws formulated by ruling classes are presented as the natural laws of society.

[P]roduction, as distinct from distribution, etc., is to be presented as governed by eternal natural laws which are independent of history, and at the same time *bourgeois* relations are clandestinely passed off as irrefutable natural laws of society *in abstracto*. This is the more or less conscious purpose of the whole procedure. (Marx & Engels [1932] 1970, 127)

Thus, according to Marx, society must move beyond the freedom of the democratic republic and the state as it has evolved. A new revolution is required, a social revolution designed to overcome class differences, as opposed to the political revolution which had already occurred.

The attempt to apply values like rights equally to everyone came from the need to defuse growing class conflict arising out of incompatible interests.[7]

Focusing on economic forces rather than ideas, led Marx to clarify his views regarding true *human emancipation*. To experience human emancipation, the alienation present under a capitalist mode of production must be overcome. Under capitalism, human beings are unable to develop and actualize their full potential; both capitalist and laborer function within a system which dictates how they must operate to survive. It is impossible for a person to become a whole being under capitalism; the person is deformed by the society of which she or he is a part. Despite political emancipation, human emancipation is denied, and individuals exist in a state of alienation.

According to Ollman, Marx presents alienation as covering four broad areas: peoples' relation to their productive activity, their product, other humans, and the species—that is, the whole of human existence. As a result of this process, there is little left in human activity that enables one to grasp the peculiar qualities of one's species.

In each instance, a relation that distinguishes the human species has disappeared and its constituent elements have been reorganized to appear as something else.

What is left of the individual after all these cleavages have occurred is a mere rump, a lowest common denominator attained by lopping off all those qualities on which is based his claim to recognition as a man. Thus denuded, the alienated person has become an "abstraction."

Alienated man is an abstraction because he has lost touch with all human specificity. He has been reduced to performing undifferentiated work on humanly indistinguishable objects among people deprived of their human variety and compassion. (Ollman 1971, 134)

In sum, under capitalism, according to Marx, human beings are not free, rather they are trapped in a system which denies their humanity. This reality is obscured by the language of rights. Rights can serve to allow, facilitate, and mask exploitation by presenting values which are unattainable for the majority as the supposed pillars upon which society is constructed.[8]

Human beings are more likely to be deprived of what they desperately need under capitalism—certainty and dignity of work, full use of human potential, and a cooperative social order.[9]

So-called natural rights symbolized for Marx this alienation of the human being from the "species being," for example, the fulfillment of life in and through social activity and social enjoyment. This is because natural rights appear to protect freedom, whereas in reality they do not address the aspects of life that would be necessary for true liberty. Instead, they present social life "as a framework exterior to individuals, a limitation of their original self-sufficiency." The preoccupation with the "rights of man" arose in the context of processes which "tear asunder all the species-bonds of man, put egoism and selfish need in the place of those species-bonds and dissolve man into a world of atomistic individuals with hostile attitudes towards each other" (Marx, quoted in Waldron 1987, 129).

Marx looked beyond this political revolution to a much more profound social revolution. This would inaugurate the true beginning of history as a record of full human self-realization, that is, human emancipation.[10]

A democratic socialist study of collective human rights seeks to develop an analysis and political program that addresses the entire social fabric of life (family, nation, gender, etc.) while understanding that a pivotal aspect of social life is class. One of the most notable features of political theory in the West, in discussions of conservatism, liberalism, equality, justice, and so on, is the lack of any serious regard for class structures and divisions. The mythology that "we are all middle class" is widely promoted and believed in the United States. In addition, many advocates within social movements (racial, sexual, ethnic, environmental, health care, etc.) often dismiss class in their organizing efforts.

In many respects, a democratic socialist conception of collective human rights recognizes the reality of class society and challenges these divisions within society. The existing world system of sovereign nation-states has been unwilling to substantively incorporate and act on the concerns of social movements, especially the claims of their working-class members. Many demands of these movements, however, are not concerned with changing the economic structures of society. For example, class analysis is of little relevance to feminists or gays concerned with access to executive corporate jobs. But for working-class members of these movements who are interested in the creation of a new society, where bigotry and discrimination can be overcome, class analysis is critical.[11]

On the other hand, a democratic socialist theory of collective human rights could confront structures of domination and exploitation through its advocacy of certain group rights. This theory could expose how the structures of class society violate these rights and thereby create pressure for fundamental change.

In fact, the ideas of collective human rights, argued for in this book, can be formulated in a manner which incorporates many of the criticisms that Marx held of rights theory.

- First, this conception of collective human rights is primarily concerned with group or social rights, as opposed to the rights of the atomized, egoistic individual.

- Second, this collective formulation of rights attempts to reinforce human sociality and break down the forced separation of human from human present under a capitalist mode of production.

- Third, collective human rights attempt to go beyond the democratic demands of political emancipation and lay a framework for human emancipation by addressing economic and structural factors ignored in liberal political rights theory.

- Fourth, the theory of collective human rights is committed to the development of "rich individuality" and the self-development of each individual.

- Fifth, the objective of collective human rights is to empower people within their own communities. Marx and Engels wrote: "Only in community [with others has each] individual the means of cultivating his gifts in all directions; only in the community, therefore, is personal freedom possible" ([1932] 1970, 83).

A democratic socialist conception of collective human rights can be seen as a means of pursuing the Marxian notion of true human freedom. Collective human rights are concerned with those economic and structural factors which cause human suffering despite political emancipation.

2. THE METHODOLOGY OF DIALECTICS

Dialectics is a way of looking at the world which incorporates *change and interaction* into one's understanding of reality. Too often, the social sciences approach knowledge as an accumulation of isolated facts without exploring the *relationship* of these facts to the world that created them in the first place.

Dialectics attempts to study the actual relationships that exist within society and how these relationships impact on behavior and knowledge.

The dialectical approach encompasses a process of "internal relations," that is, things are the sum of their relations and can only be understood as part of a larger system. To comprehend anything, it is necessary to examine how it arose, and developed, and how it fits into the larger context or system of which it is a part. A dialectical investigation of collective human rights thus examines how these ideas developed and explores their interactions in today's world. In addition, such an undertaking includes looking at the historical development of these ideas and a projection of where they seem to be headed.[12]

Internal relations are necessary relationships between entities in the sense that the entities depend upon the relation for their very identity. Classic examples include—parent-child, boss-worker, master-slave—where neither entity is conceivable without the existence of the other. The implication of this is that one cannot reduce an internal relation to its own properties, rather, the relationship itself explains the key properties of each entity.[13] For Marxists, of course, the economic relationships within a capitalist society are significant due to their decisive impact.

What is being suggested here is not that a philosophy of internal relations and dialectics explains every major event, or that economic struggles supersede all others. And it is true that certain crucial phenomena of the modern world—racism, gender oppression, homophobia, ecological devastation—have not been adequately understood by Marxist theorists. Yet can these complex phenomena be understood without the insights of Marxist theory? We may need other theories to account for them fully, but in capitalist societies, the manner in which the dynamic processes of capital accumulation and the commodification of labor *condition* social and cultural practices must be fully evaluated (see West 1991, xxiii).

Understanding dialectics and the philosophy of internal relations takes Marxism out of the category of a universal narrative, seeking universal forms, essences, substances, or categories. A dialectical world outlook rejects this type of essentialism and views human existence as contradictory and changing, undergoing processes of opposition and integration, primarily composed of the working out of the internal relationships of subjects.

Cornel West places Marxism in the framework of "radical historicism," which claims that moral truths or facts are always relative to specific aims, goals, or objectives of particular groups, communities, cultures, or societies. The universalizability of such moral truths or facts is *relative* to specific aims, goals, objectives of the particular group, community, culture, or society. The radical historicist view of ethics is to *reject* the vision of philosophy as a quest for philosophic certainty. He argues that this is exactly where we should place Marx. Marx, disenchanted with the quest for certainty, became "preoccupied with the opposition between what is and what ought to be, between facts and values, and ultimately between science and ethics" (West 1991, 10, 12, 14).

For example, in place of production for exchange, Marx proposes production for human needs; in place of domination of the worker by private owners, he proposes the freedom of the laborer by mutual ownership of products. Alienation is dehumanizing and *not* a part of human nature. Truth-searching is not a search for universals or essences, but rather an activity of "solving problems, responding to dilemmas, or overcoming quagmires" (West 1991, 65). Marx was interested in piercing the veil of appearances and disclosing what had previously been concealed. In pursuing this course, he stressed the political status of ethics in society. An adequate account of notions such as right or just, needs to incorporate an understanding of the requirements of the system of production dominant in that society.

Critical to dialectical research are what Marx called "contradictions." Contradiction here refers to the "incompatible development of different elements within the same relation, that is to say between elements that are also dependent on one another" (Ollman 1993, 15). Dialectical thinkers look to the inner contradictions of the system to find the main forces for change.

Dialectics will be used in the following way in this investigation of collective human rights:

A. Contradictions in liberal rights theories will be explored, from which the ideas of collective human rights emerged. Liberal views of rights can be used to hide and facilitate inequality and thus remain an unrealizable ideal. What are the implications of these contradictions for socialist advocates of collective human rights?

B. An examination of the content of collective human rights reveals certain "preconditions" of the future within the present. Examples include: cooperation within conflict, social consciousness within a selfish society, global economic planning within a free market. The implications of these preconditions will be examined.

From a dialectical point of view, knowledge is value-based. Attempts to present theories as scientific and objective, that is neutral, is misleading. The fact/value distinction is often spurious as an absolute distinction (Ollman 1971, 41–52). This is so because "the process of cognition has to be seen within a social context;" knowledge is socially produced. R. W. Cox makes this explicit: "Theory is always *for* someone and *for* some purpose. All theories have a perspective. Perspectives derive from a position in time and space, specifically social and political time and space"[14] (Cox 1986, 207).

Contradictions in Liberal Rights Theories

The basic contradictions in liberal theories of rights are that:

1. They are based on a right of inequality while proclaiming equality.

2. They are based on the assumption that the human species is composed of isolated individuals, whereas in reality we are a very social species.

3. They *cannot* be met by the majority of humanity within a capitalist world system.

Right of Inequality.   Marx believed that liberal rights under capitalism consist of an equal standard applied to unequal individuals. They are bourgeois rights because they presuppose inequality. Each person is unique, with different needs, weaknesses, and strengths (especially material advantages), yet none of this is taken into account in the application of rights because everyone is supposedly equal.

This was a revolutionary concept. Hobbes and Locke had written of the individual right to unlimited accumulation and the inalienable right to private property. Rousseau had discussed the abuses of greed and luxury, but granted the middle class the right to accumulate, so long as political rights were respected. *Marx wrote that right within capitalism itself results in inequality and abrogates justice.* Human beings are not born equal and class differences, in particular, should be recognized. As Marx wrote:

> But one man is superior to another physically or mentally and so supplies more labor in the same time, or can labor for a longer time.... This *equal* right is an unequal right for unequal labor. It recognizes no class differences ... it tacitly recognizes unequal individual endowment.... *It is, therefore a right of inequality, in its content, like every right.* Right by its very nature can only consist in the application of an equal standard; but unequal individuals (and they would not be different individuals if they were not unequal) are only measurable by an equal standard in so far as they are brought under an equal point of view, ... everything else being ignored. Further, one worker is married, another not; one has more children than another and so on and so forth. Thus with an equal output, and hence an equal share in the social consumption fund, one will in fact receive more than another, one will be richer than another, and so on. To avoid all these

defects, right, instead of being equal, would have to be unequal. (Marx [1891] 1966a, 9–10)

Isolated Individuals. Marx also criticized the fundamental assumption behind liberal rights theory, that humans are isolated individuals, set apart from each other and from society as a whole, with protective rights guaranteed for the individual. Such a view of humankind may fit civilized society under capitalism, but it is not a description of a person's natural and inherent nature. The social nature of humankind is denied in the liberal ideology of individual rights. For Marx, rights were part of the ruling ideas of the day, allowing for and even justifying the supreme individualism and competition necessary for the existing mode of production. Political rights and political equality were easily translated into the guarantee of economic rights of property, social inequality, and the brutality of the factory. In this way, rights are used to protect a system, which turns work into forced and alienated labor.

The liberal conception of rights is based on the idea that individuals are independent of others and therefore owe nothing to others. From a socialist perspective, this is an insidious ideology. It encourages the notion that those who succeed in society do so because of their own individual attributes (and, likewise, that those who fail do so because of innate weaknesses) rather than as the result of the social system of rampant competitive individualism. The concept of collective human rights rejects this individualism, and *begins* from a premise of the socialized existence of humanity. A socialist conception of collective human rights focuses on the needs of humanity as they arise within a world capitalist system, rather than beginning with an ahistorical approach of natural and self-evident rights.

Most socialists would probably agree that the conception of absolute, inherent, and inalienable rights based on man's origin and nature prior to society is a myth and that alleged natural rights, such as the right to property, are expressions of class interests (Campbell 1983, 4). Marx and Engels were primarily concerned with exposing the ideological and deceptive nature of bourgeois ideas and institutions. The very idea of individual rights primarily meant the equal right of all to buy and sell their labor and their products. It is thus distinctive to the capitalist period, but not to feudalism or to the postcapitalist, socialist society.

For Marx, the liberal ideal is an illusion. Pursuing selfish or egotistical ends in isolation from or in opposition to others, is not a form of freedom.[15]

To the socialist, then, liberal rights theory is the embodiment of an ahistorical bourgeois individualism, and as such, forms part of the ruling ideas of the day. These ideas divert our attention away from the actual needs of human beings and the ability to meet these needs, and instead focus on rights which cannot be met.

The Myth of Justice. The third tenet of the Marxist critique of liberal rights is that these rights cannot be met under a world system dominated by a capitalist mode of production. Freedom, liberty, justice, the pursuit of happiness, are, for the most part, privileges of class, and beyond the reach of the majority. The concepts provide ideological pillars for the system, but they do not address what is objectively needed to improve the conditions of life for most people. In chapter 6 (see pages 117–120) I cite extensive official statistics to document the impact of class in the United States on rights. In chapter 4 (see page 78–79), UN statistics demonstrate the global effect of class and power on all human rights for most of the world's people. From a Marxist perspective, these figures are clear evidence of the discriminatory nature in which rights are protected in the world today. What does "freedom" mean to individuals and groups caught in these dire circumstances? What does the pursuit of happiness mean? These rights in reality too often ring hollow.

Negation of the Negation: The Concept of "Precondition"

Of fundamental importance in the conception of collective human rights are economic, social, and cultural rights; the needs of human beings in their social groupings. Socialists argue that guaranteeing these rights requires the abolition of class exploitation and class privilege, an objective impossibility under the present mode of production. Collective human rights can therefore be viewed as a precondition[16] to a socialist society—by demanding these rights today, the contradictions within the present mode of production become apparent. Raising the world's consciousness of these issues contributes to strengthening the movement toward a more just and equitable world order.

Socialist advocates of collective human rights see such rights as ground rules (preconditions) for a cooperative society, detachable from the context of natural rights, and therefore a progressive development. The ideas of collective human rights contain certain general values and norms necessary for the equitable development of groups and individuals in any human community. These rights may be distorted and often of limited use under the capitalist mode of production, but they present a framework within which to begin the formulation of a new society. In particular, such advocates argue with liberals about the impossibility of divorcing the political from the social and economic sphere, that is, political rights alone often are of limited value for the dispossessed.

The ideas of collective human rights are useful during the current period. Group protections are necessary due to structural inequalities and inequities present in the capitalist world system. In addition, such rights are also seen as necessary in a socialist society, in that socialist ideals can only be met through the protection of these norms and values. The ideas of collective human rights present a framework of fundamental norms and values around which international civil society could be organized.

The argument is as follows: Collective human rights can be seen as a precondition for socialism, in that these rights provide a value-based framework within which it may be possible to build the necessary ideological support for the construction of an egalitarian society. Socialism can also be seen as a precondition for collective human rights, as only in a society built upon socialist values do these rights become real for the majority of people. Socialism has been defined as a condition in which all human beings share in the various aspects of economic and social life on the same footing; where all members of a society are in a position to freely engage in purposeful communal activity of a creative and fulfilling nature unencumbered by divisions of class, wealth, sex, race, or religion; where resources are available to all in equal parts; where full and equal participation exists for all in the political and economic activities of the community; where all experience equality of importance; and where all receive that which is necessary to play a full and equal part in society (Campbell 1983, 112). Fundamentally, it seeks to abolish the strict class differentiation and class privilege present in today's world.

Socialism can be seen as a precondition for the realization of the ideas of collective human rights because capitalism is based on the counter-values of competition and supreme individualism. Unfortunately, under capitalism, persons and things are treated similarly, as commodities with exchange values and capital accumulation as the principle business of society. As Levine puts it: "Our sense of fundamental human worth is therefore put in jeopardy by the requirements of capital accumulation." The concept of right challenges this direction and serves to articulate claims independent of the market. "They set off an area in which market exigencies—including even the requirements of capital accumulation—may not intrude" (Levine 1984, 145). Rights recognize a value-based sphere, in which it is possible to create other ordering priorities besides those of the market. Socialism is thus a precondition for these rights to be realized, because they so directly conflict with the value-based ideology of a capitalist mode of production (e.g., the right to food, housing, health care).

At the same time, for socialism to succeed, political thinking and acting must incorporate some of these ideas. Magdoff, for example, believes that a central purpose of socialism is to combat racism, ethnic and nationalist rivalry, and patriarchal hierarchy, but goes on to note that in postrevolutionary societies, as political and economic difficulties mount, "the social and human revolution not only takes a back seat but often seriously backslides." He writes that changes in consciousness will require a long, long process, and "real progress depends on the nature of revolutionary practice" (Magdoff 1991, 5–6). In other words, to prevent social and human revolutions from backsliding, certain values must constantly inform the process of social change. The ideas of collective human rights are potentially central to such a process of social transformation. In fact, for socialism to have any hope of succeeding, the dialectical relation of gender, ethnicity, sexuality, and class must be addressed.

The primary overlap between socialist theory and collective human rights lies in the principle of equal satisfaction of need at the highest level of fulfillment. The socialist principle of distribution in accordance with need impacts on rights. The equal satisfaction of needs requires an intermediate set of rules, for example, the allocation of available food according to the degree of hunger felt gives rise to a whole series of claims (see Campbell 1983, 142–43). The economic and structural factors addressed in the ideas of collective human rights begin to legitimate these claims by placing them in the communities people identify with and putting them in political language many people have come to accept.

Socialist advocates of collective human rights believe that such rights are designed to further recognition of collective, socially integrated communities. They are not designed to defend the private space and conflicting interests of isolated individuals. These rights are often regarded as positive rights, as ways to facilitate action by government, rather than as defenses against government. An example of such action would be for the government to place at the disposal of working people (group) access to printing presses in order to guarantee freedom of speech for each individual; or to insure freedom from hunger through direct action by the state.

Seen in this way, collective human rights are tools to secure the benefits which can be derived from harmonious communal living. Such rights, if claimed now, serve not only to undermine the old system, but to create elements of the new system within the framework of the old. This vision of a new system includes the protection of working-class rights as well as other group rights based on ethnicity and gender. Democratic socialist advocates of collective human rights believe that such rights are a step on the road to a world of equity and authentic equal opportunity. This undertaking is an attempt to move the theoretical concept of rights beyond exclusively liberalism, which is seen as too limited, and toward a vision of egalitarian justice.

3. A FUTURE VISION

Democratic socialists see the seeds of a future socialist society in the content of collective human rights today. They argue that only in a socialist society can certain ideals be realized (for example, the right to food and other basic needs). Socialism removes the masks and ideological illusions which prevent us from understanding inequality and injustice.

Socialists try to free the concept of collective human rights from the state of nature theory. They argue that, in practice, rights have evolved out of concrete historical conditions and are no longer historically linked, for instance, the inclusion of rights which are specific to a modern industrial society. For example, the right to food is unique to the modern period of agricultural abundance—the right is not historically linked to the past when it was unrealizable.

Most socialists and liberals agree that collective human rights ought to be secured for all without regard to race, gender, sexual preference, religion, or nationality. Socialists, however, emphasize those rights which focus on economic and material needs, arguing for the abolition of economic classes, and ultimately the transcendence of rights in a future egalitarian society. The task of this period is to identify which rights should be fought for and protected.

Becoming Fully Human

Marx's primary goal was the eventual liberation of each individual human being, to allow her or him to be fully human. Only with the elimination of classes, the end of exploitation, the overcoming of alienation, and the fulfillment of the individual's ability to relate to herself or himself, to others and to nature, will humans be emancipated. Thus, Marxist thought is deeply concerned with the individual. Within a genuine cooperative community (i.e., communism), the individual can fully emerge, freely, and in an all-around way.

Central to this understanding is that it is the nature of the community that determines the rights of human beings. Under the capitalist mode of production, even with political rights, the majority of humanity exists in conditions of alienation and exploitation. Economic forces control human freedom, and existence is mainly determined by class.[17]

"Man" is independent only "if he affirms his individuality as a total man in each of his relations to the world, seeing, hearing, smelling, tasting, feeling, thinking, willing, loving—in short, if he affirms and expresses all organs of his individuality" (Marx, quoted in Fromm 1966, 38). For Marx, emancipation meant self-realization and socialism meant the development of the individual personality.[18]

Marx anticipates that, in the future, society will take differences between individuals into account in order to face up to the needs of the less gifted and prevent the emergence of any kind of hierarchy. The hope is that by recognizing disadvantages it becomes possible to prevent "unequal individual attributes" to operate "as natural privileges" (Marx & Engels [1932] 1970, 47). The point is not to abolish natural differences, but to prevent individuals from gaining privileges based on them.

Antonio Gramsci and the Concept of Hegemony

Antonio Gramsci stressed similar themes to those articulated in this book. Thus, this chapter concludes with a brief examination of the relevant aspects of his work on Marxism and rights. The Gramscian concepts of ideological hegemony and counter-hegemony are of particular importance to those concerned with changing the status quo. A democratic socialist conception of collective human rights draws from this heritage.

In at least three broad areas, Gramsci directly addressed the issues surrounding a democratic socialist conception of collective human rights.

First, he was concerned with the ideological hegemony exercised by those in power and how this was maintained not through coercion, *but with consent*. One mechanism by which ideological dominance is maintained is through the language and theories of rights. The conception of collective human rights presented here challenges this ideological hegemony by developing a new understanding of rights that takes into account issues of class and power. Gramsci's focus on consciousness led him to the position that the left needed to articulate new belief systems which challenge existing paradigms. The normative framework of collective human rights can be seen as a continuation of that process.

Second, Gramsci was attentive to the relationship of the superstructure (which includes issues of culture and social relations) to the base (which refers to the mode of production). He thus sought out an ethical-political-cultural approach toward socialist theory, without losing site of the centrality of class. The framework of collective human rights outlined here expresses similar preoccupations.

Third, Gramsci's focus on civil society led him to examine the role of national and cultural experiences in the formulation of political strategy and tactics. A similar approach is found in collective human rights, which attempts to articulate norms and goals from the vantage point of groups that form due to the social nature of the human species.

The similarities between a democratic socialist framework of collective human rights and Gramsci's writings can be seen in his examination of the preconditions and contradictions within twentieth-century capitalism. For example, Gramsci was concerned with the multifaceted reality of life—culture, social relations, the family, as well as work—which is also the focus of collective human rights. He was interested in how these aspects of life determined consciousness. He sought to develop a new Marxist theory, adequate to the modern era, that would meet the requirements of a socialist transformation. Critical to his thinking was the creation of a new consciousness among people from a variety of classes about modern structures of power. Despite the existence of dire economic conditions, such an understanding of power relationships is not automatically clear to most people. The concept of collective human rights is also intended to clarify relations of power and privilege.

Gramsci believed that class rule was carried out as much through popular consensus as through physical coercion by the state. This was especially true in Western capitalist societies, where mass consciousness is formed by mass media, mass education, and mass culture. Gramsci articulated the concept of ideological hegemony—"the system's ability to reproduce itself despite its persistent economic contradictions" (Boggs 1984, 156). Neither force nor capitalist production could explain the consent that existed among the subordinate classes. He searched for the explanation in the power of consciousness and ideology.[19]

By focusing on the superstructure (culture, politics, ideology, etc.) Gramsci broke with traditional Marxists (who focused almost exclusively on the base, i.e., the capitalist mode of production). The absence of revolutionary consciousness among the working class was in part due to the fact that the majority of people internalized the dominant ideological and cultural values. Therefore, for the Marxian project of self-emancipation to succeed, the issue of consciousness had to be addressed and cultural transformation confronted. A strategy could be built aimed at gaining the active consent of the working-class majority through civil society and its hegemonic apparatuses—the factory, the schools, the family, and so on (Carnoy 1984, 69).

Gramsci's biographer Giuseppe Fiori but it this way:

> Gramsci's originality as a Marxist lay partly in his conception of the nature of bourgeois rule (and indeed of any previous established social order), in his argument that the system's real strength does not lie in the violence of the ruling class or the coercive power of its state apparatus, but in the acceptance by the ruled of a "conception of the world" which belongs to the rulers. The philosophy of the ruling class passes through a whole tissue of complex vulgarizations to emerge as "common sense": that is, the philosophy of the masses, who accept the morality, the customs, the institutionalized rules of behavior of the society they live in. The problem for Gramsci then is to understand *how* the ruling class has managed to win the consent

of the subordinate classes in this way; and then, to see how the latter will manage to overthrow the old order and bring about a new one of universal freedom. (1970, 238)

Culture, to Gramsci, meant the entire realm of social consciousness— popular ideas, attitudes, habits, myths, folklore—which functioned to mediate the class struggle, either holding back or accelerating its development. The struggle was, therefore, about changing the quality of life, and reclaiming mass culture, in order to transform society. To change the world meant elaborating a system of moral principles that could inform the process of change. Scholars have pointed out that the main difference between Gramsci's analysis of capitalist society and the Marxist-Leninist analysis, was the former's concern with the ethical-political element in development.

To be clear, Gramsci does not attempt to negate the effect of the economy on the maintenance of hegemony. In fact, this hegemony is closely connected to the relations of production, "for though hegemony is ethical-political, it must also be economic, must necessarily be based on the decisive function exercised by the leading group in the decisive nucleus of economic activity" (Gramsci 1971, 161). As Carnoy then summarizes, it is not the *separation* of superstructure from structure that Gramsci stresses, rather the dialectical relation between them (1984, 75). Thus, hegemony comes from *both* an ideologically dominant class and its position of economic power in society. Consciousness is seen as a key ingredient of change.[20]

Today it can be argued that the events leading to the demise of the former Soviet Union and other totalitarian states in Eastern Europe prove the correctness of the Gramscian position that the control of consciousness is as much an area of political struggle as is the control of the forces of production. The bankruptcy of the governing regimes in the East was the result of many factors, including of course, economic stagnation and relentless pressure from the West. However, the lack of a normative framework to justify their actions significantly weakened their legitimacy. Across these societies, there did not appear to be a commonly accepted ethical-moral framework to understand the world. The corrupt and scandalous hypocrisy of the governing elite, in acting solely out of blatant self-interest, compounded this ideological vacuum. The lack of apparently any moral values within the leadership of the ruling Communist parties, led to widespread cynicism and hopelessness within the population. The nonviolent revolutions could move so quickly to undermine these governing rulers because the social fabric of society was not held together by any common framework—the consent that Gramsci wrote so much about was missing. Coercion alone was not enough to maintain control.

The ideas of collective human rights presented here stress similar themes: the importance of uniting with the historical and cultural experiences of people in their concrete conditions in the world today, and of challenging the ideological hegemony held through customs, habits, myths, common knowledge, and so on. Socialist advocates of collective human rights assert that a strategy for change must take into account the ideological and cultural mediations that Gramsci articulated, including values, attitudes, beliefs, cultural norms, and legal precepts that serve to solidify class society and domination.[21]

In *The Prison Notebooks*, Gramsci explains how popular consciousness is transformed, how ruling ideas become deeply embedded, how they are internalized by the majority and appear as common sense and the "traditional popular conception of the world" (Gramsci 1971, 199). He challenges the left to develop strategies for confronting the falsity and irrationality of the social appearances of the dominant world order; to strive for the new belief systems, values, and social relations that would make up democratic socialism. There exists a necessity to struggle for fundamental structural change by creating a new concept of society based on new cultural and moral norms.

To Gramsci, in developed countries where hegemony was a decisive force in the hands of the bourgeoisie, the ideological-cultural arena of civil society stood behind the state as a "powerful system of fortresses and earthworks: more or less numerous from one state to the next, it goes without saying—but this precisely necessitated an accurate reconnaissance of each individual country"[22] (Gramsci 1971, 238).

In sum, Gramsci wrote that political strategy and tactics would have to take into account the historically specific conditions in which the working class finds itself.[23] The transition to socialism would therefore be very different than the transition from feudalism to capitalism. The repressive consciousness of the masses has to be transformed into its opposite; "into an emancipatory consciousness which gives meaning to socialist politics within the sphere of 'lived social relations' " (Boggs 1983, 284).

The focus on consciousness was important to Gramsci, because ultimately, even with an economic crisis caused by a declining rate of profit, if there was no change in mass consciousness, there would be no fundamental revolutionary change.[24] Therefore, there must be not only an economic crisis, but also an ideological crisis in the belief system of the state.

The ideas of collective human rights emphasize issues of class *and* culture, including ethnicity/race, gender, and sexuality, and attempt to incorporate these factors into strategies for change. In this way, socialist advocates of collective human rights are attempting to develop the themes presented by Gramsci and to confront dominant ideological beliefs. Collective human rights proponents assert that any theory of rights must incorporate an understanding of both the social nature and the natural social groups of the human species. Using the Gramscian meaning of cultural rights, the attempt is made to formulate principles that might be useful to all those oppressed groups engaged in the struggle to claim their common culture.

8

Poststructuralist, Postmodernist, and Post-Marxist Theories and Collective Human Rights

This chapter examines the concept of collective human rights in relation to poststructuralist, postmodernist, and post-Marxist theories. These approaches are useful in breaking out of fossilized conceptions of power and frozen ways of thinking about the future. Of particular importance, poststructuralism, postmodernism, and post-Marxism give voice to the "other" in society (e.g., minorities, women, gays). However, they can also result in disabling rather than empowering groups to politically confront structures of power. These theoretical approaches often fail to adequately incorporate issues of political economy and class into their analysis, thus serving to exacerbate fragmentation, rather than to build toward a new Gramscian ideological hegemony.

The new "post" writers and theorists are not afraid to challenge traditional ways of thinking and teaching, and they often expose the politically biased nature of so-called scientific behaviorialist methodology. In addition, these writers effectively demonstrate how discourse frequently constructs rather than reflects reality. The concerns of the powerless and the disenfranchised are forcefully voiced through these new approaches with their stress on communication and interaction within cultural traditions.

Nonetheless, many of these writers pay scant attention to political economy, class exploitation, and the concept of "totality," reflecting the primary difference between these perspectives and the conception of collective human rights argued for in this book. As previously discussed, without reference to the global political economy, the ideas of human rights can serve regressive causes as well as progressive convictions. In fact, given that rights in liberal theory often disguise suffering, it is potentially dangerous to promote such rights in and of themselves, divorced from the economic world system of which they are an organic part.

The components of each "post" paradigm that relate to theories of rights will now be briefly summarized; following which, an attempt is made to analyze these approaches in relation to the conception of collective human rights presented in this book.

151

POSTSTRUCTURAL ANALYSIS

One of Foucault's major concerns is to identify the mechanisms of power in modern society and to move beyond a singular focus on the state as the Hobbesian Leviathan operating through repression, terror, and fear. To Foucault, power is more than a set of institutions and apparatuses; rather, it presents itself as a "multiplicity of relations of force" within society. While the six-teenth- and seventeenth-century view of sovereignty is that it reduces issues of power almost solely to the state, Foucault writes:

> Between every point of a social body, between a man and a woman, be-tween the members of a family, between a master and his pupil, between every one who knows and every one who does not, there exist relations of power which are not purely and simply a projection of the sovereign's great power over the individual; they are rather *the concrete, changing soil in which the sovereign's power is grounded, the conditions which make it possible for it to function.* . . . For the state to function in the way that it does, there must be, between male and female or adult and child, quite specific relations of domination which have their own configuration and relative autonomy. (Foucault 1980, 187–88, emphasis added)

Foucault's concern is with relations, not of sovereignty, but of domina-tion. He refers to the "system of right," the domain of the law, as "agents of these relations of domination," the "polymorphous techniques of subjuga-tion." "Right should be viewed, I believe, not in terms of a legitimacy to be established, but in terms of the methods of subjugation that it instigates" (1980, 96). One such method is to establish a universal moral code leading to mutual antagonisms. For example, oppressed peoples are divided from each other with "the proletariat see[ing] the non-proletarianised people as marginal, dangerous, immoral, a menace to society as a whole, the dregs of the population, trash, the 'mob' " (1980, 15).

He asserts that the essential role of the theory of right from medieval times onwards, was to fix the legitimacy of power. The theory of sovereignty allowed a system of right to be superimposed upon the actual mechanisms of discipline "in such a way as to conceal its actual procedures, the element of domination inherent in its techniques." The so-called democratization of sovereignty through individual sovereign rights, was "fundamentally deter-mined by and grounded in mechanisms of disciplinary coercion" (Foucault 1980, 105).

> When we say that sovereignty is the central problem of right in Western societies, . . . the essential function of the discourse and techniques of right

has been to *efface the domination intrinsic to power* in order to present the latter at the level of appearance under two different aspects: on the one hand, as the legitimate rights of sovereignty, and on the other, as the legal obligation to obey it. (1980, 95, emphasis added)

Foucault, therefore, feels that we should conduct our research on the nature of power;[1] not on sovereignty, the state apparatuses and the ideologies which accompany them, but on the techniques and tactics of domination. "[I]t is not towards the ancient right of sovereignty that one should turn, but towards *the possibility of a new form of right*, one which must indeed be anti-disciplinarian, but at the same time liberated from the principle of sovereignty" (1980, 108, emphasis added).

Part of the focus of collective human rights, as presented here, is to examine these other relations of domination which serve as the backbone of the state. In addition, the ways in which right has been used to efface or erase "the domination intrinsic to power," speaks clearly to the need for a reconceptualization of rights to serve progressive ends.

Moving in the direction Foucault describes, Richard Ashley develops the concept of "transversal struggles," to describe "conflicts that traverse all political boundaries because they are conflicts over the interpretation of the sovereign man in whose terms states, domestic societies, and their political boundaries shall be defined" (Ashley 1989, 270). Ashley notes that there have been many "sovereign men" in political theory: the classical liberal's "possessive individual man," the welfare liberal's "man with basic needs," the Marxist "laboring man in his sociality," the romantic ecologist's "man in harmony with nature," the Christian humanist's "man of brotherhood," the Freudian's "man of basic drives," Habermas' "communicatively competent man," and so on (1989, 266). In modern discourse, the sovereign figure of man provides the "constitutive principle" of the modern state, as sovereign subject who willingly gives this sovereignty to the absolute state.

The sovereignty of the state is derived from reasoning man, who sees the necessity for order, and not from anything external. The result is a social compact between reasoning man and the state, a "paradigm of sovereignty."

[A] historically fabricated, widely circulated, and practically effective interpretation of man as sovereign being. Sparse in detail, a paradigm of sovereignty is an interpretation that does no more than privilege certain historical limitations on what man knows and does as the transcendental foundations of man's free use of reason and, hence, as the limitations that man, in the name of his freedom, has a duty never to question and always to obey. (Ashley 1989, 269–70)

Ashley believes that the critical task is to expose the limits in the paradigms of the sovereignty of man, their arbitrariness and political content, in order to resist these practices and establish "new cultural connections and new modes of political seeing, saying and being" (Ashley 1989, 284). Transversal struggles reject the absolute boundaries used to establish sovereignty in political science. This allows us to look at movements and local struggles with a new understanding and awareness.[2]

Why is such an approach important? Because current modern political discussion often accepts the limitations of the social compact, and sees no alternatives to the state. The state is seen as a product of historical necessity, and the domination that it perpetuates and the exploitation that it supports, cannot fundamentally be challenged or changed. Modern political theory often acknowledges that total freedom and total knowledge will only be achieved when history is completely and finally subordinated to humanity's sovereign will. But this is postulated as occurring only at the end of time, in some future humanist or communist vision. There is thus often a sense of futility about the current period.

So what does a poststructural analysis do? It attempts to take the givens in international relations theory and deconstruct their meaning.[3] We have inherited language, concepts, and texts that have come to constitute privileged discourse in international relations. A poststructural approach attempts (1) to show how some of this discourse constructs rather than simply reflects reality; (2) to dismantle fixed oppositions and hierarchies, such as between fact and fiction, male and female, the self and other; and (3) to challenge the positivist practice of scientific manipulation of facts yielding objective truths (Der Derian 1989, 4). As Shapiro points out, the "meaning and value imposed on the world is structured not by one's immediate consciousness but by the various reality-making scripts one inherits or acquires from one's surrounding cultural/linguistic condition" (Shapiro 1989, 11).

Poststructuralist social theories share the proposition that social life is constructed in and through discourse. It is through discourse that classes and ideology are realized. Meaning is thus relative and relational, depending on the limits that discourse imposes. Discourse mediates between consciousness and praxis. A successful political discourse "diagnoses the problems of those it seeks to reach, providing a clear and encompassing analysis of their grievances and a ready vocabulary for collective alternatives." Therefore, a poststructuralist views class and conflict as "discursive constructions." It is discourse that defines people's interests, and through it, change can be brought about (Steinberg 1991, 263).

On a local and regional level, poststructuralists feel that claims of universality are often spurious. Neither a realist appeal to the eternity of states nor the liberal, idealist appeal to a universal community is very helpful to understanding the political and cultural forces in society.

Poststructuralists question the assumption of some Marxists that the internal development of capitalism creates not only the objective conditions but also the subjective conditions for a transformation of society. This position is criticized for its obsession with economic exploitation at the expense of other sociocultural dimensions of human society. A theory of social transformation must correct this weakness.

Habermas describes this as the failure of classical Marxism to develop a "reflective theory of knowledge," in that there exists a tendency in mechanical Marxism to reduce the "self-generative act" of the human species to labor, "to eliminate in theory, if not in practice, the structure of symbolic interaction and the role of cultural tradition." Habermas sees this as a fundamental indecision in Marx's writings. Marx took account of both the productive activity *and* the organization of the interrelations of individuals in society, yet emphasized the dimension of social labor and processes of production as central to the development of the human species (McCarthy 1978, 68).

Habermas posits the "fundamental condition of our cultural existence" as work *and* interaction. As a result, the formation and transformation of modes of thought and action are linked not only to developments in the sphere of production but simultaneously (and interdependently) to developments in the organization of social relations (McCarthy 1978, 103). Emphasis is then placed on the hermeneutic goal of cultural science, that is, the analysis of the "phenomena of life in terms of their cultural significance."

Habermas stresses the elements of domination, repression, and distortion, that are incorporated into the relations of production.

> Whereas Marx located the learning process that release epochal developments . . . in the *forces of production*, there are in the meantime good reasons for assuming that learning processes also take place in the dimension of moral insight, practical knowledge, communicative action and the consensual regulation of conflicts—processes which are precipitated in maturer forms of social integration, in new *relations of production*, and which in turn first make possible the introduction of new forces of production. (Habermas, in McCarthy 1978, 234)

POSTMODERNISM

Habermas thus puts a foot in the postmodern camp, in that he questions the progress of the Enlightenment project. Modernism, having arisen out of the Enlightenment, is said to represent the belief in linear progress, absolute truths, the rational planning of ideal social orders, and thus the standardization of knowledge and production (Harvey 1989, 9). The pillars of modernism have been defined as: the state as the focus for political loyalty; nationalism as the mobilizing ideology; the market as the basis for allocating resources; war potential as the fulcrum of international stability; nuclear weapons as providing the basis for deterrence (Falk 1992a, 9).

Following World War I some academics and critical thinkers feared that the Enlightenment project was doomed and could transform itself from a quest for human emancipation into a system of universal oppression in the name of human liberation. Nazism brought these fears to dreadful reality. Foucault demonstrates how, in the name of freedom, this oppression occurs constantly on a micro-level, in all of our lives. To many observers, the core of postmodernist philosophical thought is the abandonment of the Enlightenment project entirely.

Postmodernism promotes heterogeneity and difference as liberative forces and rejects "meta-narratives," that is, large-scale theoretical interpretations purportedly of universal application. The "grand" and totalizing principles of modernity, for instance, appeals to universal justice and universal right, are no longer considered valid. In general, postmodernism rejects such foundational arguments altogether. For example, Foucault believed that Soviet repression was the outcome of a meta-theory (Marxism) appealing to the same techniques and knowledge systems as those embedded in the capitalist system it sought to replace. He therefore felt that for change to occur, we need to "eliminate the fascism in our heads," look at where knowledge is produced and localize (as opposed to universalize) struggles—feminism, gay liberation, ethnic rights, and so forth (Harvey 1989, 45–46). Critical to the postmodernist stance is the belief that groups have the right to represent their own interests, to speak in their own voice, and to have that voice accepted as legitimate.

One's sense of self in postmodern society is not with a class, but with a particular identity (Latina, African-American, gay, lesbian, etc.) that is not economically defined. Postmodernist theory, to a degree, represents a backlash against class-based political struggle. The unifying principles revolve around a privileged notion of "difference," and a focus on the "discursive construction of the real." Such a politics focuses on particular and localized points of struggle and rejects Marx's notion of unity in difference.

The concern of postmodernism for the difficulties of communication, and for respecting and valuing the subtlety of cultures and individual particular interests, has exerted a positive influence on political debate. Postmodernists have pushed the importance of acknowledging "the multiple forms of otherness as they emerge from differences in subjectivity, gender and sexuality, race and class, temporal (configurations of sensibility) and spatial geographic locations and dislocations" (Huyssens quoted in Harvey 1989, 113). In these ways, postmodernism has maintained a radical edge.

The postmodern possibility had been described as "the human capacity to transcend the violence, poverty, ecological decay, oppression, injustice, and secularism of the modern world. The failures of the modern world are here overwhelmingly associated with artificial and constraining boundaries on *imagination* and *community*, which then become springboards for conflict, inducing violence and massive suffering" (Falk 1992a, 6).

POST-MARXISM

In addition to poststructuralism and postmodernism, the concept of post-Marxism has also been developed. Post-Marxists maintain that there exists a crisis in the conception of socialism revolving around (1) the centrality of the working class, (2) the role of Revolution as the founding moment, and (3) the illusory prospect of a unitary collective will. Post-Marxists maintain that the conception of subjectivity and classes elaborated by Marxism, its vision of the course of capitalist development, and its conception of communism as a society from which antagonisms will disappear, can no longer be maintained (Laclau & Mouffe 1985, 2, 4). For the post-Marxist, the objectives of socialism become universal human goals, based on a new ideological formulation which transcends class. Rather than a process of class struggle, socialism becomes a product of radical democracy, an extension of liberal democracy.

The most well-known writer on the concept of hegemony was Gramsci. As outlined above (pp. 146–50), Gramsci felt strongly that moral and intellectual leadership required that a grouping of ideas and values be shared by a number of class sectors. Such leadership constitutes a higher synthesis, a collective will. The role of ideology is pivotal in holding this historical bloc together. It is part of the "organic, rational whole, embodied in institutions and apparatuses." Thus, for example, Gramsci stresses the "national-popular" in which the dominant sector modifies its very nature and identity. "For Gramsci a class does not *take state power*, it *becomes* [the] State." The Gramscian war of position involves the "progressive disaggregation of a civilization and the construction of another" (Laclau & Mouffe 1985, 67–70).

Post-Marxist authors attempt to go beyond Gramsci in their questioning of the position of class in Gramsci's framework. These writers are particularly critical of Lenin's pursuit of working-class political leadership within a class alliance. They believe that this presents a paradoxical situation for a communist militant who, while "[o]ften in the vanguard of a struggle for democratic liberties, . . . nevertheless could not identify with them since he would be the first to abolish them once the 'bourgeois-democratic' stage was completed." The paradox is that at the moment when the "democratic dimension of the mass struggle was being enlarged, an ever more vanguardist and anti-democratic conception asserted itself in socialist political practice" (Laclau & Mouffe 1985, 55–56).

These writers believe that to overcome this legacy, the left must abandon the "class ghetto," and reject the base/superstructure model. Mass democratic practice does not necessarily have a class character. In fact, these writers believe that it is critical to break with the view that democratic tasks are bound to a bourgeois stage, rather we should strive for a permanent articulation between socialism and democracy. Social agents are no longer chiefly linked to their position in the relations of production, challenging the Marxist focus on the role of the proletariat. In other words, the working class is displaced from the center of revolutionary theory.

To make this argument, it is necessary for these authors to dismiss the concept of material interest. In the Marxist paradigm, the working class has a clear, material interest in confronting capitalist exploitation and moving toward a socialist world. In countering this view, post-Marxists state categorically that there are no common objective interests that can be imputed to workers by virtue of their common position in the relations of production. Popular forces who maintain multiple social identities (or no such identities at all), and not the working class, will bring about fundamental, socialist change (Wood 1986, 61–63).

These scholars are critical of Marxism for dissolving the people into an amorphous and imprecise category, and the reduction of every antagonism to a class confrontation which exhausts itself. The consequences of this analysis are, first, as stated above, that the link between socialism and the working class is broken in that "a variety of other points of rupture and democratic antagonisms can be articulated on an equal footing with workers' demands." Second, the political meaning of new social movements (women, gay, ethnic), is given equal footing with working-class movements. Their role in a socialist political practice depends upon their integration and articulation with other struggles and demands.[4]

As with the poststructuralists and postmodernists, the post-Marxists also stress these new social movements. The post-Marxist emphasizes the limited role of the working class in today's world, in comparison with other relations that have emerged. The individual is not only subordinate to capital through the sale of her or his labor power, but also through her/his incorporation into a multitude of other social relations: culture, free time, gender, education, and so on. The new struggles express resistance to the commodification, bureaucratization, and alienation of social life and they play a novel role in articulating new levels of conflict. This theoretical view results in the noncorrespondence between the economic and the political, a dissociation of politics from class. In its place is a plurality of democratic struggles, which are to lead the fight for socialism. The impetus for socialism no longer comes from the exploitation and alienation present within a capitalist mode of production, the economic sphere, but rather from the dissatisfaction occurring throughout the social sphere.[5]

Post-Marxists see the emergence of new social movements as a result of both transformed social relations of the post–World War II period *and* the effect of the "egalitarian imaginary" constituted around the liberal-democratic discourse. This discourse has led to the demand for new rights of economic and social equality, referred to as "positive liberties."

Post-Marxists are critical of the "traditional dogmatism of the left," which attributes secondary importance to superstructural forces (culture, gender, ethnicity), which they put at the center of political philosophy. With this understanding, liberal, democratic demands should not be ignored, but should be deepened in the direction of a radical, pluralist democracy. A subversive potential exists within the "articulations of liberalism and democracy," as "more and more subjects demand these rights."

The post-Marxist analysis thus sidesteps the connection between the economic interests of the working class and the politics of socialism. Post-Marxists do not question the fact that the economic sphere under capitalism is dominated by class relations, but, they do not look at how these class relations manifest themselves in other social areas and in politics.

According to Wood, the post-Marxists thus attempt the impossible task of separating the organization of production from social relations. However, the fundamental antagonism at the core of capitalist production is inseparable from the relations of domination in other arenas. These connections are organic—as are the connections between socialism and the interests of the working class. Therefore, the problem of the post-Marxist analysis is that it separates new social movements from the organic connection that exists with the economic sphere (Wood 1986, 86).

The logic of the post-Marxists is that since material interests do not exist independently, but are constructed by politics and ideology, there is no connection between material conditions and political forces. Therefore, no social group is better situated than any other to undermine the structure of capitalism, and all have an equal capacity to become a collective agent in that project (Wood 1986, 100).

INTEGRATING KNOWLEDGE AND UNDERSTANDING

What does all of this mean about the conception of collective human rights in relation to poststructuralism, postmodernism and post-Marxism? To begin with, there are two broad areas of agreement/overlap between the "post" trio and the conception of collective human rights presented here.

First, all of these paradigms are concerned with giving voice to the "other." The purpose of collective human rights is also to empower those groups in modern society who are oppressed and exploited and to provide a language through which their voices can be heard. The argument is that by reconceptualizing rights to specifically address the claims of individuals and groups, we will hopefully be able to engage in meaningful, progressive politics at the end of the twentieth-century. Perhaps the voice of the "other" can be reflected in such an elaboration of rights.

The language of rights is not accidental. Habermas points out that there is an "evolutionary relevant" learning process that finds its way into cultural tradition. Rights are part of this evolution of cultural tradition and modern discourse that can be utilized in a liberatory manner by social movements. Most nation-states today face certain problems of legitimation. For example, quality of life is often dependent on collective commodities (transportation, health care, education, etc.) that private appropriation often does not address. Basic human needs continue to be unmet for millions. The conception of group rights addresses some of these collective needs that Lockean individual rights ignores.

Second, along with the "post" theories discussed above, proponents of collective human rights also point to the incompleteness of the Enlightenment project, and question the modernist drive for advancement. Given the systematic exclusion of certain groups from the equality of opportunity promised under liberal democracy, the modernist drive is not only incomplete but systemically and structurally discriminatory. Market efficiency standards alone do not produce freedom and justice for the majority, despite the visions of modernist utopians. Therefore, both "post" theories and advocates for collective human rights call for a new normative framework to guide development.

Collective human rights are posited as values, or a set of norms, which encompass the demands of certain groups. The point is to develop norms that are not only morally acceptable, but are potent and effective in exposing the often brutal contradictions present under a capitalist mode of production. For a democratic socialist, the aim of such a theory is to show the discrepancy between the existing normative framework and the realities of society. In capitalist society there is a huge discrepancy between an egalitarian ethos and actual class inequality, between libertarian ideas and actual social relations (see West 1991, 156).

However, a difference between the conception of collective human rights articulated here, and the "post" trio, lies in the theoretical concept of "internal relations." As explained in chapter 7, internal relations refers to a dialectical approach toward knowledge in which things are the sum of their relations and can only be understood as part of a larger system. There is a critical necessity to understand collective human rights within their social context, that is, the global economic system. This system impacts on their effectiveness, in that as with any rights theory, they can be utilized to disguise, rather than expose, exploitation and oppression.

Lukacs concept of "totality" helps to clarify this point. To Lukacs, "objectively grounding norms" (which is what an articulation of collective human rights attempts to do) means two things. First, it exposes reification, by describing and explaining the dehumanizing concrete realities that must be overcome in a capitalist society. And, second, it points to the historical tendencies existing within social reality. In this process, the category of "totality" is central, in that most current social science research in the academy separates the parts of reality into isolated, atomic components and, as a result liquidates meaning or true understanding (West 1991, 159). Collective human rights, as an attempt at objectively grounding norms, must also be put in the context of this totality, (e.g., a global mode of production) or these norms could also become isolated components that serve to mask rather than reveal reality. For example, to continue to talk about the "freedom" Americans enjoy because of the individual rights that are protected under the constitution, hides the reality that for many Americans such rights are often limited in effectiveness. To avoid this, all conceptions of rights must be evaluated within the totality of society.

In fact, writers in the poststructural, postmodern, and post-Marxist frameworks often do not address this critical issue. The argument here is that it is imperative that these group rights be put within the framework of a larger understanding of how society works. For example, some academics argue that a weakness of Foucault is that he leaves open the entire question of how localized struggles fit into a broader picture of progressive social change. In fact, these academics assert that under Foucault's paradigm it is unclear why local struggles would necessarily end up being progressive at all (rather than localized, reactionary, and separatist movements). It has been argued that struggles organized around localist politics (feminist, gay, ethnic, regional autonomist) have not only not been effective in challenging the central mechanisms and structures creating suffering for the majority, but have in general shown little interest in doing so.

Michael Burawoy believes that under advanced capitalism, hegemonic regimes manufacture consent, and that Marxism has too easily removed questions of politics and ideology to the superstructure while confining the base to its "economic moment" (1991, 315). The new social movements are a response to the discrepancy between the ideals and the reality of democracy. The failed promises of democratic rights brought forth the civil rights movement, the women's movement, the ecology movement, the peace movement.

But under liberalism, the pursuit of political emancipation is quite compatible with capitalist expansion and the denial of human emancipation. The new social movements, important as they are, do not challenge the fabric of capitalism. Burawoy thus notes that by making capitalism a better place to inhabit, they may actually protect it from its tendencies toward self-destruction (1991, 327). Therefore, it is of critical importance for social movements to incorporate an understanding of political economy into their work—to challenge the manufacturing of consent, rather than adapting to it.

In the 1980s and 1990s, new methods of capitalist organization and patterns of work have meant less insurance coverage, lower pension rights and wage levels, and a loss of job security for the working class (see Phillips 1990; Wolff 1995). Women and ethnic minorities bear the brunt of these changes. For women concerned with patriarchal structures and the organization of the family, or for African-Americans concerned with cultural racism, to *not* incorporate the relationship between the modern system of capitalist production and its impact on the organization of the family and cultural life, is to block these movements from understanding major components of their suffering.

Harvey describes the problem of organizing "in place" as opposed to "over space." Oppositional movements have gained degrees of power in specific locations (in place), but have been disempowered when it comes to organizing outside of their locale (over space). In fact, by clinging to a "place-bound identity," these movements "become a part of the very fragmentation which a mobile capitalism can feed upon." Capitalism is becoming more resilient through dispersal, geographic mobility, and flexible responses to changes in labor markets, labor processes, products, and technological innovation. Central to this success was the complete reorganization of the global financial system and the formation of a single world market for money and credit supply (Harvey 1989, 159–60). It is now beyond the power of any nation-state to adequately control the world's financial markets. Social movements are only beginning to adapt to these changing circumstances and remain, for the most part, localized. Formulating the concept of collective human rights may contribute to movements breaking out of this fragmentation by drawing global connections between certain groups.

The collective human rights framework, elaborated in this book, attempts to address some of the concerns of the "post" writers, such as the importance of giving voice to the "other" in society and of exposing the limitations of the modernist drive for development. Yet the trio of poststructuralist, postmodernist, and post-Marxist theories, should not minimize the importance that a class analysis has in any egalitarian vision of the future. Advocates for collective human rights need to maintain a deep understanding of the critical role the global economic system has on the objective conditions facing all individuals and groups.

CONCLUSION

9

The Case for Collective Human Rights

The relevance of collective human rights emerged in the United States when issues of class, race, and gender exploded into the national psyche during the 1991 Senate Judiciary Committee hearings on the Clarence Thomas nomination to the Supreme Court. The hearings posed the question of whether "race" should hold more weight than other factors, such as gender or class, in evaluating an individual's behavior. Hill's charges of sexual harassment raised issues of gender and women's rights. Thomas defended himself with imagery of a racist lynching, evoking the group rights of African-Americans. Thomas' race was used by conservative Republicans to defend their nominee from charges of class blindness at the EEOC (Equal Employment Opportunities Commission). Thomas wrapped himself in "blackness" to successfully sidetrack charges of sexual harassment. Thus, America witnessed these three characteristics—class, race, and gender—played off each other for reasons of political expediency.

James Baldwin commented, "You can't tell a black man by the color of his skin, either" (Thelwell 1992, 91). Cornel West raises the same issue in posing the question: "What is black authenticity? Who is really black?" (1992, 393). On the one hand, all people with black skin are subject to potential white-supremacist abuse and hence have some interest in resisting racism. Yet, on the other hand, that common interest is mediated by divisions of class, gender, and sexual orientation. Thus individuals within a group will define the group's interests differently. In this case, the "closing of the ranks" in support of a black man, was at the expense of a black woman, and thus was of dubious value to the African-American community as a whole. For many African-Americans, "black authenticity" is to be evaluated in each case, and not assumed because of the color of one's skin (see West 1992, 390–401).

Issues of race, class, gender, and sexuality continually manifest themselves at all levels of political activity in the United States and around the world. The conception of collective human rights presented in this book attempts to incorporate these contradictions into its analysis, arguing that any conception of rights must take into account divisions of race, class, gender, and sexuality. To address only one is often at the expense of the other. And to ignore these issues limits, and often totally cripples, the usefulness of a rights framework as a tool in organizing against injustice.

The review of political theory in the previous three chapters illustrates the limitations in liberal, Marxist, and post-modernist approaches to collective human rights. The Western liberal tradition of rights, while contributing substantially to the development of civil and political rights and individual liberty, inadequately recognizes the effect of economic inequality and deprivation on human dignity. Marxist theory enhances our understanding of the impact of power and class on rights, but pays insufficient attention to issues of gender, sexuality, race, and personal freedom. And the postmodernists' focus on the politics of difference, too often fragments and divides individuals and groups who share common dilemmas. In addition, as documented in chapters 3 and 4, the international system of nation-states hesitates to pressure states to fully implement such collective human rights as the right to self-determination and the right to development. And finally, we have seen how international organizations and nation-states take a limited approach to economic rights, women's rights, and gay and lesbian rights.

"Rights" evolve over time. The grievances and intolerabilities of the eighteenth century brought forth the "Rights of Man" which formed the basis of Western individualist philosophies. Around the world today grievances continue to include the denial of personal liberty, but also relate to economic deprivation and the prohibition of all sorts of social rights. The conception of rights emerging in the late twentieth century relate to new collective grievances; and thus, international human rights norms today refer to an expanded set of ideals that are *not* solely synonymous with Western liberal theory, but include economic rights and other collective human rights as well. This historical advance in human rights theory greatly strengthens the view that these norms have become international and no longer solely reflect Western liberal political theory.

Collective human rights remain controversial in the West, with such claims often labeled "special rights" by majority groups. Yet certain groups have achieved some success in having their group rights recognized by working within a democratic framework. Western liberal democracies have been debating and acting on these issues since the end of World War II, and even more so, since the end of the Cold War. What has been the result of this political debate? It would be a mistake to either not recognize progress, or to overstate the degree to which states pursue collective human rights.

This final chapter attempts to sort through these issues with a review of post Cold War approaches to implementing collective human rights within the international system overall and, specifically, within the United States. The attempt here is to acknowledge the pressures at work and discover if the state system has been responsive to this tension. I conclude that it is necessary to seek both a new paradigm in political theory and a new international normative standard to evaluate state practice. A central focus of this theory and these norms must be on the importance of proclaiming and *implementing* collective human rights. There are particularist and universalist components to all of our identities which inform a new articulation of these issues. Perhaps, with the end of the Cold War, a window of opportunity exists for a new attempt to formulate a "third way" between individualist liberalism and collectivist statist socialism.

COLLECTIVE HUMAN RIGHTS
IN THE INTERNATIONAL SYSTEM

Eleanor Roosevelt, the first U.S. Representative to the UN Human Rights Commission, played a key role in focusing the human rights debate on the protection of individual human rights. Scholars at the time noted how with few exceptions minority rights were not considered a proper subject of international law. The way to deal with minorities was thought to be assimilation within existing states. Catering to specific group identities, on the other hand, might encourage self-determination movements which could disrupt the state system itself.

Minority rights were, however, clearly articulated in article 27 of the 1966 International Covenant on Civil and Political Rights, which states: "In those states in which ethnic, religious or linguistic minorities exist, persons belonging to such minorities shall not be denied the right, in community with the other members of their group, to enjoy their own culture, to profess and practice their own religion, or to use their own language" (Brownlie 1981, 137). Yet, again, the beneficiary is the individual member of the minority group and not the group as a whole.

In the aftermath of the Cold War, a number of important documents have stressed the importance of collective group minority rights. These include a 1991 draft Declaration on the Rights of Minorities (prepared by a working group of the UN Sub-Commission on Prevention of Discrimination and Protection of Minorities); the 1990 Copenhagen Document, from the Conference on the Human Dimension organized by the Conference on Security and Cooperation in Europe (CSCE); the Charter of Paris for a New Europe, signed by CSCE heads of state and government in November 1990; the Report of the Geneva CSCE Meeting of Experts on National Minorities in 1991; and the Draft "European Convention for the Protection of Minorities" prepared in 1991 by the European Commission for Democracy through Law, a consultative body of the Council of Europe (see Halperin, Scheffer, and Small 1992, 57–60).

The "European Convention for the Protection of Minorities" includes protection "against any activity capable of threatening their existence" (article 3[1]), "the right to freely preserve, express and develop their cultural identity in all its aspects, free of any attempts at assimilation against their will" (article 6[1]), schooling in the minority's mother tongue (article 9), effective remedies before national authorities for violations of minority rights (article 11), and the "effective participation of minorities in public affairs" (article 14[1]). Article 13 requires that states "refrain from pursuing or encouraging policies aimed at the assimilation of minorities or aimed at intentionally modifying the proportions of the population in the regions inhabited by minorities" (Halperin, Scheffer, and Small 1992, 59).

Yet, despite the advances represented in these documents, governments have consistently been hesitant to enforce issues of peoples' rights under national law. Some governments are fearful of secessionist movements, while others see attempts to guard peoples' rights as movements for "special rights" beyond those granted the majority. The result in numerous countries has been minority discontent, as their legitimate claims are either ignored or rejected. And, in fact, the right to self-determination in the modern period is organized around principles of state sovereignty, rather than the protection of a people's cultural heritage. By 1990, politically active communal groups numbered some 900 million people, about one-sixth of the world's population, most of them disadvantaged. Since 1945, more than fifty of these groups have fought protracted campaigns of protest, terrorism, and rebellion against the states that govern them (Gurr 1993, ix). Despite the rhetorical advances of numerous documents of international law and the public positions of statesmen, there are almost no effective protections of minority rights in the international system.

For example, the human rights provisions of international law have long upheld the rights of indigenous (or "native" or "tribal") peoples to protection from cultural dismemberment. Yet attempts at enforcing these norms have been meager at best. No matter what standards of measurement one uses, the results are startling: human cultures are disappearing at unprecedented rates. Experts note that there have been more extinctions of tribal peoples in this century than in any other in history. In the first half of this century, Brazil alone lost eighty-seven tribes. In North America one-third of indigenous languages have disappeared since 1800—the overwhelming share of them since 1900. Two-thirds of Australian languages have disappeared in the same time period. University of Alaska linguist Michael Krauss projects that half the world's languages—the storehouses of peoples' intellectual heritages—will disappear within a century (Durning 1993, 83).

The problem appears not to be one of norm articulation or the lack of codification of human right principles in international law. The problem is an unwillingness on the part of nation-state elites to seriously address the structural changes needed to protect minority rights and indigenous cultures. A further problem is a lack of enforcement capability within international society to compel adherence to human rights standards.

Unfortunately, similar problems of enforcement hamper the development and implementation of other collective human rights.

CAN ECONOMIC, SOCIAL AND CULTURAL RIGHTS BE ENFORCED?

It is unquestionably true that Western liberal democracies have emphasized civil and political rights almost to the exclusion of economic, social and cultural rights. However, as of 1 June 1994, 129 nations had ratified the 1966 International Covenant on Economic, Social and Cultural Rights.[1] These ratifications suggest that the world's nation-states have committed themselves to the promotion and protection of economic, social and cultural rights.

In 1985 the Economic and Social Council (ECOSOC) of the United Nations voted to establish a new Committee on Economic, Social and Cultural Rights to operationalize the implementation procedures in part IV (articles 16–23) of the covenant on these rights. The hope was that this new committee would prove to be less superficial, less politicized, and more substantive than the previous body administering the implementation provisions. Only the United States opposed the establishment of this new committee.

The committee resembles the Human Rights Committee, with its members designated as "experts with recognized competence in the field of human rights, serving in their personal capacity." They do not operate as representatives of governments. A potentially significant difference, however, is that the committee only exists at the pleasure of ECOSOC, whereas the Human Rights Committee is a treaty-based organ whose mandate is laid down in the covenant itself. The committee approaches its work by attempting to (1) clarify the norms contained in the covenant; (2) expand its information base; and (3) design an effective monitoring system to evaluate states' performance in the area of economic, social, and cultural rights (see Alston 1992).

The Committee on Economic, Social and Cultural Rights may yet prove to be an important step in the process of establishing mechanisms to hold states accountable to meeting economic and other collective human rights. However, to date we have witnessed an international community unwilling to seriously approach these issues with any thoroughness. The result is that despite the good intentions of the experts on the committee there has been painfully slow movement by the international community to clarify and implement economic and other collective human rights.

Many observers have commented on the vagueness of the rights recognized in the 1966 Covenant on Economic, Social and Cultural Rights. Such vagueness allows for continuous, vitriolic, and contentious debate on the exact meaning of rights to food, clothing, shelter, health care, and education. Since 1966 there has been a failure on the national and international levels to resolve this debate and develop the meaning and precise policy implications of these normative goals—a failure to develop any significant jurisprudence on the principal economic rights.

As a result, the relevant UN reports admirably call attention in great detail to the statistics of infant mortality, homelessness, and death by starvation, but continuously fail to identify the core requirements stemming from recognition of particular rights. For example, progress was made by the Committee on Economic, Social and Cultural Rights in their third "General Comment" in clarifying some of the normative expectations of states. Explicit statements are made regarding the obligations of states toward the covenant. The committee notes that the covenant is not merely aspirational, but does impose "various obligations which are of immediate effect." Two such obligations are the nondiscrimination provisions and the undertaking "to take steps" toward meeting this set of rights. Regarding the latter, the committee states that appropriate steps "must be taken within a reasonably short time after the Covenant's entry into force for the States concerned" and that they should be "deliberate, concrete and targeted as clearly as possible towards meeting the obligations recognized in the Covenant" (Alston 1992, 495).

Most importantly of all, the committee observes that "a minimum core obligation to ensure the satisfaction of, at the very least, minimum essential levels of each of the rights is incumbent upon every State Party." This leads it to the conclusion that "a State Party in which any significant number of individuals is deprived of essential foodstuffs, of essential primary health care, of basic shelter and housing, or of the most basic forms of education is, prima facie, failing to discharge its obligations under the Covenant" (Alston 1992, 495).[2] Clearly this is an important normative clarification of state responsibilities under the covenant.

Yet, at the same time, the committee was struggling for normative clarity, the states themselves were pursuing economic policies which ignored these obligations. For example, UN economists note that despite economic growth no progress has been made in reducing poverty in Latin America in the last decade. In fact, these UN economists predict that despite projected economic growth through the end of the century, reliance solely on neoliberal economics will mean that no progress will be made in reducing poverty. They even predict that poverty will increase. As of 1986,

37 percent of all families in Latin America were living in poverty; by 2000, the economists say the figure will be 38 percent, or 192 million people (*New York Times*, 7 September 1994). Further, the UNDP notes that Egypt, South Africa, Nigeria, and Brazil are in danger of joining the world's list of "failed states" because of wide income gaps between sections of their populations. They fear the result could be disastrous social upheavals and explosions (*New York Times*, 2 June 1994).[3]

Many other statistics could be summarized, but the point should be clear. Despite progress in the international community on defining normative goals and rights, there has not been similar success in pushing states to actually change the conditions faced by those trapped at the bottom of the global division of labor. Objectively there has been little done to meet the duties and obligations (outlined in chapter 4 above) to respect, to protect from deprivation, and to aid the deprived. This lack of action leads to cynicism about the UN and other IGOs. Normative proclamations and declarations are continuously *not* followed up with significant action to alleviate suffering. This type of diplomatic hypocrisy led Sartre to call such high-sounding principles as liberty, equality, fraternity . . . little more than "chatter, chatter" (Sartre 1963, 22).

WHAT ABOUT THE INTERNATIONAL
LABOR ORGANIZATION AND THE EEC?

More than any other international organization, the International Labor Organization (ILO) has since its founding consistently attempted to implement an integrated understanding of human rights. The dichotomy in the UN between economic rights on the one hand, and civil and political rights on the other, has been avoided. Instead, the ILO has adopted a broad conception of human rights, establishing essentially the same systems of supervision for all rights.

For example, the 1944 Declaration of Philadelphia states: "all human beings, irrespective of race, creed, or sex have the right to pursue both their material well-being and their spiritual development in conditions of freedom and dignity, of economic security and equal opportunity" (Brownlie 1981, 173).[4] The ILO from the beginning focused on "social justice," the intrinsic links between the material advancement of peoples and their civil and political rights. This broader philosophical approach to human rights avoids the distinctions and priorities among different types of rights, giving equal value to material well-being, economic security, freedom, and nondiscrimination.

As a result, the same ILO supervisory system is used for monitoring the implementation of all conventions, those covering civil rights and economic rights. As we have seen, the UN divided human rights into two covenants with two separate reporting/implementing systems—the end result being a weaker UN implementation system for economic, social, and cultural rights. The ILO has not made this distinction. It has refused to divide these interrelated rights and has attempted more than other organizations to show that economic rights as well as civil and political rights may be subject to precise definition and enforcement.

But how effective is this ILO system of supervision which is often held up as a model for others attempting to implement human rights? The view from the ILO is that their supervision of the implementation of conventions has been relatively successful. The ILO system has been in operation over seventy years.[5] Of particular importance is the ILO system of reporting which consists of a two-tier examination of reports on ILO conventions: first by a committee of experts, and, second, by a larger committee composed of representatives of governments, employers, and workers. Reports of all 171 ILO conventions are examined by the same two committees.

The committee of experts is perceived to be selected objectively rather than politically, and undertakes its technical examination of reports in a closed session without the presence of representative states. Closed meetings, lack of publicity, and the lack of presence of government representatives have depoliticized the ILO procedure and enhanced the reputation of the committee of experts. The second stage involves the ILO conference committee, a political body composed of some 200 members, of whom one-third are government delegates, one-third representatives of workers' organizations, and one-third representatives of employer organizations. Two aspects of the ILO conference committee procedure are particularly noteworthy: the active participation of employer and worker representatives in addition to the government delegates, and the reference in the committee's report to certain governments who have failed to implement ratified conventions (Leary 1992b, 599). The nongovernmental participation has been critical to the citing of governments for failure to implement conventions in its reports. It is highly unlikely that a committee composed of governments only would have done so.

Has this "blacklist" of delinquent governments (in the form of "special paragraphs") successfully brought about a change in a state's policies? States cited in the list increasingly object and consider it a form of censure. They do not want to be publicly tagged as not living up to their international obligations under human rights law. This "mobilization of shame" does appear to have some effect. The procedures of naming the violating governments has withstood attacks only because of the long-term credibility of the ILO.

Yet does this change policy? Has the ILO, for example, positively impacted on the employment policies of its members? ILO members must provide information and report on their employment policies. From this information, the ILO has voiced some rather sharp criticisms of national performance concerning employment policy. Further, the ILO and the UN have become leading centers of communication, research, and policy experimentation. Conclusions are then shared with national governments, which has resulted in an increasing acceptance of norms. To some degree, the responsibilities of governments and employers to their employees has evolved as a result. Yet acceptance of norms and principles in the area of employment rights has been limited in all regions of the world.

And here we come back to the failures at the international level to clarify the content of economic, social, and cultural rights. For example, what are employment rights? What is the content of the right to work? What does it mean to strive for full employment? And if we cannot agree on these definitions, what are we enforcing? The answers to most of these questions remain vague.

As a global process, ILO employment norms have had a *limited impact*, particularly in relation to the Third World and Eastern Europe. Third World unemployment and underemployment stood at roughly 40–50 percent in 1987, according to the Overseas Development Council, who went on to say: "In the next two decades, at least 600 million new jobs—more than the total number of jobs in all the industrial market economies—will have to be created just to accommodate new entrants into the labor force who are already alive today" (Siegel 1994, 127–28).

In a review of the work of the ILO's expert committee in 1989 and 1990, Richard Siegel found a rather "benign approach" to the responsibility of most states for employment, with moderate criticism of selected Western European states (including Ireland, Italy, and France) standing as the exceptions to this pattern. He found the committee willing to accept imposed structural adjustment as a sufficient excuse for Third World failures to deal with unemployment and give East-Central European countries a substantial grace period. "Such leniency was even extended to the absence of meaningful estimates of national unemployment and underemployment by many governments, an approach that seems unduly generous in some cases and a clear retreat from the Committee's posture less than a decade earlier" (Siegel 1994, 169). The result overall has been a substantial weakening of the ILO supervisory role.[6]

Unfortunately, similar patterns are found within the European Community. It is unquestionably true that the legislative and judicial powers of the European Community are unmatched by other regional or international organizations throughout the world. Rights and obligations of individuals throughout the Community are protected regionally through founding treaties. Member states must legislate in conformity with common standards in order to carry out treaty obligations. The European Court of Justice has developed authoritative case law.

Yet even the European Economic Community (EEC) has primarily produced only *nonbinding* resolutions and recommendations on unemployment and other economic rights. Nonbinding measures within the EEC have dealt with the promotion of opportunities for young workers, the reorganization of working time, and harmonization of national vocational training policies. Despite their nonbinding nature, these instruments were very difficult for the EEC to agree to, let alone promote (Siegel 1994, 136).

In fact, the EEC has very few major binding full-employment measures to implement. As a result, commentators have found it necessary to distinguish between the Council of Europe's weaker enforcement of the European Social Charter and the employment-oriented conventions from its fairly impressive system for implementing the mostly political and civil rights in the European Convention for the Protection of Human Rights and Fundamental Freedoms. One expert concludes that the Council of Europe "is able to do little more than keep an eye on the effectuation of conventions and agreements at a fairly superficial level" (Siegel 1994, 134).

A profound unwillingness to confront the structural constraints hampering the realization of collective human rights is exposed through an objective analysis of state practice within regional and global IGOs. The UN, the ILO, and the EEC have not been effective in establishing mechanisms for implementing the collective human rights found within the Covenant on Economic, Social and Cultural Rights. There is a continuing inclination to view these rights as separate issues for each country. Problems such as unemployment are often believed to be problems that are impossible to solve at a global, or even regional, level. And at the national level, elites resist change and problems of definition and implementation remain unresolved. As a result, the majority of the world's peoples live without the protections found within these rights.

COLLECTIVE HUMAN RIGHTS IN THE UNITED STATES

Under the Bush administration, the United States ratified the Covenant on Civil and Political Rights, and his representative to the United Nations Commission of Human Rights, Ambassador Kenneth Blackwell, called for the United States to ratify the Economic and Social Covenant. At the 1993 World Conference on Human Rights held in Vienna, Secretary of State Christopher stated that the Clinton administration would push for the ratification of the Covenant on Economic, Social and Cultural Rights (at the moment it has been pushed behind the racial and women's treaties).

The political climate in the United States, however, is such that attempts to actually address economic, social, and cultural rights are often attacked as "socialist" or "communist" measures that can supposedly only be funded with huge tax increases. The recent debate on the Clinton health care proposal is a case in point. In fact, the purported differences between civil and political rights on the one hand, and economic, social, and cultural rights on the other, are less than they appear. Some cast civil and political rights as negative restraints on governments, while economic, social, and cultural rights are characterized as affirmative obligations. The former, therefore, do not cost money while the latter do. This is a false distinction. You can run down the list of civil and political rights and demonstrate in the United States, and in other countries, that great expenditures have been required, often as the result of litigation. A few examples: as a result of the Eighth Amendment prohibition on cruel and unusual punishment, states have been required to upgrade prison facilities and even build new ones; since *Gideon v. Wainwright*, the state and federal governments have been required to provide lawyers and other professions to indigents charged with felonies—at great expense; one can even argue that the entire due process and fair trial provisions require enormous expenditures by the government to establish a judicial system (Lockwood, Owens, & Severyn 1993, 24–28).

A further argument against economic rights is that they are amorphous and not susceptible to judicial definition, whereas civil and political rights can be clearly defined. There are difficulties with both parts of this argument. First, civil and political rights are hardly easy to define. In the classic First Amendment area, whole law courses are devoted to the study of how courts have struggled with the meaning of freedom of speech. And second, basic economic needs can be defined. In fact, the federal government requires every state to define the poverty line in concrete terms: they do not have to meet it but they have to define it.

In the United States, activists and academics have pursued an agenda of collective human rights in the post–Cold War world. In chapter 2 above, we examined aspects of the movements for women's rights, gay and lesbian rights, and cultural rights of ethnicity/race. In addition, organizers have pursued programs of economic rights and African-American rights, which will now be explored. Will liberal democracy in the United States accommodate these efforts? To date the answer is mixed.

ECONOMIC RIGHTS: UTILIZING STATE CONSTITUTIONS

Despite the growth of the overall U.S. economy, the typical American household continues to see its income decline and the 1990s appear to be consolidating the long-term growth in inequality in the United States. Since there is no federal constitutional right to basic needs, the U.S. Constitution is of limited use in the enforcement of minimum standards of care for the poor.

To resolve this dilemma, the poor and their advocates in Ohio have developed a unique new legal strategy that holds great potential. They are examining the utility of state constitutional and statutory law in the protection of basic needs. Lockwood, Owens, and Severyn point out that many state constitutions contain substantive provisions that deal explicitly with poverty, housing, shelter, and nutrition. For example, New York's requirement that the legislature provide for "aid, care and support of the needy" and Alabama's obligation to provide "adequate provision for the maintenance of the poor." The plaintiffs in *Daugherty v. Wallace* argue that Ohio's constitutional guarantee of the right of "obtaining . . . safety" encompasses the right of poor citizens to receive subsistence assistance from the state, in an amount sufficient to enable them to avoid homelessness and to obtain basic health care.

This litigation in Ohio is noteworthy because many states have safety and/or happiness provisions in their constitutions. The plaintiffs in this case argue that state constitutional language such as this can serve as the basis for a constitutional right to public assistance sufficient to meet basic needs. In their view, the right to obtain happiness and safety is meaningless for the unemployed, disabled, and poor unless interpreted as imposing an affirmative right to assistance sufficient to provide shelter and medical care. The Urban Morgan Institute for Human Rights also framed the scope of the right more broadly, urging that the Ohio constitutional rights to happiness and safety encompass a right to basic subsistence, defined as protection against deprivations of the food, clothing, shelter, and medical care necessary for a decent life. Given that many state constitutions have clauses declaring as inalienable the right to seek and/or obtain happiness and/or safety, these clauses may serve as a source of a positive right to basic needs. The ultimate success of the plaintiff's claims in Ohio remains to be seen. But their strategy of litigating the happiness and safety clauses of state constitutions may be adapted by advocates of the poor in other states facing serious reductions in public assistance. State constitutions may serve as a better vehicle than the U.S. Constitution for responding to the needs of the impoverished (Lockwood, Owens, & Severyn 1993, 4, 5, 8, 9, 28).

A strategy for justice based on the necessity of economic rights, the right to basic needs, clearly must be formulated. The arguments make sense, but they have yet to be accepted by either the American public or the judicial branch.

What about the rights of ethnicity and race? Has America successfully adopted these collective human rights, since the advances of the Civil Rights movement of the 1960s? Do the equal protection clauses of the Fourteenth Amendment address our concerns of collective human rights?

ETHNIC RIGHTS: LANI GUINIER AND AFRICAN-AMERICAN REPRESENTATION

In the spring of 1993, President Bill Clinton withdrew his nomination of Lani Guinier to be assistant attorney general in charge of the Justice Department's civil rights division. After reading her legal writings he decided he could not support many of her views on bolstering the political power of African-Americans. What were the issues that Lani Guinier wrote about that President Clinton found objectionable?

Guinier attempted to tackle one of the most difficult political questions confronting a democracy, that is, how to create a fair and just political system that does not solely reflect the wishes of the numerical majority (often at the expense of various numerically smaller groups). She argued that majority rule is often insufficient to provide African-Americans with a fair share of political power. To overcome this, she proposed a variety of voting schemes to enhance the power of black voters and black lawmakers.

Guinier interprets the 1965 U.S. Voting Rights Act to mean the right to effective representation, which implies more than merely the right to vote. The "opportunity . . . to participate [equally] in the political process" has not adequately been addressed, and instead the focus has been on securing the "opportunity . . . to elect the representatives of [the protected group's] choice" (1991a, 1093). She notes that this has resulted in issues of voter participation, effective representation, and policy responsiveness being, for the most part, ignored.

The real goal of the Civil Rights movement in America was to alter the material condition of the lives of America's subjugated minorities. Single-district black electoral success has not achieved this goal. Such representation is not meaningless, but is limited in effectiveness. As Guinier wrote, authentic black representation is "a limited empowerment tool."

It is limited for many reasons, including the fact that there is no ongoing relationship between the representative and the represented. There exists no mechanism, other than electoral ratification, for measuring representativeness. The election of black officials is interpreted as equalling black empowerment, even when the officials do not respond to constituent needs. Guinier maintains that such a process does not generate "sustained, empowering participation in the political process" (1991a, 1110–12).

Guinier is posing the fundamental problem confronting peoples' rights in a constitutional democracy, when the "people" in question do not constitute a majority. How are peoples' rights protected under national law? Pluralist theories of democracy envision a degree of "checks and balances" to control "factions" (as Madison put it) including both minority "special interests" and the tyranny of a hostile majority.

Guinier believes that majority tyranny is not checked when black political rights are focused solely on electing black candidates in black districts. This system expects these individuals (who may not share the original civil rights vision) to transform the status of the group as a whole. Suddenly these individuals become group spokesmodels, "without continuously articulating either the basis for a cohesive, community agenda or the responsibility to develop any agenda" (1991a, 1130–31). She goes on to explain how this system overestimates the transformative possibilities of electoral activity, which "may fail as a means of creating and redistributing political power and wealth" (1991a, 1131). For the assumption that elections provide the policy issue control by constituents of representatives is inaccurate. It is often difficult for constituents to punish unresponsive representatives at the polls. There are problems in organizing collective action and for poor constituents such activity may prove too costly. "Unless the concept of political participation transcends election day activity, a constituent is not providing much substantive direction simply by casting a ballot"[7] (1991a, 1133).

A society that is concerned about collective human rights, peoples' rights, being protected and minority interests being represented must address these concerns. Physical representation is not enough if the majority continues to ignore the vital interests and basic rights of the minority.

What Guinier is arguing is that black electoral success presents both progress and a paradox. The progress, of course, is the increase in the number of black elected officials and the large number of blacks who vote. "The paradox is that by winning, blacks ultimately lose; as soon as they achieve one electoral success, the focus of the discrimination shifts to the legislative arena" (1991b, 1446–47). And in this arena, white majority rule continues unabated. "[E]ffective representation is not just the process of reelection; it is the policy-centered process of governing responsibly. . . . Sustained black voter participation is a necessary condition to ensuring that black representatives remain substantively accountable to constituent policy preferences" (1991a, 1448).

Solutions are not easy. Guinier reaches back to the proposals of John Calhoun, who in the mid-nineteenth century wrote of the "concurrent majority," designed to protect minority interests in the South. Under Calhoun's proposals, legislation would need both the support of the majority of the minority representatives, and the majority of the majority representatives (1991a, 1140). Such a system would give the "minority" certain "veto" rights, which is why the majority opposes these schemes.

Yet if a minority veto is not fair, what is legitimate about a winner-take-all system of majority rule? Why should 51 percent of the people control 100 percent of the outcomes?

Guinier proposes a "proportionality principle of collective decision-making." Her principles are as follows:

1. Each group has a right to have its interests represented.

2. Each group has a right to have its interests satisfied a fair proportion of the time (1991b, 1481).

One proposal for interest representation is through cumulative voting. In a city that now has five districts, for example, each citizen would have five votes in a citywide race so the five people elected would have to think about various groups of supporters instead of representing just whites or blacks (1991b, 1436–37). Cumulative voting has been used by corporate boards for years, and by local jurisdictions in five states to solve voting rights disputes.

Early in 1994, Federal Judge Joseph Young, in a Maryland case, ordered the adoption of cumulative voting rather than race-conscious districting as the most effective way to facilitate the representation of African-American voters in Maryland's Worcester county. This marked the first time that a federal court has sought to impose this type of remedy. It is then up to the voters, and not the courts or legislators, to decide to what extent they want to be race conscious. In Worcester county's at-large election for five county commissioners, cumulative voting would enable voters to cast more than one of their five votes for a single candidate. If the county's African-American voters decided to give all five of their votes to one candidate, for example, their candidate's vote total would quickly reach the minimum quota required for election. Cumulative voting has helped break the racial barriers for the election of African-Americans in Chilton county, Alabama; Latinos in Alamogordo, New Mexico; and Native Americans in Sisseton, South Dakota. In addition, twenty-one school boards and city councils in Texas have adopted cumulative voting and the state legislature is currently considering it for judicial elections (Pillsbury 1994, 445).

In sum, Guinier presents interest representation as accomplishing the following: (1) Neither the majority nor the minority always dominate; (2) each voter has an equal opportunity to cast a meaningful vote; (3) the decisional rules use principles of proportional power to induce consensual approaches to problem solving (1991b, 1484).

TAKING SUFFERING SERIOUSLY

Is there a "third way," between liberalism and Marxism, toward a world that takes suffering seriously—with decisions made on the basis of meeting basic human needs? The late Christian Bay believed that there is such a new movement already well on its way, in the countless organizations and agencies seeking to make governments and other powerful agencies more accountable for abusive treatment of human rights in disregard of human needs and rights, including the needs and rights of future generations. "Provided we take the universality of basic human needs and of need-based rights seriously enough, we may envisage an expanding world-wide human rights movement as a viable third way toward a more humane and sustainable world, post-liberal and post-Marxist" (1990, 236).

One approach toward this "third way" is to attempt to develop a new paradigm of rights which overcomes the limitations of both the Western liberal tradition of rights as well as the failures of a Marxist understanding of rights. Since the 1930s, numerous intellectuals have made desperate efforts to find a "third way" between capitalism and communism. For example, a group of "personalists" in France during the Nazi occupation, drafted a declaration of rights. The final draft published in 1945, entitled "Declaration of the Rights of Persons and Communities," specifically addresses group rights. Part 2 is labelled "Rights of Communities." Article 27 states: "There exist natural communities. Born outside the State, they cannot be subject to it. Their spontaneous powers limit the power of the State. They should be represented as such within the State." The twelve articles included under the heading of rights of communities relate to the rights of families, the nation, economic and work communities, and the international community[8] (Leary 1992a, 118).

Liberal social contract theory does not respect collective human rights, that is, it includes no theoretical justification for protecting women, African-Americans, lesbians and gays, or any other group as a group. As Sigler points out, Rawls' modern theory of contractual, individual rights ignores group rights and therefore "fails to account for reality." Groups, "in fact do have status and rights at an intermediate level between the individual and the state, and it is imperative for a theory of justice to take this fact into account" (1983, 25). If societies are to thrive, individual rights must be supplemented by group rights.

Assimilation is not the answer for most groups. African-Americans do not wish to be white. Jews do not wish to be Catholics. Croats do not want to be Serbs. Native Americans do not want to lose their ethnic heritage. Women do not wish to be men. And lesbians and gays do not wish to be heterosexual. The group demands its own preservation rather than assimilation and commands respect.

To emphasize, as I have throughout this book, the importance of class, is not to denigrate sexual or ethnic oppression in all their manifestations. It is not a question of hierarchy, with class at the top and other oppressions fighting for their position on the list. Rather, it is a question of relationships, processes, and interactions that occur within the social body—how they are manifested and intertwined.

Liberal democracy involves the separation of political rights and powers from economic and social ones. The point of emphasizing the impact of economics is to highlight the falsity of that separation. If rights are talked about independently of class, they often serve to obfuscate and hide, rather than to clarify oppression and exploitation. Therefore, the economic context must always be considered.

Rights alone are not necessarily progressive and, in fact, can serve to disguise exploitation rather than help end it. Genocide has been committed under the banner of group rights, and therefore the *context* of these rights must be made explicit. What is the vision of the world these rights are trying to create and how can this be brought about? This question cannot be avoided, and leads directly to an analysis of political economy. A strong argument can be made that only under a radically modified market system is it possible for these individual and collective rights to be implemented in any meaningful way.

Current mainstream ideology and "common sense" ways of thinking maintain to a large degree the fiction of the separation of economics from politics and society. The expansion of freedom and equality in the political and social sphere can supposedly take place without touching economic exploitation. Capitalist relations of production depend upon economic coercion alone, and are therefore compatible with liberal democracy, and a neutral state. Equality and equity have very little to do with a liberal view of economics, and thus often become distant abstractions to the majority.[9] Our task is to crystallize the relationship between class and all rights theories, including collective human rights, to make these rights meaningful for the majority.

But, liberal democracy is not only a false or misleading ideology. Liberal theory's resilience is partially due to the fact that its claims contain vital and indispensable elements of truth. In fact, the political freedoms adhered to by liberal democracy perhaps make it possible to transform the nation-state into an instrument for the creation of a more egalitarian society. More serious attention needs to be taken of proposals like Lani Guinier's to make democracy meaningful for those without wealth and power. If that is done, perhaps then a liberal democratic state can become a vehicle for the protection of individual and group rights. Perhaps a democratic state will then accept globalist priorities of global justice, ecological balance, peace, and human rights. Perhaps a democratic state can then become the means to enforce the moral vision outlined in this book. But such a transformation of the state will require an expansion of democracy to those individuals and groups currently locked into positions on the bottom of society. A truly democratic state would not only provide means for all peoples and groups to voice their claims, but would also be responsive to the needs of those who suffer. True democracy requires that politics be guided by a moral normative framework of individual *and* group rights rather than wealth. The nonviolent, normatively based, mass movements for human rights that brought down oppressive governments in the Philippines, Eastern Europe, and the former Soviet Union demonstrate the power of values and rights in bringing about dramatic change. Rather than the Marxist vision of the "proletariat" as the "agent" for change, perhaps our "agency" is the power of a radical, normative framework embracing collective human rights, and thus reconceptualizing a future vision of true egalitarianism. Hopefully, this will represent the beginning of a normatively based, nonviolent movement for humane governance.[10]

GLOBAL HUMANE GOVERNANCE

This movement for humane governance also has a global dimension. As reviewed above in chapter 5, to a large degree nation-states can be considered morally and geopolitically obsolete since they can no longer provide security for their citizens. Security is now conceived only on a global level, and includes not just quantities of military power, but issues of economic and environmental interdependence. We saw that these new interpretations and understandings of international society directly challenge premises of realist theory on the functioning of the international system.

Can a global civilization truly emerge? Unlike the idea of a world government, the notion of an emerging global civilization can perhaps be better envisioned as a loosely integrated form of world order that might have the following characteristics: gradual development, coexistence with rich cultural and political diversity, less reliance on the centralization of power characteristic of the modern state (Bateson 1990, 145), and some normative values embodied in collective human rights around which global expectations hopefully can converge.

It is noteworthy that poststructuralist and Gramscian themes were found in the published writings on new thinking by Gorbachev's foreign policymakers before the dissolution of the USSR. These individuals called for a new hegemony within international relations around the values embodied in a world society. Scholars pointed to the connection between Soviet new thinking and the Kantian or universalist tradition, in which the dominant theme among states is really the relationships among all human beings in the human community. The interests of all humankind are identical, and eventually will present a challenge to the supremacy of the state system. There is a moral imperative for the overthrow of the conflictual state system and its replacement by a cosmopolitan society which reflects these common interests. Gorbachev therefore declared "a world society" as a vision of the future.

This new direction emerged from the recognition of worldwide problems such as environmental destruction and nuclear holocaust and de-emphasized the state-system. Over the socioeconomic structure of states there was said to exist an interdependent world society: "an all-human morality and a hierarchy of values headed by peace, reflecting the right and responsibility of every individual to live on the planet as his/her common home." A moral code was found in the "common heritage of mankind," the "democratization of international relations," and the "balance of interests" (as opposed to the "balance of power"). All of these proposals (if implemented) would lead to severe limitations on the sovereignty of states. These Soviet writers emphasized not only the gradual disarmament of states, but the need to investigate the implications of national and cultural diversity in a world made up of nonsovereign societies (Kubalkova & Cruickshank 1989, 71).

Proponents of the ideas of collective human rights address globalization and domestic fragmentation in a number of ways. They challenge the notion that political authority is exercised exclusively or even primarily within clearly demarcated territorial boundaries, and question the state's unlimited authority within its defined territory. And second, they point to the growing disjuncture between state and civil society, between economic organization and political authority, between cultural identification and social cohesion (Camilleri 1990, 29). Such an articulation is an attempt at a process of redefining the meaning and boundaries of civil society, and reaffirming the priority of civil society over the state, of popular sovereignty over state sovereignty.

As we enter the twenty-first century, it is clear now that such a vision must include rights of gender, sexuality, ethnicity, and race within a dialectical framework of class analysis, to create a society based upon ideals of freedom, justice, and equality. The norms of both individual and collective human rights can potentially help establish such a framework.

There are particularist and universalist components to one's identity. The conception of rights presented here celebrates both the Marxist and "Enlightenment" conception of the universal moral worth of the individual and the postmodernist image of difference and fragmentation. We must draw on the best of both the universalist tendencies of Marxism and liberalism *and* the postmodern defense of the centrality of particular identities to human emancipation. If various oppressed groups are to build a potentially powerful coalition, a common platform is needed which begins to forge the bonds of common citizenship which can mediate (and also, at times, transcend) particularist identities. We are not defending "special interests" or "special rights"; rather we are building a common human interest based on collective human rights. Common sources of suffering unite the divergent particular identities, and thus it would be a mistake to abandon class analysis in the name of a "politics of difference." It is in the interest of all but a small elite to create political, civil, and socioeconomic rights which enable all individuals through group membership to develop a valuable, independent life in civil society. Democratic state authority and cooperation will be key, but it will not be enough. We live in an era of globalized capital and an emerging globalized society.

Collective human rights are thus also part of the movement from geopolitics to global humane governance. The realist worldview accepts international warfare and wide economic disparities as "inevitable" in an "anarchic" political order with no centralized world government. A rival normative world order based on values that promote a peaceful, equitable, sustainable, just, and participatory humane governance is needed for the new millennium.

APPENDIX A

Universal Declaration of the Rights of Peoples
Algiers, 4 July 1976

PREAMBLE

We live at a time of great hopes and deep despair;

— a time of conflicts and contradictions;

— a time when liberation struggles have succeeded in arousing the peoples of the world against the domestic and international structures of imperialism and in overturning colonial systems;

— a time of struggle and victory in which new ideals of justice among and within nations have been adopted;

— a time when the General Assembly of the United Nations has given increasing expression, from the Universal Declaration of Human Rights to the Charter on the Economic Rights and Duties of States, to the quest for a new international, political and economic order.

But this is also a time of frustration and defeat, as new forms of imperialism evolve to oppress and exploit the peoples of the world.

Imperialism, using vicious methods, with the complicity of governments that it has itself often installed, continues to dominate a part of the world. Through direct or indirect intervention, through multinational enterprises, through manipulation of corrupt local politicians, with the assistance of military regimes based on police repression, torture and physical extermination of opponents, through a set of practices that has become known as neo-colonialism, imperialism extends its stranglehold over many peoples.

Aware of expressing the aspirations of our era, we met in Algiers to proclaim that all the peoples of the world have a equal right to liberty, the right to free themselves from any foreign interference and to choose their own government, the right if they are under subjection, to fight for their liberation and the right to benefit from other peoples' assistance in their struggle.

Convince that the effective respect for human rights necessarily implies respect for the rights of peoples, we have adopted the UNIVERSAL DECLARATION OF THE RIGHTS OF PEOPLES.

May all those who, throughout the world, are fighting the great battle, at times through armed struggle, for the freedom of all peoples, find in this Declaration the assurance of the legitimacy of their struggle.

SECTION 1. — RIGHT TO EXISTENCE

ARTICLE 1.—Every people has the right to existence.

ARTICLE 2.—Every people has the right to the respect of its national and cultural identity.

ARTICLE 3.—Every people has the right to retain peaceful possession of its territory and to return to it if it is expelled.

ARTICLE 4.—None shall be subjected, because of his national or cultural identity, to massacre, torture, persecution, deportation, expulsion or living conditions such as may compromise the identity of integrity of the people to which he belongs.

SECTION II.—RIGHT TO POLITICAL SELF-DETERMINATION

ARTICLE 5.—Every people has an imprescriptible and unalienable right to self-determination. It shall determine its political status freely and without any foreign interference.

ARTICLE 6.—Every people has the right to break free from any colonial or foreign domination, whether direct of indirect, and from any racist regime.

ARTICLE 7.—Every people has the right to have a democratic government representing all the citizens without distinction as to race, sex, belief or colour, and capable of ensuring effective respect for the human rights and fundamental freedoms for all.

SECTION III.—ECONOMIC RIGHTS OF PEOPLES

ARTICLE 8.—Every people has an exclusive right over its natural wealth and resources. It has the right to recover them if they nave been despoiled, as well as any unjustly paid indemnities.

ARTICLE 9.—Scientific and technical progress being part of the common heritage of mankind, every people has the right to participate in it.

ARTICLE 10.—Every people has the right to a fair evaluation of its labor and to equal and just terms in international trade.

ARTICLE 11.—Every people has the right to choose its own economic and social system and pursue its own path to economic development freely and without any foreign interference.

ARTICLE 12.—The economic rights set forth above shall be exercised in a spirit of solidarity amongst the peoples of the world and with due regard for their respective interests.

SECTION IV.—RIGHT TO CULTURE

ARTICLE 13.— Every people has the right to speak its own language and preserve and develop its own culture, thereby contributing to the enrichment of the culture of mankind.

ARTICLE 14.—Every people has the right to its artistic, historical and cultural wealth.

ARTICLE 15.—Every people has the right not to have an alien culture imposed upon it.

SECTION V.—RIGHT TO ENVIRONMENT AND COMMON RESOURCES

ARTICLE 16.—Every people has the right to the conservation, protection and improvement of its environment.

ARTICLE 17.—Every people has the right to make use of the common heritage of mankind, such as the high seas, the sea-bed, and outer space.

ARTICLE 18.—In the exercise of the preceding rights every people shall take account of the necessity for coordination the requirements of its economic development with solidarity amongst all the peoples of the world.

SECTION VI.—RIGHTS OF MINORITIES

ARTICLE 19.—When a people constitutes a minority within a State it has the right to respect for its identity, traditions, language and cultural heritage.

ARTICLE 20.—The members of a minority shall enjoy without discrimination the same rights as the other citizens of the State and shall participate on an equal footing with them in public life.

ARTICLE 21.—These rights shall be exercised with due respect for the legitimate interests of the community as a whole and cannot authorize impairing the territorial integrity and political unity of the State, provided the State acts in accordance with all the principles set forth in this Declaration.

SECTION VII.—GUARANTEES AND SANCTIONS

ARTICLE 22.—Any disregard for the provisions of this Declaration constitutes a breach of obligations towards the international community as a whole.

ARTICLE 23.—Any prejudice resulting from disregard for this Declaration must be totally compensated by whoever caused it.

ARTICLE 24.—Any enrichment to the detriment of the people in violation of the provisions of this Declaration shall give rise to the restitution of profits thus obtained. The same shall be applied to all excessive profits on investments of foreign origin.

ARTICLE 25.—Any unequal treaties, agreements or contracts concluded in disregard of the fundamental rights of peoples shall have no effect.

ARTICLE 26.—External financial charges which become excessive and unbearable for the people shall cease to be due.

ARTICLE 27.—The gravest violations of the fundamental rights of peoples, especially of their right to existence, constitute international crimes for which their perpetrators shall carry personal penal liability.

ARTICLE 28.—Any people whose fundamental rights are seriously disregarded has the right to enforce them, especially by political or trade union struggle and even, in the last resort, by the use of force.

ARTICLE 29.—Liberation movements shall have access to international organizations and their combatants are entitled to the protection of the humanitarian law of war.

ARTICLE 30.—The re-establishment of the fundamental rights of peoples, when they are seriously disregarded, is a duty incumbent upon all members of the international community.

APPENDIX B

African Charter on Human and Peoples' Rights (Preamble and Part I). Banjul, 26 June 1981. Entered into force, 21 Oct. 1986. O.A.U. Doc. CAB/LEG/67/3 Rev. 5.

PREAMBLE

The African States members of the Organization of African Unity, parties to the present convention entitled "African Charter on Human and Peoples' Rights";

Recalling Decision 115 (XVI) of the Assembly of Heads of State and Government at its Sixteenth Ordinary Session held in Monrovia, Liberia, from 17 to 20 July 1979 on the preparation of a "preliminary draft on an African Charter on Human and Peoples' Rights providing *inter alia* for the establishment of bodies to promote and protect human and peoples' rights";

Considering the Charter of the Organization of African Unity, which stipulates that "freedom, equality, justice and dignity are essential objectives for the achievement of the legitimate aspirations of the African peoples";

Reaffirming the pledge they solemnly made in Article 2 of the said Charter to eradicate all forms of colonialism from Africa, to coordinate and intensify their cooperation and efforts to achieve a better life for the peoples of Africa and to promote international cooperation having due regard to the Charter of the United Nations and the Universal Declaration of Human Rights;

Taking into consideration the virtues of their historical tradition and the values of African civilization which should inspire and characterize their reflection on the concept of human and peoples' rights;

Recognizing on the one hand, that fundamental human rights stem from the attributes of human beings, which justifies their national and international protection and on the other hand that the reality and respect of peoples rights should necessarily guarantee human rights;

Considering that the enjoyment of rights and freedoms also implies the performance of duties on the part of everyone;

Convinced that it is henceforth essential to pay a particular attention to the right to development and that civil and political rights cannot be dissociated from economic, social and cultural rights in their conception as well as universality and that the satisfaction of economic, social and cultural rights is a guarantee for the enjoyment of civil and political rights;

Conscious of their duty to achieve the total liberation of Africa, the peoples of which are still struggling for their dignity and genuine independence, and undertaking

189

to eliminate colonialism, neo-colonialism, apartheid, zionism and to dismantle aggressive foreign military bases and all forms of discrimination, particularly those based on race, ethnic group, color, sex, language, religion or political opinions;

Reaffirming their adherence to the principles of human and peoples' rights and freedoms contained in the declarations, conventions and other instruments adopted by the Organization of African Unity, the Movement of Non-Aligned Countries and the United Nations;

Firmly convinced of their duty to promote and protect human and peoples' rights and freedoms taking into account the importance traditionally attached to these rights and freedoms in Africa;

HAVE AGREED AS FOLLOWS:

PART I: RIGHTS AND DUTIES

CHAPTER I

HUMAN AND PEOPLES' RIGHTS

ARTICLE 1.—The Member States of the Organization of African Unity parties to the present Charter shall recognize the rights, duties and freedoms enshrined in this Charter and shall undertake to adopt legislative or other measures to give effect to them.

ARTICLE 2.—Every individual shall be entitled to the enjoyment of the rights and freedoms recognized and guaranteed in the present Charter without distinction of any kind such as race, ethnic group, color, sex, language, religion, political or any other opinion, national and social origin, fortune, birth or other status.

ARTICLE 3

1. Every individual shall be qual before the law.
2. Every individual shall be entitled to equal protection of the law.

ARTICLE 4.—Human beings are inviolable. Every human being shall be entitled to respect for his life and the integrity of his person. No one may be arbitrarily deprived of this right.

ARTICLE 5.—Every individual shall have the right to the respect of the dignity inherent in a human being and to the recognition of his legal status. All forms of exploitation and degradation of man particularly slavery, slave trade, torture, cruel, inhuman or degrading punishment and treatment shall be prohibited.

ARTICLE 6.—Every individual shall have the right to liberty and to the security of his person. No one may be deprived of his freedom except for reasons and conditions previously laid down by law. In particular, no one may be arbitrarily arrested or detained.

ARTICLE 7

1. Every individual shall have the right to have his cause heard. This comprises:

    (a) the right to an appeal to competent national organs against acts of violating his fundamental rights as recognized and guaranteed by conventions, laws, regulations and customs in force;
    (b) the right to be presumed innocent until proved guilty by a competent court or tribunal;
    (c) the right to defence, including the right to be defended by counsel of his choice;
    (d) the right to be tried within a reasonable time by an impartial court or tribunal.
2. No one may be condemned for an act or omission which did not constitute a legally punishable offence at the time it was committed. No penalty may be inflicted for an offence for which no provision was made at the time it was committed. Punishment is personal and can be imposed only on the offender.

ARTICLE 8.—Freedom of conscience, the profession and free practice of religion shall be guaranteed. No one may, subject to law and order, be submitted to measures restricting the exercise of these freedoms.

ARTICLE 9

1. Every individual shall have the right to receive information.
2. Every individual shall have the right to express and disseminate his opinions within the law.

ARTICLE 10

1. Every individual shall have the right to free association provided that he abides by the law.
2. Subject to the obligation of solidarity provided for in Article 29 no one may be compelled to join an association.

ARTICLE 11.—Every individual shall have the right to assemble freely with others. The exercise of this right shall be subject only to necessary restrictions provided for by law in particular those enacted in the interest of national security, the safety, health, ethics and rights and freedoms of others.

ARTICLE 12

1. Every individual shall have the right to freedom of movement and residence within the borders of a State provided he abides by the law.
2. Every individual shall have the right to leave any country including his own, and to return to his country. This right may only be subject to restrictions, provided for by law for the protection of national security, law and order, public health or morality.
3. Every individual shall have the right, when persecuted, to seek and obtain asylum in other countries in accordance with laws of those countries and international conventions.

4. A non-national legally admitted in a territory of a State Party to the present Charter, may only be expelled from it by virtue of a decision taken in accordance with the law.

5. The mass expulsion of non-nationals shall be prohibited. Mass expulsion shall be that which is aimed at national, racial, ethnic or religious groups.

ARTICLE 13

1. Every citizen shall have the right to participate freely in the government of his country, either directly or through freely chosen representatives in accordance with the provisions of the law.

2. Every citizen shall have the right of equal access to the public service of his country.

3. Every individual shall have the right of access to public property and services in strict equality of all persons before the law.

ARTICLE 14.—The right to property shall be guaranteed. It may only be encroached upon in the interest of public need or in the general interest of the community and in accordance with the provisions of appropriate laws.

ARTICLE 15.—Every individual shall have the right to work under equitable and satisfactory conditions, and shall receive equal pay for equal work.

ARTICLE 16

1. Every individual shall have the right to enjoy the best attainable state of physical and mental health.

2. States parties to the present Charter shall take the necessary measures to protect the health of their people and to ensure that they receive medical attention when they are sick.

ARTICLE 17

1. Every individual shall have the right to education.

2. Every individual may freely, take part in the cultural life of his community.

3. The promotion and protection of morals and traditional values recognized by the community shall be the duty of the State.

ARTICLE 18

1. The family shall be the natural unit and basis of society. It shall be protected by the State which shall take care of its physical health and moral.

2. The State shall have the duty to assist the family which is the custodian of morals and traditional values recognized by the community.

3. The State shall ensure the elimination of every discrimination against women and also censure the protection of the rights of the woman and the child as stipulated in international declarations and conventions.

4. The aged and the disabled shall also have the right to special measures of protection in keeping with their physical or moral needs.

ARTICLE 19—All peoples shall be equal; they shall enjoy the same respect and shall have the same rights. Nothing shall justify the domination of a people by another.

ARTICLE 20

1. All peoples shall have the right to existence. They shall have the unquestionable and inalienable right to self-determination. They shall freely determine their political status and shall pursue their economic and social development according to the policy they have freely chosen.
2. Colonized or oppressed peoples shall have the right to free themselves from the bonds of domination by resorting to any means recognized by the international community.
3. All peoples shall have the right to the assistance of the States parties to the present Charter in their liberation struggle against foreign domination, be it political, economic or cultural.

ARTICLE 21

1. All people shall freely dispose of their wealth and natural resources. This right shall be exercised in the exclusive interest of the people. In no case shall a people be deprived of it.
2. In case of spoliation the dispossessed people shall have the right to the lawful recovery of its property as well as to an adequate compensation.
3. The free disposal of wealth and natural resources shall be exercised without prejudice to the obligation of promoting international economic cooperation based on mutual respect, equitable exchange and the principles of interna-- tional law.
4. States parties to the present Charter shall individually and collectively exercise the right to free disposal of their wealth and natural resources with a view to strengthening African unity and solidarity.
5. States parties to the present Charter shall undertake to eliminate all forms of foreign economic exploitation particularly that practiced by international monopolies so as to enable their peoples to fully benefit from the advantages derived from their national resources.

ARTICLE 22

1. All peoples shall have the right to their economic, social and cultural development with due regard to their freedom and identity and in the equal enjoyment of the common heritage of mankind.
2. States shall have the duty, individually or collectively, to ensure the exercise of the right to development.

ARTICLE 23

1. All peoples shall have the right to national and international peace and security. The principles of solidarity and friendly relations implicitly affirmed by the Charter of the Untied Nations and reaffirmed by that of the Organization of African Unity shall govern relations between States.
2. For the purpose of strengthening peace, solidarity and friendly relations, States parties to the present Charter shall ensure that:

(a) any individual enjoying the right of asylum under Article 12 of the present Charter shall not engage in subversive activities against his country of origin or any other State party to the present Charter;

(b) their territories shall not be used as bases for subversive or terrorist activities against the people of any other State party to the present Charter.

ARTICLE 24.—All peoples shall have the right to a general satisfactory environment favorable to their development.

ARTICLE 25.—States parties to the present Charter shall have the duty to promote and ensure through teaching, education and publication, the respect of the rights and freedoms contained in the present charter and to see to it that these freedoms and rights as well as corresponding obligations and duties are understood.

ARTICLE 26.—States parties to the present Charter shall have the duty to guarantee the independence of the Courts and shall allow the establishment and improvement of appropriate national institutions entrusted with the promotion and protection of the rights and freedoms guaranteed by the present Charter.

CHAPTER II

DUTIES

ARTICLE 27

1. Every individual shall have duties towards his family and society, the State and other legally recognized communities and the international community.

2. The rights and freedoms of each individual shall be exercised with due regard to the rights of others, collective security, morality and common interest.

ARTICLE 28.—Every individual shall have the duty to respect and consider his fellow beings without discrimination, and to maintain relations aimed at promoting, safeguarding and reinforcing mutual respect and tolerance.

ARTICLE 29.—The individual shall also have the duty:

1. To preserve the harmonious development of the family and to work for the cohesion and respect of the family; to respect his parents at all times, to maintain them in case of need;

2. To serve his national community by placing his physical and intellectual abilities at its service;

3. Not to compromise the security of the State whose national or resident he is;

4. To preserve and strengthen social and national solidarity, particularly when the latter is threatened;

5. To preserve and strengthen the national independence and the territorial integrity of his country and to contribute to its defence in accordance with the law;

6. To work to the best of his abilities and competence, and to pay taxes imposed by law in the interest of the society;

7. To preserve and strengthen positive African cultural values in his relations with other members of the society, in the spirit of tolerance, dialogue and consultation and, in general, to contribute to the promotion of the moral well being of society;

8. To contribute to the best of his abilities, at all times and at all levels, to the promotion and achievement of African unity.

APPENDIX C

CONVENTION ON THE ELIMINATION OF ALL FORMS OF DISCRIMINA-
TION AGAINST WOMEN. New York, 18 December 1979. Entered into force, 3
September 1981. UNGA Res. 34/180 (XXXIV), 34 UN GAOR, Supp.
(No. 46) 194, UN Doc. A/34/830(1979), reprinted in 19 I.L.M. 33 (1980)
(Note: The Introduction, article 2, and parts V and VI are omitted here.)

PART I

ARTICLE 1. For the purposes of the present Convention, the term "discrimination
against women" shall mean any distinction, exclusion or restriction made on the basis
of sex which has the effect or purpose of impairing or nullifying the recognition,
enjoyment or exercise by women, irrespective of their marital status, on a basis of
equality of men and women, of human rights and fundamental freedoms in the political, economic, social, cultural, civil or any other field.

ARTICLE 3. States Parties shall take in all fields, in the political, social, economic
and cultural fields, all appropriate measures, including legislation, to ensure the full
development and advancement of women, for the purpose of guaranteeing them the
exercise and enjoyment of human rights and fundamental freedoms on a basis of
equality with men.

ARTICLE 4.

(1) Adoption by States Parties of temporary special measures aimed at accelerating *de
    facto* equality between men and women shall not be considered discrimination as
    defined in this Convention, but shall in no way entail, as a consequence, the
    maintenance of unequal or separate standards. These measures shall be discontin-
    ued when the objectives of equality of opportunity and treatment have been achieved.

(2) Adoption by States Parties of special measures, including those measures con-
    tained in the present Convention, aimed at protecting maternity shall not be
    considered discriminatory.

ARTICLE 5. States Parties shall take all appropriate measures:

(a) To modify the social and cultural patterns of conduct of men and women, with
    a view to achieving the elimination of prejudices and customary and all other
    practices which are based on the idea of the inferiority or the superiority of
    either of the sexes or on stereotyped roles for men and women.

197

(b) To ensure that family education includes a proper understanding of maternity as a social function and the recognition of the common responsibility of men and women in the upbringing and development of their children.

PART II

ARTICLE 6. States Parties shall take all appropriate measures, including legislation, to suppress all forms of traffic in women and exploitation of prostitution of women.

ARTICLE 7. States Parties shall take all appropriate measures to eliminate discrimination against women in the political and public life of the country and, in particular, shall ensure, on equal terms with men, the right:

(a) To vote in all elections and public referenda and to be eligible for election to a publicly elected bodies;
(b) To participate in the formulation of government policy and the implementation thereof and to hold public office and perform all public functions at all levels of government;
(c) To participate in non-governmental organizations and associations concerned with the public and political life of the country.

ARTICLE 8. States Parties shall take all appropriate measures to ensure to women on equal terms with men and, without any discrimination, the opportunity to represent their Governments at the international level and to participate in the work of international organizations.

ARTICLE 9.

(1) States Parties shall grant women equal rights with men to acquire, change or retain their nationality. They shall ensure in particular that neither marriage to an alien nor change of nationality by the husband during marriage shall automatically change the nationality of the wife, render her stateless of force upon her the nationality of the husband.
(2) States Parties shall grant women equal rights with men with respect to the nationality of their children.

PART III

ARTICLE 10. States Parties shall take all appropriate measures to eliminate discrimination against women in order to ensure to them equal rights with men in the field of education and in particular to ensure, on a basis of equality of men and women:

(a) The same conditions for career and vocational guidance, for access to studies and for the achievement of diplomas in educational establishments of all categories in rural as well as in urban areas; this equality shall be ensured in pre-school, general, technical, professional and higher technical education, as well as in all types of vocational training;

(b) Access to the same curricula, the same examinations, teaching staff with qualifications of the same standard and school premises and equipment of the same quality;

(c) The elimination of any stereotyped concept of the roles of men and women at all levels and in all forms of education by encouraging coeducation and other types of education which will help to achieve this aim and, in particular, by the revision of textbooks and school programmes and the adaptation of teaching methods;

(d) The same opportunities to benefit from scholarships and other study grants;

(e) The same opportunities for access to programmes of continuing education, including adult and functional literacy programmes, particularly those aimed at reducing, at the earliest possible time, any gap in education existing between men and women;

(f) The reduction of female student drop-out rates and the organization of programmes for girls and women who have left school prematurely;

(g) The same opportunities to participate actively in sports and physical education;

(h) Access to specific educational information to help ensure the health and well-being of families, including information and advice on family planning.

ARTICLE 11.

(1) State Parties shall take all appropriate measures to eliminate discrimination against women in the field of employment in order to ensure, on a basis of equality of men and women, the same rights, in particular:

(a) The right to work as an inalienable right of all human beings;

(b) The right to the same employment opportunities, including the application of the same criteria for selection in matters of employment;

(c) The right to free choice of profession and employment, the right to promotion, job security and all benefits and conditions of service and the right to receive vocational training and retraining, including apprenticeships, advanced vocational training and recurrent training;

(d) The right to equal remuneration, including benefits, and to equal treatment in respect of work of equal value, as well as equality of treatment in the evaluation of the quality of work;

(e) The right to social security, particularly in cases of retirement, unemployment, sickness, invalidity and old age and other incapacity to work, as well as the right to paid leave;

(f) The right to protection of health and to safety in working conditions, including the safeguarding of the function of reproduction.

(2) In order to prevent discrimination against women on the grounds of marriage or maternity and to ensure their effective right to work, State Parties shall take appropriate measures:

(a) To prohibit, subject to the imposition of sanctions, dismissal on the grounds of pregnancy or of maternity leave and discrimination in dismissals on the basis of marital status;

(b) To introduce maternity leave with pay or with comparable social benefits without loss of former employment, seniority or social allowances;

(c) To encourage the provision of the necessary supporting social services to enable parents to combine family obligations with work responsibilities and participation in public life, in particular through promoting the establishment and development of a network of child-care facilities.

(d) To provide special protection to women during pregnancy in types of work proved to be harmful to them.

(3) Protective legislation relating to matters covered in this article shall be reviewed periodically in the light of scientific and technological knowledge and shall be revised, repealed or extended as necessary.

ARTICLE 12.

(1) States Parties shall take all appropriate measures to eliminate discrimination against women in the field of health care in order to ensure, on a basis of equality of men and women, access to health care services, including those related to family planning.

(2) Notwithstanding the provisions of paragraph 1 above, States parties shall ensure to women appropriate services in connexion with pregnancy, confinement and the post-natal period, granting free services where necessary, as well as adequate nutrition during pregnancy and lactation.

ARTICLE 13. States Parties shall take all appropriate measures to eliminate discrimination against women in other areas of economic and social life in order to ensure, on a basis of equality of men and women, the same rights, in particular:

(a) The right to family benefits;

(b) The right to bank loans, mortgages and other forms of financial credit.

(c) The right to participate in recreational activities, sports and in all aspects of cultural life.

ARTICLE 14.

(1) States Parties shall take into account the particular problems faced by rural women and the significant roles which they play in the economic survival of their families, including their work in the non-monetized sectors of the economy, and shall take all appropriate measures to ensure the application of the provisions of the Convention to women in rural areas.

(2) States Parties shall take all appropriate measures to eliminate discrimination against women in rural areas in order to ensure, on a basis of equality of men and women, that they participate in and benefit from rural development and, in particular, shall ensure to such women the right:

(a) To participate in the elaboration and implementation of development planning at all levels;

(b) To have access to adequate health care facilities, including information, counselling and services in family planning;

(c) To benefit directly from social security programmes;

(d) To obtain all types of training and education, formal and non-formal, including that relating to functional literacy, as well as the benefit of all community and extension services, *inter alia*, in order to increase their technical proficiency;

(e) To organize self-help groups and co-operatives in order to obtain equal access to economic opportunities through employment or self-employment;

(f) To participate in all community activities;

(g) To have access to agricultural credit and loans, marketing facilities, appropriate technology and equal treatment in land and agrarian reform as well as in land resettlement schemes;

(h) To enjoy adequate living conditions, particularly in relation to housing, sanitation, electricity and water supply, transport and communication.

PART IV

ARTICLE 15.

(1) States Parties shall accord to women equality with men before the law.

(2) States Parties shall accord to women, in civil matters, a legal capacity identical to that of men and the same opportunities to exercise that capacity. They shall in particular give women equal rights to conclude contracts and to administer property and treat them equally in all stages of procedures in courts and tribunals.

(3) States Parties agree that all contract and all other private instruments of any kind with a legal effect which is directed at restricting the legal capacity of women shall be deemed null and void.

(4) States Parties shall accord to men and women the same rights with regard to the law relating to the movement of persons and the freedom to choose their residence and domicile.

ARTICLE 16.

(1) States Parties shall take all appropriate measures to eliminate discrimination against women in all matters relating to marriage and family relations and in particular shall ensure, on a basis of equality of men and women:

(a) The same right to enter into marriage;

(b) The same right to choose a spouse and to enter into marriage only with their free and full consent;

(c) The same rights and responsibilities during marriage and at its dissolution;

(d) The same rights and responsibilities as parents, irrespective of their marital status, in matters relating to their children. In all cases the interests of the children shall be paramount;

(e) The same rights to decide freely and responsibly on the number and spacing of their children and to have access to the information, education and means to enable them to exercise these rights;

(f) The same rights and responsibilities with regard to guardianship, wardship, trusteeship and adoption of children, or similar institutions where these concepts exist in national legislation. In all cases the interest of the children shall be paramount;

    (g) The same personal rights as husband and wife, including the right to choose a family name, a profession and an occupation;

    (h) The same rights for both spouses in respect of the ownership, acquisition, management, administration, enjoyment and disposition of property, whether free of charge or for a valuable consideration.

(2) The betrothal and the marriage of a child shall have no legal effect and all necessary action including legislation, shall be taken to specify a minimum age for marriage and to make the registration of marriages in an official registry compulsory.

NOTES

INTRODUCTION

1. The conventional name for the International League for the Rights and Liberation of Peoples (ILRLP). The ILRLP was founded in 1976 by an Italian member of Parliament, Lelio Basso, and has central offices in Rome and Geneva, as well as chapters in Western Europe and Latin America and supporters around the world. The ILRLP is completely independent of any government, political party, or special ideology. In 1979, the United Nations granted the ILRLP status as a Non-Governmental Organization and accredited it to the UN Economic and Social Council.

2. Forsythe makes this point explicit: "In a behavioral or empirical sense, rights exist only if they are recognized as such by public authorities" (1991, 11).

3. See Donnelly 1989, 143–54.

4. Paul Kennedy describes these trends as follows: "As we know, the world of the late twentieth century is being moved by two currents. One, driven by technology and communications and trade, tends toward ever greater economic integration. The second is the revived tendency toward ethnic separatism, currently exacerbated by the collapse of a transcendent creed (Communism), the rise of religious fundamentalism, and increasing internal questioning (from Croatia to Somalia) of national borders that were superimposed, often from outside, upon very different ethnic groups; it is also exacerbated at times by economic fears" (1993, 287).

1. CONCEPTUALIZING COLLECTIVE HUMAN RIGHTS

1. The "Westphalian system" refers to the Peace of Westphalia, signed in 1648, which "is widely recognized as the dividing line between the time when medieval Europe was dominated by small, localized political units, under the comprehensive authority of the Holy Roman Empire and/or the pope, and modern Europe, where states are recognized as sovereign." Since 1648, the nation-state has been recognized in international relations as the primary "sovereign" unit (Ray 1995, 168).

2. Separately, Nickel and Szabo add the following to this discussion: First, Nickel outlines six characteristics of human rights: (1) they are rights, i.e. definite, high priority norms whose pursuit is mandatory; (2) they are alleged to be universal; (3) they exist independently of recognition or implementation in the customs or legal systems of particular countries; (4) they are held to be important norms; (5) they

imply duties for both individuals and governments; and (6) they establish minimal standards of decent social and governmental practice (Nickel 1987, 3–4).

Imre Szabo presents the notion of human rights as follows: "The notion of human rights falls within the framework of constitutional law and international law, the purpose of which is to defend by institutionalized means the rights of human beings against abuses of power committed by the organs of the State and, at the same time, to promote the establishment of humane living conditions and the multi-dimensional development of the human personality" (Szabo 1982, 11).

3. For example, Joel Feinberg writes: " To have a right is to have a claim against someone whose recognition as valid is called for by some set of governing rules or moral principles. To have a *claim* in turn, is to have a case meriting consideration, that is, to have reasons or grounds that put one in a position to engage in performative and propositional claiming. The activity of claiming, finally, as much as any other thing, makes for self-respect and respect for others, gives a sense to the notion of personal dignity, and distinguishes this otherwise morally flawed world from the even worse world or Nowheresville" (Feinberg 1980, 155).

4. Richard Falk places human rights within the struggle against structural violence: "Human rights are not, in the main, legal or moral abstractions. They are embedded in historical process. More concretely, this process at this time is closely intertwined with the ongoing anti-imperial struggle against political, economic, and cultural structures of international domination" (1981, 6).

5. One way to conceptualize international human rights is in relation to Rawls' levels of moral and political deliberation in his *Theory of Justice*. He outlines the first level as being the most abstract and philosophical, the "original position," the place where one attempts to formulate and defend transhistorical principles of morality and justice. Next comes the "constitutional stage," at which one formulates specific rights and duties that apply abstract principles to particular countries. This is followed by the "legislative stage," and finally, constitutional and legal norms are applied at the "judicial stage." In moving from the grand principles to the judicial stage, the norms become less abstract and more directly applicable to particular events (Rawls 1971, 195–201). Nickel inserts an "international human rights stage" between the level of abstract principles and the constitutional stage, "recognizing the importance of international politics and organizations and partially correcting Rawl's excessively narrow focus on the nation-state" (Nickel 1987, 43–44 and 107–8).

6. For a discussion of the limited U.S. conception of rights, see Elias 1986, 193–228.

7. Lelio Basso, an important developer of some of the ideas of peoples' rights, expressed this conception as follows: "We are concerned with man as he is in real life, wholly involved in his social and community relations from which he cannot be divorced without losing his personal identity and being transformed into an anonymous and impersonal being. . . . Man only exists as a social being, as a member of a community whose language, culture, forms of expression he shares, in short, whose

'language' he speaks in the broadest sense of the term, and hence the medium through which he has to communicate in order to experience his being a man" (Basso 1978).

8. Christian Bay and John Burton argue that basic human needs are powerful facts which should inform the content of human rights. "A society or government that keeps on violating basic needs of large numbers will encourage violent crime in the streets—and more so when the wealth of the affluent glaringly contrasts with dire poverty and other indignities for the less privileged classes" (Bay 1990, 248).

9. Or, as Bay puts it: "the only kind of world order that is good enough to struggle for is one that requires no more victims of structural violence or deprivation elsewhere so that ample liberties may prosper for privileged classes and individuals in our 'advanced' parts of the world" (Bay 1981, 108–9).

10. Within the literature on peoples' rights, the holder, the subject of such rights is often not clearly defined, or is defined in an extremely narrow manner. In many cases, no attempt is even made to define peoples, while listing such and such rights as essential to peoples' interests. Scholars point to the dangers of not attempting a definition: "The precise identification of the holders of peoples' rights is an undertaking that must go hand in hand with the definition of the rights themselves. If they remain too long 'in search of subjects' these rights are in great danger of being taken over by entities, which, in contrast, are well-structured and defined, such as States" (Marie 1986, 201).

11. Partsch outlines five ways in which the term "peoples" was used during the period between the two world wars:

1. Peoples living entirely as a minority (or even as a majority) group inside a state ruled by another people (as the Irish before 1919 and the Mongols before 1911/1921);

2. Peoples living as minority groups in more than one state without their own statehood (as Poles in Russia, Austria and Germany before 1919);

3. A people living as a minority group in a state but understanding itself as part of the people of a neighboring state (Mexicans in California and Hungarians in Romania);

4. Peoples or "nations" forced by external influences to live in separate states (as the German nation within several states);

5. A people living as the majority (or also as a minority group) inside a territory with a special status under foreign domination (for example, colonial regimes). (Partsch 1982, 63–64)

12. For a discussion of article 2, section 7 of the UN Charter, see McKean 1983, 56–57, and Renteln 1990, 21–25.

13. The declaration has gained in acceptance and authority since its adoption over forty years ago. It is almost universally considered to be one of the cornerstones of the United Nations structure. It is referred to in preambles of nation-state

constitutions and in most national and international documents that deal with human rights. "Despite all the criticisms and all the value judgments, it can be asserted that the Declaration has been a success rarely encountered in the history of international law" (Szabo 1982, 23–24).

14. The text of the African Charter on Human and Peoples' Rights had been concluded at an OAU Ministerial Meeting in January 1981, in Banjul, The Gambia. The charter is therefore often referred to as the "Banjul Charter."

15. Issa Shivji makes the important point that the role of imperialism is hardly discussed in the massive literature on human rights violations in Africa. "To cite a quick example, in the dominant literature one again and again sees references to Bokassa, Amin and Nguema as gruesome perpetrators of human rights violations, which indeed they were; but these citings go without the mention of the fact that Bokassa was France's protégé, that Nguema received support from Spain and the U.S. while Amin was installed by . . . Israel" (Shivji 1989, 52–53).

16. Many argue, however, that the major problem with the charter is its reliance on the state. Economic rights are conditional and depend upon the progressive achievement of future benefits without any target dates or precise goals. State action has unfortunately been minimal (Scoble 1984, 195).

As a document in the hands of governments of existing nation-states, the charter's usefulness and potential for misuse must be analyzed carefully. Many of the provisions contain "clawback" clauses that allow a nation-state to restrict rights to the extent permitted by domestic law, either by local law or by the existence of a national emergency—two vague and broad standards. For example, regarding freedom, the charter states: "No one may be deprived of his freedom except for reasons and conditions previously laid down by law." As a result of the clawback clauses, the individual is in actuality given no greater protection than she or he would have under domestic law (Gittleman 1984, 157–62).

17. The "Declaration of Principles of Indigenous Rights" is reprinted in Crawford 1988, 205–7.

18. Harold J. Laski describes these rights as follows: "The rules . . . imply claims against the state. For what the state can do is obviously limited by its end; and that end involves rights for the citizen against the state in order that the end may be safeguarded. What do we mean by the idea of rights? It is a condition without which, in the light of historic experience, the individual lacks assurance that he can attain happiness. We cannot, that is, say that the rights of the individual are constant; they are obviously relative to time and place. But, granted that relativity, the individual is entitled to expect their recognition from the state as the condition of his obedience to its commands" (Laski 1962, 26–27).

19. Falk places peoples' rights within an anti-statist framework, maintaining that they provide "normative coordinates to assess claims on the basis of a world order logic." He outlines three versions of peoples' rights. First, governments are the au-

thoritative representatives of peoples, as assumed in formal international instruments, such as the UN Charter. Second, the use of peoples' rights in international civil society has provided a means for peoples to put public pressure on governments for the protection of their rights; states are not the only actors in the international arena working to create a new normative order. The third version of peoples' rights identifies a specific framework to protect, "both the individual and group rights that pertain to the special circumstances of indigenous peoples" (Falk 1988, 17–37).

Nettheim offers ten classes of claims of peoples rights: physical survival; cultural survival and cultural identity; sovereignty; land rights; self-determination; self-government; control of land and its resources; compensation; nondiscrimination; and affirmative action (Nettheim 1988, 116–24).

Prott's list of peoples' rights overlaps with Nettheim's, but makes two additions: the right to peace and security and the right to development (Prott 1988, 96–97).

Sieghart and Crawford also present a list of seven "collective rights," which overlap with Nettheim and Prott's list. In addition, they include rights in relation to the environment (Crawford 1988, 56–57).

20. Throughout the world distinctive national and cultural entities, including the Basques, Samis, Tamils, Sikhs, Kurds, Maoris, Miskitos, Quebecois, Karens, Native Americans, and others, have rejected absorption into the majority culture. The fulfillment of these aspirations and claims is most often seen as occurring within the borders of existing states through respect for individual rights *and* the rights of minority groups seeking to promote their separate identity. In some cases, where ethnic rights are continually abused and denied, new states are called for. But secession is most often seen as the last option. For a global survey of self-determination movements, see the appendix in Halperin, Scheffer, & Small 1992, 123–60.

21. The United States faces notable class polarization, as most dramatically demonstrated in the 1992 riots in Los Angeles and across the United States. Over 36.9 million people are officially classified as poor according to the Census Bureau's 1993 report (which is widely believed to be a significant under count) (*New York Times*, 18 October 1993). Conservative political strategist Kevin Phillips cites the following statistics: "since 1977, the average after-tax family income of the lowest 10 percent, in current dollars, fell from $3,528 to $3,157. That's a 10.5 percent drop. During the same period, average family income of the top 10 percent increased from $70,459 to $89,783—up 24.4 percent. The incomes of the top 1 percent, which were 'only' $174,498 in 1977, are up to $303,900—a whopping 74.2 percent increase over the decade." Phillips draws these figures from a 1977–87 study of income trends by Ross LaRoe and John Charles Pool, who analyzed data from the Congressional Budget Office. See Phillips 1990, 14.

22. The environment provides a clear case in point. The state system is organized by the logic of social Darwinism, that is, each attempting to maximize its own immediate gains. Environmental problems today, however, defy national boundaries. Ozone depletion, the buildup of carbon dioxide in the atmosphere, and oceanic pollution, are literally global in scope. The competitive nature of the international system often

prevents global cooperation on these issues, and thus negatively impacts on ecological balance. See Falk, Kim, & Mendlovitz 1982, 435–36.

2. ETHNICITY/RACE, GENDER, AND SEXUALITY

1. The American Anthropological Association submitted a statement to the United Nations Commission on Human Rights in 1947, which included the following concern about the Universal Declaration of Human Rights: "It will not be convincing to the Indonesian, the African, the Indian, the Chinese, if it lies on the same plane as like documents of an earlier period. The rights of Man in the Twentieth Century cannot be circumscribed by the standards of any single culture or be dictated by the aspirations of any single people. Such a document will lead to frustration, not realization of the personalities of vast numbers of human beings" (quoted in Renteln 1990, 83).

2. Pollis writes, "Whatever the diversity among third world countries . . . individuals still perceive themselves in terms of their group identity. Who and what an individual is has been conceptualized in terms of the kinship system, the clan, the tribe, the village. . . . The concept of the autonomous individual possessed of inherent, inalienable rights has been meaningless, just as it was meaningless in the West prior to the modern political philosophers and the atomization attendant upon industrialization. . . . If the concept of rights has any relevance, it is derived from relations with others. They are 'rights with' " (Pollis 1982, 16).

3. Keba M'Baye and Birame Ndiaye point out that the Universal Declaration of Human Rights of 1948 "did not have the effect of putting an end to the discriminatory practices resulting from colonization." The declaration and the structures established at the United Nations were designed to put an end to racism practiced "by white men against white men," (i.e., Nazism) and thus were "of very small interest to Africa" (1982, 585).

In fact, at the time, Africans warned the UN founders against applying Western morality to the globe. Leopold Sedar Senghor, then a member of the French Parliament, cautioned the negotiators of the European Convention of 4 November 1950, to beware lest they prepare a Declaration of the Rights of "the European Man" (quoted in M'Baye & Ndiaye 1982, 583–84).

4. Internal and external self-determination are defined and examined in length in chapter 3.

5. Buchanan asserts that the nationalistic principle of self-determination is "one of the least plausible justifications" for secession. He writes that perhaps the strongest argument for secession is to rectify past injustices. In such cases, "secession is simply the reappropriation, by the legitimate owner, of stolen property." He also asserts that a group may have a right to secede from a state "in order to protect its members from extermination by that state itself." Buchanan views secession as a group right (1991, 48, 65, 67, 74).

6. "Basic indicators of caloric intake and life expectancy measured by the Indian government's 1991 census reveal a growing gender gap in several states since 1980. In fact, contrary to sex ratios found in most countries, the ratio of women to men in India has actually been declining since the early part of the century. There are now only 929 women for every 1,000 men, compared with 972 in 1901. Dr. Veena Mazumdar, director of the Delhi-based Center for Women's Development Studies, notes that 'the declining sex ratio is the final indicator that registers [that] women are losing out on all fronts—on the job market, in health and nutrition and economic prosperity' " (Jacobson 1993, 65).

7. For example, in New York State, the Governor's Task Force on Bias-Related Violence reported in 1988 that thirty-one percent of the students surveyed said they had witnessed anti-gay attacks in school. In its study of 2,823 high school students, the task force concluded that "one of the most alarming findings [was] the openness with which the respondents expressed their aversion and hostility toward gays and lesbians." Surveyors found that students concealed racist attitudes, "aware that bias based on race and ethnicity can no longer be overtly condoned." By contrast, "students were quite emphatic about their dislike [for gays and lesbians], and frequently made violent, threatening statements. Gays and lesbians, it seems, are perceived as legitimate targets which can be openly attacked" (Minkowitz 1991, 12).

8. See "Order Issuing Permanent Injunction," United States District Court, Southern District of Ohio, Western Division, C-1-93-773. Signed by Judge S. Arthur Speigel, United States District Judge, on 9 August 1994. Note, in particular, "Findings of Fact," pp. 17–19.

3. THE RIGHT TO SELF-DETERMINATION

1. Article III states: "The Contracting Powers unite in guaranteeing to each other political independence and territorial integrity." Wilson added the following proviso: "But it is understood between them that such territorial readjustments, if any, as may in the future become necessary by reason of changes in present racial conditions and aspirations or present social and political relationships, pursuant to the principle of self-determination, and also such territorial readjustments as may . . . be demanded by the welfare and interest of the people concerned, may be effected, if agreeable to those peoples" (quoted in Schaeffer 1990, 51).

2. The significance of this endorsement is clearly stated by Richard Falk: "However many times governments might insist that the mention of peoples is to be understood as subsumed beneath the basic affirmation of the territorial unity of sovereign states, an important conceptual wedge helpful for the assertion of the most drastic forms of group claims—relating to collective and separatist rights of autonomy, even secession—has been validated, at least provisionally" (Falk 1989b, 13).

3. The statist bias of the United Nations was also demonstrated in a report initiated by the Sub-Commission on Prevention of Discrimination and Protection of

Minorities, published in 1980. Authored by Hector Gros Espiell, the study suggested that the right to self-determination was confined to "peoples under colonial and alien domination" from an external source. A concern for the preservation of territorial integrity was and remains the prevailing consideration (Nettheim 1988, 119).

4. In fact, Ismail-Sabri Abdalla asserted: "National liberation was practically reduced to a flag, an airline and some prestige constructions. . . . [C]lass differentiation led to the emergence of a [new] mixed bourgeoisie constituted by state officials and other bureaucrats maintained in power by imperialist subsidies. . . . [C]orruption and abuse of state power are at the base of the new wealth" (Abdalla 1988, 383).

5. As Nyerere wrote, "Everyone wants to be free, and the task of the nationalist is simply to rouse the people to a confidence in their own power of protest. But to build the real freedom which socialism represents is a very different thing. It demands a positive understanding and positive actions, not simply a rejection of colonialism and a willingness to cooperate in noncooperation" (quoted in Davis 1978, 54).

6. Lenin *Collected Works*, 21: 273–74, as quoted in Davis 1978, 79. See also V. I. Lenin, "The Right of Nations to Self-Determination," *Lenin: Selected Works* (Moscow: Progress Publishers, [1914] 1970), 595–647.

According to historian Roy Medvedev, the Bolsheviks advocated the self-determination of nations up to and including their complete governmental separation from Russia as independent nation-states. The Bolsheviks sought an alliance of free peoples and nations as the first step in a worldwide socialist revolution. "In the first decade after the formation of the USSR the union republics still enjoyed considerable autonomy in resolving their internal problems. Stalin did not like this, and under the guise of a struggle against nationalism he began a systematic restriction of the rights of the union republics, a violation of the nationalities policy that had been worked out under Lenin. This caused many party members to protest, whereupon these internationalists were arbitrarily reviled as 'national deviationists' " (Medvedev 1989, 293).

7. Marx makes this point very clear in *The German Ideology:* "how absurd is the conception of history held hitherto, which neglects the real relationships and confines itself to high-sounding dramas of princes and states. . . . Civil society embraces the whole material intercourse of individuals within a definite stage of the development of productive forces. It embraces the whole commercial and industrial life of a given stage and, insofar, transcends the State and the nation, though, on the other hand again, it must assert itself in foreign relations as nationality, and inwardly must organize itself as State" (Marx & Engels [1932] 1970, 57).

8. "However much the individual bourgeois fights against the others, as a *class* the bourgeois have a common interest, and this community of interest, which is directed against the proletariat inside the country, is directed against the bourgeois of

other nations outside the country. This the bourgeois calls his *nationality*" (Marx [1971] 1975, 281; quoted in Szporluk 1988, 35).

9. See, for example, the proposals in Gottlieb 1993.

4. THE MORALITY OF THE DEPTHS

1. For example, see Samir Amin, Maldevelopment: *Anatomy of a Global Failure* (Tokyo: United Nations University Press, 1990); Robin Attfield & Barry Wilkins, eds., *International Justice and the Third World* (New York: Routledge, 1992); Brian Barry, "Humanity and Justice in Global Perspective," in Pennock & Chapman, eds., *Ethics, Economics and the Law* (New York: New York University Press, 1982); Charles Beitz, *Political Theory and International Relations* (Princeton: Princeton University Press, 1979); Willy Brandt, *North-South: A Program for Survival* (Cambridge, Mass.: MIT Press, 1980); Partha Dasgupta, *An Inquiry into Well-Being and Destitution* (Oxford: Clarendon Press, 1993); Rajini Kothari, *Rethinking Development* (New York: New Horizons Press, 1989); Ellen Paul, Fred Miller, & Jeffrey Paul, eds., *Economic Rights* (Cambridge: Cambridge University Press, 1992); Peter Singer, *Practical Ethics* (New York: Cambridge University Press, 1979); Edward Weisband, ed., *Poverty amidst Plenty: World Political Economy and Distributive Justice* (Boulder: Westview Press, 1989).

2. For example, see Kunanayakam, "Historical Analysis of the Principles Contained in the Declaration on the Right to Development," U.N. Doc. HR/RD/1990/ CONF.1 (1990); Roland Rich, "The Right to Development: A Right of Peoples?," in James Crawford, ed., *The Rights of Peoples* (Oxford: Clarendon Press, 1988), 39–54; Ved P. Nanda, "Development as an Emerging Human Right under International Law," *Denver Journal of International Law and Policy* 13.2–3 (1984); Roland Rich, "The Right to Development as an Emerging Human Right," *Virginia Journal of International Law* 23.2 (1983): 287–327. International Commission of Jurists, *Development, Human Rights and the Rule of Law* (Oxford: Pergamon Press, 1981); Karel de Vey Mestdagh, "The Right to Development," *Netherlands International Law Review* 28 (1981): 30; W. D. Verwey, *The Establishment of a New International Economic Order and the Realization of the Right to Development and Welfare: A Legal Survey*, HR/ Geneva, 1980/BP.3; *Report of the Secretary General: The International Dimensions of the Right to Development as a Human Right* . . . , E/CN.4/1334 Jan. 1979.

3. For example, see Donnelly 1985b and Forsythe 1993, 1–11.

4. As Thomas J. Biersteker writes: "Development is defined as a self-generating process whereby a highly integrated economy and society are created which are capable of substantially providing for basic needs of the masses of its population" (1981, 166).

5. Judge Tanaka, for example, in his dissenting opinion in the *South West Africa Cases* in 1966 wrote:

A State, instead of pronouncing its view to a few States directly concerned, has the opportunity, through the medium of the organization, to declare its position to all members of the organization and to know immediately their reaction on the same matter. In former days, practice, repetition and *opinio juris sive necessitatis*, which are the ingredients of customary international law, might be combined together in a very long slow process extending over centuries. In the contemporary age of highly developed techniques of communication and information, the formation of a custom through the medium of international organizations is greatly facilitated and accelerated. (*ICJ Reports* 1966: 248 at 291, quoted in Higgins 1994, 23)

6. See T. Gruchalla-Wisierski, "A Framework for Understanding 'Soft Law'," *Revue de droit de McGill* 30 (1984): 37–88. Also see Chinkin 1989, 850–66. Soft law is further discussed below in chapter five.

7. Alston 1981 and 1985; Galtung 1977 and 1979; Kothari 1989; M'Baye 1972 and 1981, 5–8; Nanda 1984 and 1985; Rich 1983 and 1988; Shepherd 1985a, 1985b, and 1990; van Boven 1982b, 20–39, 68–75, 144–51, 171–77, and 1989.

8. Nanda 1984, 176. Nanda documents the evolution of the right to development within UN bodies, and shows how the right now transcends economic growth and has both individual and collective dimensions.

9. The conclusions and recommendations of the meeting are found in UN Doc. E/CN.4/1990/9/Rev.1 (1990), para 150. See Barsh 1991, 329–30.

10. For a discussion of the critical importance of promoting economic rights while questioning the utility of the right to development, see Howard 1989, and 1985, 607–32.

11. Shue 1980, 18. Shue himself does not include development in his discussion of basic rights. I am using his methodology to make this case.

12. Shue initially called the first duty, the "duty to avoid depriving" (1980, 52). Later, in response to critiques of his book, he changed the name of this duty to the "duty to respect" (1984, 84–85).

13. IMF Assessment Project, IMF Conditionality, 1980–91 (Arlington, Va.: Alexis de Tocqueville Institution, 1992), 18. See also Walton & Ragin 1990, 877.

14. Robert E. Goodin in *Protecting the Vulnerable* argues the need to rethink the moral relations between us and strangers. He focuses on the fact that strangers are frequently dependent on us in ways that render us responsible for their well-being. In our shrinking interdependent world responsibilities move beyond the family and the nation. As he wrote: "What is crucial is that others are dependent on us. . . . The same considerations of vulnerability that make our obligations to our families, friends, clients and compatriots especially strong can also give rise to similar responsibilities toward a much larger group of people who stand in none of the special relationships to us" (1985, 11). See also Goodin 1988, 663–86.

5. COLLECTIVE HUMAN RIGHTS IN A "WORLD SOCIETY"

1. For a stimulating and thorough analysis of realism see Smith 1986.

2. As their careers have progressed, Robert Keohane and Joseph Nye have moved closer to many realist positions compared to their early writings. This change can be seen by comparing their edited work *Transnational Relations and World Politics* (Cambridge, Mass.: Harvard University Press, 1971), to Robert Keohane, *After Hegemony: Cooperation and Discord in World Politics* (Princeton: Princeton University Press, 1984).

However, I use *Power and Interdependence* as the point of reference because of the impact of the analysis within the discipline in challenging certain major realist assumptions. Further, it is generally acknowledged that this work played a pivotal role in the development of "regime theory," which continues as a major focus for transnational scholars. And finally, the authors themselves stand by their work. In 1987, in the article "Power and Interdependence Revisited" (*International Organization* 41.4 [Autumn 1987]), Keohane and Nye claim that the "analysis that we put forward in *Power and Interdependence* has not been rendered irrelevant by events." As with any analysis, further efforts toward clarity and cogency are made in this article, but the basic foundations, for the most part, remain.

3. "Consider, for instance, the shifting patterns of legitimacy, loyalty, and authority relations that might be weakening whole systems and strengthening subgroups: one's political antennae can pick up the emergence and spread of such attitudinal dynamics" (Rosenau 1990, 28–29). The growth of the women's, human rights, and environmental movements on a global scale are clear examples of new "subgroups" gaining strength.

4. Neorealists, of course, stress the impact of the international system on the behavior of nation-states, in particular focusing on the condition of "anarchy," that is, the absence of any central authority in the world. The implication of anarchy to the neorealist is that an individual state has no choice but to focus on protecting its "power" position in order to survive.

In contrast, WSA focuses on the economic ramifications of anarchy, that is, the way in which the interstate system facilitates the expansion of global capitalism as no single state is able to control the entire world economy. Thus, political anarchy is merely the backdrop for an extensive analysis of the dynamics of capitalism.

5. The use of negation here refers to "dialectical overcoming," in which "the past stage is both annulled and preserved in the succeeding stage. . . . This sense of transition" (Cox 1992, 139). In addition to the negation of hegemony described above, Cox also writes of the era as potentially "post-Westphalian" and "post-globalization" (Cox 1992, 145–46).

6. "Hegemony expands and is maintained by the success of the dominant social strata's practices and the appeal they exert to other social strata—through the process

that Gramsci described as passive revolution. Hegemony frames thought and thereby circumscribes action" (Cox 1992, 140).

7. Michel Chossudovsky presented this analysis of the distortion of World Bank figures on global poverty at the NGO forum of the World Summit for Social Development. See also conference papers by Michel Chossudovsky: "The Causes of the Social Crisis: Critique of the Declaration and Programme of Action of the World Summit for Social Development" (pp. 4–5), and "The Global Economic Crisis," both distributed at the World Summit for Social Development, Copenhagen, March 1995.

8. Clearly other causes of social disintegration are highly visible, such as ethnic passions (Bosnia) or the terror of armed groups (Somalia). Yet, outside the glare of CNN cameras, one finds a deep tragedy confronting humanity that rarely makes it into the headlines. The maldistribution of economic and political power has led to an international system that produces massive suffering.

9. Paul Kennedy points out, however, that spare agricultural capacity "lies chiefly in the developed world, especially North America and Europe, not in the countries where the food is most needed; and 'cornucopian' writings about this general reserve capacity rarely consider the problem of *global* supply and demand" (1993, 69). Thus, "rural poverty in Africa, Asia, and elsewhere will not be solved by technical fixes, if structural and cultural aspects of the problem remain unattended" (1993, 70). He further writes that "global agriculture is facing two very different—indeed, contradictory—structural crises. The rich countries suffer from overproduction; the poorest suffer from too little production" (1993, 73).

10. See chapter 2 on self-determination. However, some human rights scholars take an opposite point of view. They argue that where the nation-state is secure and stable there has been a better protection of individual civil rights in comparison with unstable states, and further, that such stability allows for certain group rights to be respected. While this argument is true for some individuals and groups, for other individuals and groups it is false and ultimately misleading. If one analyzes the position of some groups (for example, women of color in the United States), one finds extreme group suffering within strong nation-states. Individual rights alone have not provided adequate protection for these groups.

11. Richard Falk writes of the need for a new politics that is compassionate, globalist, localist, and spiritual: "The relevant point here is that we cannot, at present, view reigning ideologies as capable either of governing effectively and humanely or of providing a liberating challenge to the established authority structure. Indeed, as has been argued, the political competition now taking place in most countries does not include a serious option of liberation" (Falk 1992a, 67).

"There is no reason whatsoever to doubt that human nature is capable of developing and relying upon a far better set of practices with respect to the organization of life on the planet than those that now are dominant. . . . The challenge of political emancipation is to find *plausible pathways* that might lead from *a menaced here* to *a valued there* and thereby orient thought and action in fruitful directions that realize some of the potential for a better, more satisfying world" (Falk 1992a, 105).

12. The International Court of Justice prescribes that the Court apply "international custom, as evidence of a general practice accepted as law (*opinio juris sive necessitatis*)." A custom, according to Levi, is "a habitual behavior," and thus implies a time element. "This criterion can be discovered by examining a state's laws, treaties, statements, and behavior, as well as the repetition, volume, and consistency of state practice" (Levi 1991, 35).

13. Also see above, 211n5.

14. Kratochwil goes on to argue: "In general we can say that soft law imposes an obligation to seek a more specific and detailed solution to an issue without in itself imposing specific enforceable duties. Thus, we could say that soft law represents a weak institutionalization of the norm-creation process by prodding the parties to seek more specific law-solutions within the space laid out in the declarations of intent. Furthermore, by legitimizing conduct which might diverge from the existing practices, soft law provides an alternative which can become a legally relevant crystallization for newly emerging customs or more explicit norms" (1989, 201).

15. D'Amato goes on to write: "If human rights means anything in international law, it means that traditional state-based jurisdictional exclusivities must give way to a more fundamental realization that the rights of people count for more than the rights of states . . . substitute 'internationality' for 'nationality' " (1987, 205).

6. LIBERAL THEORY AND COLLECTIVE HUMAN RIGHTS

1. Wolff asserts that "wealth," the net worth of the household, is a better indicator of long-run economic security than "income." "Wealth is found by adding together the current value of all the assets a household owns—financial wealth such as bank accounts, stocks, bonds, life insurance savings, mutual fund shares; houses and unincorporated businesses; consumer durables like cars and major appliances; and the value of pension rights—and subtracting liabilities—consumer debt, mortgage balances, other outstanding debt. Wealth can vary from year to year as asset prices rise and fall, but it remains the foundation for a family's long-term security. Without wealth, a family lives from hand to mouth, no matter how high its income" (Wolff 1995, 1–2).

2. Classic liberal works in defense of individual freedom are John Stuart Mill's famous essay *On Liberty* (1975) and Isaiah Berlin's book *Four Essays on Liberty* (1969).

3. Collective human rights can also be distinguished from what McDonald has described as the *class action concept of collective rights*. "In the class action concept, the group as a rights-holder serves as a convenient device for advancing the multiple discrete and severable interests of similarly situated individuals. Thus, all consumers who have been disadvantaged by Bell Canada's exceeding the legal limits set on phone rates might be regarded by the courts as a single litigant, simply because it would be too expensive and inconvenient to have each Bell customer take legal action on his or her own."

The aim of collective human rights is to protect group interests that cannot be broken off into individual interests. As McDonald put it, "the rights in question benefit the group itself by providing collective benefits. Moreover, group rights paradigmatically involve the collective exercise of rights through the use of group decision-making mechanisms. Collective benefit and collective exercise are not, therefore, captured by the class action conception of collective rights" (1992, 134–35).

4. This breakdown of the liberal attitude toward group rights into three attitudes (outright hostility, moderate skepticism, guarded endorsement) is taken directly from the summary done by McDonald (1992, 143–54).

5. McDonald stated this point as follows: "For it is the welfare or interests of the community that are at stake and not just the welfare of a given member. The risks to the community's interests are increased if individual members may exercise rights on their own without prior community agreement. The chances of there being either a misconceived or even a mischievous exercise of rights are increased if the power to exercise is not subject to the beneficiary's control. Moreover, there is something perverse about the idea of collective interests being standardly vested in individuals. There is a slide from 'ours' to 'mine' that should be resisted" (1992, 149).

6. Kymlicka 1989, 190. See also Rawls 1971, 75–100; Dworkin 1981, part 2.

7. Or as McDonald puts it: "Collective autonomy for the minority will be diminished in order to advance the autonomy of individual members of the minority" (1992, 153).

8. "Just as a child replaces his or her parent as the family standard-bearer, application of the concept of generation to human rights implies that one generation gives away to and is replaced by, the next, even though it may carry on some of the characteristics of its ancestors" (Alston 1982, 316).

9. See Ian Kershaw 1995, 217–46.

10. Paul Sieghart clearly articulates the danger of nation-state abuse of abstract terms like *the people:* "abstract concepts have in the past only too often presented great dangers to the enjoyment by individuals of their human rights and fundamental freedoms. Some of the worst violations of those rights have been perpetrated in the service of some inspiring abstraction, such as 'the one true faith,' 'the nation,' 'the state' (including, as a recent example, '*das Reich*'), 'the economy' (including 'a strong dollar [or pound]') and indeed 'the masses'. . . . If any of the individual rights and freedoms protected by modern international human rights law ever came to be regarded as subservient to the rights of 'a people' . . . there would be a very real risk that legitimacy might yet again be claimed on such a ground for grave violations of the human rights of individuals" (1983, 368).

11. For example, the 1979 report of the UN secretary-general on "the international dimensions of the right to development," stated: "[the] enjoyment of the right to development necessarily involves a careful balancing between the interests of the

collectivity on one hand, and those of the individual on the other. It would be a mistake, however, to view the right to development as necessarily attaching only at one level or the other. Indeed there seems to be no reason to assume that the interests of the individual and those of the collectivity will necessarily be in conflict. A healthy regard for the right of the individual to pursue his self-realization, manifested by respect for the right within collective decision-making procedures which permit the full participation of the individual, will contribute to, rather than weaken, the efforts of the collectivity to pursue its right to development. In addition, individual development and fulfillment can be achieved only through the satisfaction of collective prerequisites" (UN doc. E/CN.4/1334 [1979], para. 85).

12. Richard Falk, for example, has placed peoples' rights in the context of the struggle of grassroots organizations to open alternative political spaces *to confront the state.* "One central insight of popular movements over the last two decades has been the imperative need to supplement the international legal efforts by governments to uphold human rights with a quite distinctive conception of standards and procedures based on the right of peoples, championing claims on behalf of individuals and groups in relation to issues of peace, justice, basic human needs, and equitable development that are put forward outside the formal state-centered framework of international relations. Governments are often the principal offenders of human rights obligations toward their own citizens. . . . To affirm the rights of peoples is an expression of legal, moral and political support on a transnational basis for popular struggles against various contemporary forms of oppression" (1989a, 58).

13. To many observers, military spending is a clear example of the necessity to redirect priorities. Wasteful military spending by the United States continues despite the end of the Cold War and no new "enemy" emerging with the military capacities of the former Soviet Union. The Joint Chiefs are preparing to fight two wars at once against "rogue states," such as Cuba, Libya, Syria, Iraq, and North Korea. The U.S. 1995 military budget of $264 billion exceeds the combined military budgets of all other NATO members ($147.6 billion).

Seymour Melman estimates that cuts in valueless military parts of the proposed 1996 to 2002 budgets would save at least $875.7 billion. "With these savings, we could improve America's infrastructure while creating two million-plus new jobs—more than enough to offset the jobs lost be ending these military programs. . . . Almost half the nation's badly damaged housing could be rebuilt for $98 billion. Education would be vastly improved by spending the $100 billion needed for public school building maintenance. And $44 billion could be spent to fully finance major Federal education programs; for $15 billion, we could raise the financing of higher education to the same annual per student rate as Japan's" (*New York Times,* 26 June 1995).

7. MARXIST THEORY AND COLLECTIVE HUMAN RIGHTS

1. "Political emancipation is of course a great progress. Although it is not the final form of human emancipation in general, it is nevertheless the final form of

human emancipation inside the present world order. It is to be understood that I am speaking here of real, practical emancipation" (Marx [1844] 1987, 141–42).

2. It has been pointed out that Marx himself spent as much of his time supporting meetings for the liberation of Poland as he spent organizing or supporting strikes (Tay 1978, 106). So, in practice, one could argue that Marx felt strongly about a people's right to self-determination.

3. According to Marx, even a monarch is sovereign only "insofar as he represents the people's unity; he himself, then, is only a representative, a symbol of the sovereignty of the people. The sovereignty of the people does not exist through him but, just the contrary, he exists through it" (quoted in Draper 1977, 85).

4. For example, political theorists Sabine and Thorson write: "In comparison with the undefined liberties which he imputed to a socialist society, he described rights like the suffrage, and political methods like representation, as mere formalities or mere concealments of an underlying class despotism. In general, however, *he assumed that socialism would continue and extend political liberty*" (1973, 691, emphasis added).

5. "Thus freedom is the right to do and perform what does not harm others. The limits within which each person can move without harming others is defined by the law, just as the boundary between two fields is defined by the fence. The freedom in question is that of a man treated as an isolated monad and withdrawn into himself. . . . But the right of man to freedom is not based on the union of man with man, but on the separation of man from man. It is the right to this separation, the rights of the limited individual who is limited to himself" (Marx [1844] 1987, 146).

6. "Security is the highest social concept of civil society; the concept of the police. The whole of society is merely there to guarantee to each of its members the preservation of his person, rights and property" (Marx [1844] 1987, 146–47).

7. Bertell Ollman writes: "To apply values equally is to abstract from the unequal conditions in which people live and the incompatible interests that result. The main effort of capitalist ideology has always been directed to dismissing or playing down this incompatibility. The abstractions with which such ideology abounds are so many attempts to sever the class-affected 'facts' from the judgments and actions that ordinarily follow upon their comprehension" (1971, 46–47).

8. "Thus, in imagination, individuals seem freer under the dominance of the bourgeoisie than before, because their conditions of life seem accidental; in reality, of course, they are less free, because they are more subjected to the violence of things" (Marx & Engels [1932] 1970, 84).

9. "But the common essence from which the worker is isolated is a common essence of quite a different reality and compass from the political collectivity. This collectivity from which his own work separates him is life itself, physical and intellectual life, human morality, human activity, human enjoyment, human essence. The human essence is the true collectivity of man. And since isolation from this essence is out of all proportion more universal, insupportable, terrifying and full of contradic-

tions than isolation from the political collectivity, the abolition of this isolation or even a partial reaction or revolt against it is the more immeasurable as man is more immeasurable than the citizen and human life than political life. An industrial revolt can therefore be as partial as it likes; it contains within it a universal soul: a political revolt can be as universal as it likes, even under the most colossal form it conceals a narrow spirit" (Marx, "The King of Prussia," quoted in Waldron 1987, 135).

10. "In place of the old bourgeois society, with its classes and class antagonisms, we shall have an association, in which the free development of each is the condition for the free development of all" (Marx & Engels [1848] 1967, 105).

11. As Miliband writes, "The question, then, is not whether new social movements can achieve certain changes in their societies: this may by now be taken for granted. The question is rather what the changes they seek, *even if they could be fully realized*, would mean in terms of the *distribution of power, property, privilege, and position* in their societies—in other words, in the structure of domination and exploitation." (1989, 100).

12. For a rigorous, sophisticated, yet accessible work on the dialectical approach towards knowledge, see Bertell Ollman", *Dialectical Investigations* (New York: Routledge, 1993).

13. For example, as cited by Ollman, Marx makes his adherence to internal relations clear in his discussion of two physical objects: the sun and a plant. "The sun," Marx writes, "is the object of the plant—an indispensable object to it confirming its life—just as the plant is an object of the sun, being an expression of the life awakening power of the sun, of the sun's objective essential power." As Ollman goes on to explain, "The sun's effect on the plant, which most of us are inclined to treat causally, is considered by Marx to be an 'expression' of the sun itself, a means by which it manifests what it is and, in this way, part of it" (Ollman 1971, 28).

14. "The world is seen from a standpoint definable in terms of nation or social class, of dominance or subordination, of rising or declining power, of a sense of immobility or of present crisis. . . . There is, accordingly, no such thing as theory in itself, divorced from a standpoint in time and space. When any theory so represents itself, it is more important to examine it as ideology, and to lay bare its concealed perspective" (Cox 1986, 207).

15. As Kain summarized this point: "Individuals separately pursuing their particular interests are not part of the eternal and natural state of things, but a historical outcome produced by a certain form of competitive exchange society. In another sense, this form of socialization simply hinders and frustrates freedom, development, and true individuality by turning the individual's theoretical and practical effort away from what is essential towards mere appearance" (Kain 1988, 60).

16. According to Ollman, precondition played a "decisive role in [Marx's] inquiry into the future." The future is an essential part of the present. "It is not only what the present becomes, but whatever happens in the future exists in the present, within all present forms, as potential" (Ollman 1993, 140).

17. According to Marx, it is only under communism that bourgeois right will be overcome: *"Right can never be higher than the economic structure of society and the cultural development thereby determined. . . .*

"In a higher phase of communist society, after the enslaving subordination of individuals under division of labor, and therewith also the antithesis between mental and physical labor, has vanished; after labor, from a mere means of life, has itself become the prime necessity of life; after the productive forces have also increased with the all-round development of the individual, and all the springs of co-operative wealth flow more abundantly—*only then can the narrow horizon of bourgeois right be fully left behind and society inscribe on its banners: from each according to his ability, to each according to his needs!"* ([1891] 1966a, 10, emphasis added).

18. Independence and freedom, for Marx, are based on the act of self-creation. "A being does not regard himself as independent unless he is his own master, and he is only his own master when he owes his existence to himself. A man who lives by the favor of another considers himself a dependent being. But I live completely by another person's favor when I owe to him not only the continuance of my life but also its *creation*; when he is its *source*. My life has necessarily such a cause outside itself if it is not my own creation" (Marx [1932] 1966b, 138).

19. According to Hobsbawm, "politics" for Gramsci, "is the central human activity, the means by which the single consciousness is brought into contact with the social and natural world in all its forms" (1982, 22–23).

Gramsci sought to show how the ruling class managed to win the active consent of those over whom it rules (Gramsci 1971, 244).

20. Giuseppe Fiori quotes Gramsci in 1916: "Man is above all else mind, consciousness—that is, he is a product of history, not of nature. There is no other way of explaining why socialism has not come into existence already, although there have always been exploiters and exploited, creators of wealth and selfish consumers of wealth. Man has only been able to acquire a sense of his worth bit by bit, in one sector of society after another. . . . And such awareness was not generated out of brute physiological needs, but out of intelligent reasoning, first of all by a few and later on by entire social classes who perceived the causes of certain social facts and understood that there might be ways of converting the structure of repression into one of rebellion and social reconstruction. This means that every revolution has been preceded by an intense labour of social criticism, of cultural penetration and diffusion" (Gramsci 1970, 103).

21. As Boggs summarizes: "The arenas of ideological-cultural transmission are infinite: the state, legal system, work place, schools, churches, bureaucracies, cultural activities, the media, the family. Hegemony quite clearly embraces far more than single, well-defined ideologies (e.g. liberalism) . . . not only competitive individualism . . . but also the social atomization and depoliticization produced by bureaucracy, the fatalism instilled by religion, the state-worship fanned by nationalism, and the sexism which grows out of the family . . . [the result] . . . securing general popular acceptance of their dominant position as something 'natural,' part of an eternal social order, and thus unchallengeable" (1984, 160–61).

22. Gramsci sought to generate a uniquely *national* role for Marxist theory. His "war of position," for example stressed that each individual country would require an "accurate reconnaissance." He believed that each individual country had to develop its own plan of how to create socialism in the particular political and cultural context in which they found themselves. The war of position involved establishing working class norms and values which challenge the existing ideological hegemony. This new ideological hegemony is later the basis on which to build a new socialist state. Therefore, the effort to build a new proletarian hegemony in the process of carrying out the war of position, becomes the foundation of the new moral and intellectual order (Carnoy 1984, 83).

23. Gramsci wrote: "In reality, the internal relations of any nation are the result of a combination which is 'original' and (in a certain sense) unique: these relations must be understood and conceived in their originality and uniqueness if one wishes to dominate them and direct them. To be sure, the line of development is towards internationalism, but the point of departure is 'national'—and it is from this point of departure that one must begin. Yet the perspective is international and cannot be otherwise" (1971, 240).

24. As Gramsci wrote, "A crisis cannot give the attacking forces the ability to organize with lightning speed in time and space; still less can it endow them with fighting spirit. Similarly the defenders are not demoralized, nor do they abandon their positions, even among the ruins, nor do they lose faith in their own strength or their own future" (Gramsci 1971, 235).

8. "POST" THEORIES AND COLLECTIVE HUMAN RIGHTS

1. The "domination intrinsic to power," is perhaps the key aspect to understanding much of Foucault's work. As biographer James Miller wrote: "he [Foucault] understood power not as a fixed quantity of physical force, but rather as a stream of energy flowing through every living organism and every human society, its formless flux harnessed in various patterns of behavior, habits of introspection, and systems of knowledge, in addition to different types of political, social, and military organization."

Miller continues: "From schools and the professions to the army and the prison, the central institutions of our society, charged Foucault, strove with sinister efficiency to supervise the individual, 'to neutralize his dangerous states,' and to alter his conduct by inculcating numbing codes of discipline. The inevitable result was 'docile bodies' and obedient souls, drained of creative energy" (1993, 15).

2. As Ashley wrote, "One analyzes how, amid the same transversal struggles, local movements that are uncertain of their identity, that speak in a quavering timbre, that would not project a sovereign voice of man in need of a state's violent protections, that know themselves to be neither domestic nor international, that find happiness in their historicity and know themselves to be always in process and in doubt—how such resistance movements might find in ambiguity not a source of peril but

enabling opportunities to explore and disseminate new strategies of resistance to the disciplining practice of 'man, the state, and war' " (1989, 312).

3. See, for example, R. B. J. Walker's discussion of Machiavelli in *Inside/ Outside: International Relations as Political Theory* (Cambridge: Cambridge University Press, 1993), 26–49.

4. As Laclau & Mouffe write: "The rejection of privileged points of rupture and the confluence of struggles into a unified political space, and the acceptance, on the contrary, of the plurality and indeterminacy of the social, seem to us the two fundamental bases from which a new political imaginary can be constructed, radically libertarian and infinitely more ambitious in its objectives than that of the classic left" (1985, 152).

5. For a Marxist critique of this agenda, see Ellen Meiksins Wood and John Bellamy Foster, eds., "In Defense of History: Marxism and the Postmodern Agenda," *Monthly Review* 47.3 (July–August 1995).

9. THE CASE FOR COLLECTIVE HUMAN RIGHTS

1. See "State of Ratifications of Major Human Rights Conventions," *Netherlands Quarterly of Human Rights* 12.3 (1994): 341–51.

2. Alston notes that the only qualification the committee adds is that a state may be able to demonstrate that resource constraints make it impossible for anything positive to be done in this regard. The burden of proving that this is the case would, however, be a difficult one to discharge and falls upon the state itself (1992, 495).

3. Another clear failure to meet the "minimum core obligation to ensure the satisfaction of, at the very least, minimum essential levels of each of the rights" found in the covenant is seen throughout Eastern Europe today. A UN study covering developments from 1989 into early 1994 in Albania, Bulgaria, the Czech Republic, Slovakia, Hungary, Poland, Romania, Russia, and the Ukraine concludes that the years of transition from Communism to free-market democracies have left the most vulnerable people of Eastern and Central Europe significantly poorer, less healthy or fed, and more prone to accidental death and homicide. The UNICEF report states that economic changes have "provoked a deterioration of unparalleled proportions in human welfare throughout most of the region." Russia has experienced a tenfold increase in families living below the poverty line and a mortality rate up by 35 percent compared with the pre-1989 rate. Iodine-deficiency disorders are endemic in all countries studied except parts of Hungary, the Czech Republic, and Slovakia. In Bulgaria the situation is as bad as in Central Africa. Such deficiencies lead to goiter, nervous system damage, growth retardation, and cretinism (*New York Times*, 7 October 1994).

4. *Declaration of the Aims and Purposes of the International Labour Organization*, known as the "Declaration of Philadelphia," attached as an annex to the text of the constitution as revised, UST No. 874, 26 *ILO Official Bulletin* 26 (1944): 1–3.

5. For a summary of the ILO experience, see Leary 1992b.

6. Further, the ILO has curtailed its previous challenges to structural adjustment programs (SAPs) designed to accelerate liberalization in Third World countries, and instead now facilitates them. Previous ILO criticisms of SAPs were based on the understanding that (1) the East Asian models for growth that SAPs are often designed to emulate, rely on strong (often authoritarian) national government intervention; and (2) the fact that even levels of $30 billion annually in combined IMF/World Bank/UN Development Program financing do not match the continuing flow of funds from the South to the North. The ILO no longer pushes these contradictions (see Siegal 1994, 167).

7. Guinier summarized the failings of the black electoral success theory as follows: "the theory abandoned the civil rights movement's transformative vision of politics. In that vision, the purpose of political equal opportunity was to ensure fairness in the competition for favorable policy outcomes, not just fairness in the struggle for a seat at the bargaining table. In addition, legislative responsiveness would not be secured merely by the election day ratification of black representatives. Rather, legislative responsiveness would depend on citizen participation, legislative presence, and legislative success in meeting the needs of a disadvantaged group" (1991a, 1134). Simply "providing technical access for minority group representatives yields very modest results at best" (1991a, 1135).

8. In adopting a "personalist vision," Jacques Maritain, a French philosopher who served on the faculty at Princeton for a number of years, wrote: "Those whom, for want of a better name, I just called the advocates of a liberal-individualist type of society, see the mark of human dignity first and foremost in the power of each person to appropriate individually the goods of nature in order to do freely whatever he wants; the advocates of a communistic type of society see the mark of human dignity first and foremost in the power to submit these same goods to the collective command of the society body in order to 'free' human labor (by subduing it to the economic community) and to gain the control of history; the advocates of a personalistic type of society see the mark of human dignity first and foremost in the power to make these same goods of nature serve the common conquest of intrinsically human, moral, and spiritual goods and of man's freedom of autonomy. . . . As far as I am concerned, I know where I stand: with the third of the three schools of thought I just mentioned" (Leary 1992a, 113–14).

The concepts of individual and group rights are essential to Maritain's personalist perspective. Individual rights are needed as protection against the tyranny of groups as well as against the tyranny of the state. Yet he also recognized the importance of collectivities on an intermediate level between the individual and the state.

9. An example of a "distant abstraction" is the "right to food," which "has been endorsed more often and with greater unanimity and urgency than most other human rights," according to Philip Alston, "while at the same time being violated more comprehensively and systematically than probably any other right" (1984, 9). The current economic system, according to UNESCO, allows approximately 40,000 children to die every day, 15 million per year. Whatever the exact numbers, it is clear that millions of people continue to be chronically malnourished. Yet the problem is not a lack of food.

Estimates are that the present world agricultural output per capita of grain alone could supply everyone with more than 3,000 calories and 65 grams of protein daily. In a detailed study of major famines over forty years, Amartya Sen demonstrates that in each one the major problem was poverty, not lack of food. In each famine vast numbers of people died, yet the total supply of food either did not decline or declined only slightly (Alston 1984, 11). Increased food production alone will not diminish hunger, unless it is accompanied with a more equitable distribution of wealth and income; some correctives to the failures of the market.

10. Professor Richard Falk was the first to employ the concept of humane governance and geogovernance as a counter to geopolitics. See *On Humane Governance* (University Park: Pennsylvania State University Press, 1995).

BIBLIOGRAPHY

Abdalla, Ismail-Sabri. 1988. "Beyond the Nation State." In *The Theory and Practice of Liberation at the End of the XXth Century*. Brussels: Bruylant.

Adam, Barry D. 1987. *The Rise of a Gay and Lesbian Movement*. Boston: Twayne Publishers.

Alker, Hayward, Thomas Biersteker, & T. Inoguchi Wars. 1989. "From Imperial Power Balancing to People's Rights: Searching for Order in the Twentieth Century." In *International /Intertextual Relations*, ed. James Der Derian & Michael J. Shapiro. Lexington: Lexington Books.

Alston, Philip. 1981. "Development and the Rule of Law: Prevention Versus Cure as a Human rights Strategy." In *Development, Human Rights and the Rule of Law*, ed. the International Commission of Jurists. Oxford: Pergamon Press.

————. 1982. "A Third Generation of Solidarity Rights: Progressive Development or Obfuscation of International Human Rights Law?" *Netherlands International Law Review* 29.3.

————. 1984. "International Law and the Human Right to Food." In *The Right to Food*, ed. P. Alston & K. Tomasevski. Utrecht: Martinus Nijhoff Publishers.

————. 1985. "The Shortcomings of a 'Garfield the Cat' Approach to the Right to Development." *California Western International Law Journal* 15.

————. 1992. "The Committee on Economic, Social and Cultural Rights." In *The United Nations and Human Rights: A Critical Appraisal*, ed. P. Alston. Oxford: Clarendon Press.

————. 1994. "The UN's Human Rights Record: From San Francisco to Vienna and Beyond." *Human Rights Quarterly* 16.2 (May).

Althusser, L. and C. Balibar. 1970. *Reading Capital*. London: New Left Books.

Amin, Samir. 1990. "The Social Movements in the Periphery: An End to National Liberation?" In *Transforming the Revolution*, ed. S. Amin, G. Arrighi, A. G. Frank, & I. Wallerstein. New York: Monthly Review Press.

Amnesty International, USA. 1994. *Breaking the Silence: Human Rights Violations Based on Sexual Orientation*. New York: Amnesty International Publications.

ANC Constitutional Committee. 1990. *A Bill of Rights for a New South Africa*. Bellville: Centre for Development Studies.

Anderson, Benedict. 1991. *Imagined Communities*. London: Verso Press.

An-Na⁽im, Abdullahi Ahmed. 1992. *Human Rights in Cross-Cultural Perspectives: A Quest for Consensus*. Philadelphia: University of Pennsylvania Press.

Arnaud, Nicole & Jacques Dofny. 1977. *Nationalism and the National Question*. Montreal: Black Rose Books.

Arrighi, Giovanni. 1990. "The Making and Remaking of the World Labor Movement." In *Transforming the Revolution*, ed. S. Amin, G. Arrighi, A. G. Frank, & I. Wallerstein. New York: Monthly Review Press.

Ashley, Richard K. 1989. "Living on Border Lines: Man, Poststructuralism, and War." In *International/Intertextual Relations*, ed. James Der Derian & Michael J. Shapiro. Lexington: Lexington Books.

Attwooll, Elspeth. 1986. "The Right to be a Member of a Trade Union." In *Human Rights: From Rhetoric to Reality*, ed. Campbell, Goldberg, McLean, & Mullen. Oxford: Basil Blackwell.

Balibar, Etienne. 1991. "Preface." In *Race, Nation, Class: Ambiguous Identities*, by Etienne Balibar & Immanuel Wallerstein. London: Verso Press.

Barnet, Richard J.. 1980. "Human Rights Implications of Corporate Food Policies." In *The Politics of Human Rights*, ed. Paula R. Newberg. New York: New York University Press.

Barnet, Richard J. & John Cavanagh. 1994. *Global Dreams: Imperial Corporations and the New World Order*. New York: Simon & Schuster.

Barnet, Richard J. & Ronald E. Muller. 1974. *Global Reach: The Power of the Multinational Corporations*. New York: Simon & Schuster.

Barsh, Russel Lawrence. 1991. "The Right to Development as a Human Right: Results of the Global Consultation." *Human Rights Quarterly* 13.3.

Bartholomew, Amy. 1990. "Should a Marxist Believe in Marx on Rights?" *Socialist Register*. London: Merline Press.

Barry, Brian. 1982. "Humanity and Justice in Global Perspective." In *Ethics, Economics, and the Law*, ed. Pennock & Chapman. New York: New York University Press.

Basso, Lelio. 1978. *La Societa*. No. 19, December.

Bateson, Mary Catherine. 1990. "Beyond Sovereignty: An Emerging Global Civilization." In *Contending Sovereignties: Redefining Political Community*, ed. R. B. J. Walker & Saul Mendlovitz. Boulder: Lynne Rienner Publishers.

Bay, Christian. 1981. *Strategies of Political Emancipation*. Notre Dame: University of Notre Dame Press.

———. 1990. "Taking the Universality of Human Needs Seriously." In *Conflict: Human Needs Theory*, ed. John Burton. New York: St. Martin's Press.

Beitz, Charles R. 1979. *Political Theory and International Relations*. Princeton: Princeton University Press.

———. 1981. "Economic Rights and Distributive Justice in Developing Societies." *World Politics* 33 (April).

Belsey, Andrew. 1992. "World Poverty, Justice, and Equality." In *International Justice and the Third World*, ed. Robin Attfield & Barry Wilkins. New York: Routledge, Chapman and Hall.

Benston, Margaret. 1989. "The Political Economy of Women's Liberation." *Monthly Review* 41.7.

Berlin, Isaiah. 1969. *Four Essays on Liberty*. Oxford: Oxford University Press.

Berman, Ruth. 1989. "The Feminization of the U.S. Workforce." *Monthly Review* 41.6.

Biersteker, Thomas. 1981. "The Limits of State Power in the Contemporary World Economy." In *Boundaries*, ed. Brown & Shue. Toronto: Rowman and Littlefield.

Birnie, Patricia. 1992. "International Environmental Law: Its Adequacy for Present and Future Needs." In *The International Politics of the Environment*, ed. Andrew Hurrell & Benedict Kingsbury. Oxford: Clarendon Press.

Blauner, Bob. 1989. *Black Lives, White Lives: Three Decades of Race Relations in America*. Berkeley: University of California Press.

———. 1990. "Black Workers and the Underclass." *New Politics* 2.4 (Winter).

Blaut, James M. 1987. *The National Question*. London: Zed Books.

Boggs, Carl. 1984. *The Two Revolutions: Gramsci and the Dilemmas of Western Marxism*. Boston: South End Press.

Bozeman, Adda. 1971. *The Future of Law in a Multicultural World*. Princeton: Princeton University Press.

———. 1984. "The International Order in a Multicultural World." In *The Expansion of International Society*, ed. Hedley Bull & Adam Watson. Oxford: Clarendon Press.

Brandt, Willy. 1980. *North-South: A Programme for Survival: Report of the Independent Commission on International Development Issues*. Cambridge, Mass.: MIT Press.

Bronski, Michael. 1984. *Culture Clash: The Making of Gay Sensibility*. Boston: South End Press.

Brownlie, Ian. 1981. *Basic Documents on Human Rights*, 2nd ed. Oxford: Clarendon Press.

————. 1984. "The Expansion of International Society: The Consequences for the Law of Nations." In *The Expansion of International Society*, ed. Hedley Bull & Adam Watson. Oxford: Clarendon Press.

————. 1988. "The Rights of Peoples in Modern International Law." In *The Rights of Peoples*, ed. James Crawford. Oxford: Clarendon Press.

Buchanan, Allen. 1991. *Secession: The Morality of Political Divorce from Fort Sumter to Lithuania and Quebec*. Boulder: Westview Press.

Bull, Hedley. 1977. *The Anarchical Society*. New York: Columbia University Press.

————. 1984. "The Revolt against the West." In *The Expansion of International Society*, ed. Hedley Bull & Adam Watson. Oxford: Clarendon Press.

Burawoy, Michael. 1991. "Painting Socialism: Working Class Formation in Hungary and Poland." In *Bringing Class Back In*, ed. McNall, Levine, & Fantasia. Boulder: Westview Press.

Burgos-Debray, Elisabeth, ed. 1984. *I, Rigoberta Menchu*. London: Verso.

Burrows, Noreen. 1986. "International Law and Human Rights: The Case of Women's Rights." In *Human Rights: From Rhetoric to Reality*, ed. Campbell, Goldberg, McLean, & Mullen. Oxford: Basil Blackwell.

Camilleri, Joseph A. 1990. "Rethinking Sovereignty in a Shrinking, Fragmented World." In *Contending Sovereignties: Redefining Political Community*, ed. R. B. J. Walker & Saul Mendlovitz. Boulder: Lynne Rienner Publishers.

Camilleri, Joseph A. & Jim Falk. 1992. *The End of Sovereignty? The Politics of a Shrinking and Fragmented World*. Aldershot, U.K.: Edward Elgar Publishing Limited.

Campbell, Tom. 1983. *The Left and Rights*. London: Routledge & Kegan Paul.

Camus, Albert. [1946] 1964. "Neither Victims nor Executioners." In *Seeds of Liberation*, ed. Paul Goodman. New York: George Braziller, Inc.

Carnoy, Martin. 1984. *The State and Political Theory*. Princeton: Princeton University Press.

Castberg, Frede. 1968. "Natural Law and Human Rights: An Idea-Historical Survey." In *International Protection of Human Rights*, ed. Eide & Schou. Stockholm: Almquist & Wiksell.

Chesneaux, Jean. 1988. "Which Fight for What Liberation?" In *The Theory and Practice of Liberation at the End of the XXth Century*. Brussels: Bruylant.

Chinkin, Christine M. 1991. "Remarks." In *American Society of International Law Proceedings of the 85th Annual Meeting*. Washington D.C.: ASIL.

——. 1989. "The Challenge of Soft Law: Development and Change in International Law. *International and Comparative Law Quarterly* 38.

Chossudovsky, Michel. 1995a. "The Causes of the Social Crisis: Critique of the Declaration and Programme of Action of the World Summit for Social Development (WSSD)." Paper presented to the NGO Forum of the WSSD. Copenhagen, Denmark.

——. 1995b. "The Global Economic Crisis." Paper presented to the NGO Forum of the World Summit for Social Development. Copenhagen, Denmark.

Claude, Inis L., Jr. 1984. *Swords into Plowshares: The Problems and Progress of International Organization*, 4th ed. New York: Random House.

Collins, Joseph. 1994. "World Hunger: A Scarcity of Food or a Scarcity of Democracy?" In *World Security: Challenges for a New Century*, ed. Michael T. Klare & Daniel C. Thomas. New York: St. Martin's Press.

Constitution of the Republic of South Africa. 1994. *Government Gazette* (Republic of South Africa) 343.15466 (28 January).

Cook, Rebecca J. 1994. *Human Rights of Women*. Philadelphia: University of Pennsyvania Press.

Coole, Diana H. 1988. *Women in Political Theory: From Ancient Misogyny to Contemporary Feminism*. Sussex: Wheatsheaf Books.

Cox, Robert W. 1986. "Social Forces, States and World Order: Beyond International Relations Theory." In *Neorealism and Its Critics*, ed. Robert O. Keohane. New York: Columbia University Press.

——. 1992. "Towards a Post-Hegemonic Conceptualization of World Order: Reflections on the Relevancy of Ibn Khaldun." In *Governance without Government: Order and Change in World Politics*, ed. James N. Rosenau & Ernst-Otto Czempiel. Cambridge: Cambridge University Press.

Crawford, James, ed. 1988. *The Rights of Peoples*. Oxford: Clarendon Press.

D'Amato, Anthony. 1987. *International Law: Process and Prospect*. Dobbs Ferry: Transnational Publishers.

Dahrendorf, Ralf. 1990. *The Modern Social Conflict*. Berkeley: University of California Press.

Davis, Horace. 1967. *Nationalism and Socialism*. New York: Monthly Review Press.

——. 1978. *Toward a Marxist Theory of Nationalism*. New York: Monthly Review Press.

Der Derian, James. 1989. "The Boundaries of Knowledge and Power in International Relations." In *International/Intertextual Relations*, ed. James Der Derian & Michael J. Shapiro. Lexington: Lexington Books.

Der Derian, James & Michael J. Shapiro. 1989. *International/Intertextual Relations*. Lexington: Lexington Books.

Dessler, David. 1989. "Agent-Structure Debate." *International Organization* (World Peace Foundation and MIT) 43.3 (Summer).

Dias, Charles J. 1981. "Realizing the Right to Development: The Importance of Legal Resources." In *Development, Human Rights and the Rule of Law*, ed. International Commission of Jurists. Oxford: Pergamon Press.

Dinstein, Yoram. 1989. "Self-Determination and the Middle East Conflict." In *Human Rights in the World Community*, ed. Richard P. Claude & Burns H. Weston. Philadelphia: University of Pennsylvania Press.

Donnelly, Jack. 1985a. *The Concept of Human Rights*. New York: St. Martin's Press.

———. 1985b. "In Search of the Unicorn: The Jurisprudence and Politics of the Right to Development" and "The Theology of the Right to Development: A Reply to Alston." *California Western International Law Journal* 15.

———. 1989. *Universal Human Rights in Theory and Practice*. Ithaca: Cornell University Press.

Draper, Hal. 1977. *Karl Marx's Theory of Revolution,* Volume 1: *State Bureaucracy*. New York: Monthly Review Press.

Duncan, Grahme. 1973. *Marx and Mill: Two Views of Social Conflict and Social Harmony*. Cambridge: Cambridge University Press.

Dunn, John. 1979. *Western Political Theory in the Face of the Future*. Cambridge: Cambridge University Press.

———. 1985. *Rethinking Modern Political Theory*. Cambridge: Cambridge University Press.

Durning, Alan. 1993. "Supporting Indigenous Peoples." In *State of the World 1993*, ed. Worldwatch Institute. New York: W. W. Norton & Co.

Dworkin, Ronald. 1977. *Taking Rights Seriously*. Cambridge, Mass.: Harvard University Press.

———. 1981. "What is Equality?" Parts I and II. *Philosophy and Public Affairs* 10.

———. 1985. *A Matter of Principle*. Cambridge, Mass.: Harvard University Press.

Elias, Robert. 1986. *The Politics of Victimization*. New York: Oxford University Press.

Elshtain, Jean Bethke. 1989. "Freud's Discourse of War/Politics." In *International/ Intertextual Relations*, ed. James Der Derian & Michael J. Shapiro. Lexington: Lexington Books.

Engels, Friedrich. [1846] 1976a. "The Festival of Nations in London." In *Collected Works (Marx and Engels)*, vol. 6 New York: International Publishers.

————. [1914] 1976b. "Principles of Communism." In *Collected Works (Marx and Engels)*, vol. 6. New York: International Publishers.

Espiritu, A. Caesar. 1981. "Keeping Human Life Human." In *Development, Human Rights and the Rule of Law*. Oxford: Pergamon Press.

Falk, Richard. 1970. *The Status of Law in International Society*. Princeton: Princeton University Press.

————. 1981. *Human Rights and State Sovereignty*. New York: Holmes & Meier.

————. 1983. *The End of World Order: Essays on Normative International Relations*. New York: Holmes & Meier.

————. 1988. "The Rights of Peoples (In Particular Indigenous Peoples)." In *The Rights of Peoples*, ed. James Crawford. Oxford: Clarendon Press.

————. 1989a. "United States Foreign Policy as an Obstacle to the Rights of Peoples." *Social Justice* 16.1.

————. 1989b. "Group Claims and the Nation-State within the United Nations System." Conference on Ethnic Conflict and the UN Human Rights System. Oxford: St. Ann's College.

————. 1990. "Evasions of Sovereignty." In *Contending Sovereignties: Redefining Political Community*, ed. R. B. J. Walker & Saul Mendlovitz. Boulder: Lynne Rienner Publishers.

————. 1991. "Theory, Realism, and World Security." In *World Security: Trends & Challenges at Century's End*, ed. Michael T. Klare & Daniel C. Thomas. New York: St. Martin's Press.

————. 1992a. *Explorations at the Edge of Time*. Philadelphia: Temple University Press.

————. 1992b. "Economic Aspects of Global Civilization: The Unmet Challenges of World Poverty." World Order Studies Program Occasional Paper, no. 22. Princeton: Center of International Studies, Princeton University.

————. 1995. *On Humane Governance*. University Park: Pennsylvania State University Press.

Falk, Richard, S. Kim, & Saul H. Mendlovitz. 1982. *Toward a Just World Order*. Boulder: Westview Press.

Faludi, Susan. 1991. *Backlash: The Undeclared War against American Women.* New York: Crown Publishers.

Fanon, Frantz. 1966. *The Wretched of the Earth.* New York: Grove Press.

Feinberg, Joel. 1980. *Rights, Justice, and the Bounds of Liberty.* Princeton: Princeton University Press.

Felice, William. 1989. "Rights in Theory and Practice: An Historical Perspective." *Social Justice* 16.1.

Fiori, Giuseppe. 1970. *Antonio Gramsci: Life of a Revolutionary.* New York: Schocken Books.

Foster, Phillips. 1992. *The World Food Problem.* Boulder: Lynne Rienner Publishers.

Forsythe, David P. 1983. *Human Rights and World Politics.* Lincoln: University of Nebraska Press.

———. 1991. *The Internationalization of Human Rights.* Toronto: Lexington Books.

———. 1993. *Human Rights and Peace.* Lincoln: University of Nebraska Press.

Foucault, Michel. 1979. *Power, Truth, Strategy.* Sydney: Feral Publications.

———. 1980. *Power/Knowledge: Selected Interviews and Other Writings.* New York: Pantheon Books.

———. 1982. "The Subject and Power." In *Michel Foucault: Beyond Structuralism and Hermeneutics*, ed. Hubert Dreyfus & Raul Rabinow. Chicago: University of Chicago Press.

Frank, Andre Gunder & Marta Fuentes. 1990. "Civil Democracy: Social Movements in Recent World History." In *Transforming the Revolution*, ed. S. Amin, G. Arrighi, A. G. Frank, & I. Wallerstein. New York: Monthly Review Press.

Fromm, Erich. 1966. *Marx's Concept of Man.* New York: Continuum.

Galtung, Johan. 1977. "Is the Legal Perspective Structure-Blind?" In *Declarations on Principles: A Quest for Universal Peace*, ed. Akkerman, Van Krieken, & Pannenborg. Leyden: A. W. Sijthoff.

———. 1979. *Development, Environment and Technology: Towards a Technology for Self-Reliance.* Geneva: United Nations Conference on Trade and Development.

———. 1980. "Self-Reliance: Concepts, Practice and Rationale." In *Self-Reliance: A Strategy for Development*, ed. Galtung, O'Brien, & Preiswerk. London: Bogle-L'Ouverture Publications.

———. 1990. "International Development in Human Perspective." In *Conflict: Human Needs Theory*, ed. J. Burton. New York: St. Martin's Press.

———. 1994. *Human Rights in Another Key.* Cambridge: Polity Press.

Galtung, Johan & Anders Wirak. 1976. "Human Needs, Human Rights and the Theories of Development." UNESCO. SHC.75/ws/55.

Gellner, Ernest. 1983. *Nations and Nationalism*. Ithaca: Cornell University Press.

Geras, Norman. 1976. *The Legacy of Rosa Luxemburg*. London: Verso Press.

Gill, Stephen. 1993. *Gramsci, Historical Materialism and International Relations*. Cambridge: Cambridge University Press.

Gittleman, Richard. 1984. "The Banjul Charter on Human and Peoples' Rights: A Legal Analysis." In *Human Rights and Development in Africa*, ed. Claude E. Welch, Jr. & Ronald I. Meltz. Albany: SUNY Press.

Glahn, Gerhard von. 1992. *Law Among Nations*, 6th ed. New York: Macmillan Publishing Co.

Goodin, Robert E. 1985. *Protecting the Vulnerable*. Chicago: University of Chicago Press.

———. 1988. "What Is So Special about Our Fellow Countrymen?" *Ethics* 98 (July): 663–86.

Gottlieb, Gidon. 1993. *Nations against State: A New Approach to Ethnic Conflicts and the Decline of Sovereignty*. New York: Council on Foreign Relations.

Gramsci, Antonio. 1971. *Prison Notebooks*. New York: International Publishers.

Green, James & Enrique Asis. 1993. "Gays and Lesbians: The Closet Door Swings Open." *Report on the Americas* 26.4.

Grinspun, Ricardo & Maxwell Cameron. 1993. "Mexico: The Wages of Trade." *Report on the Americas* 26.4.

Guinier, Lani. 1991a. "The Triumph of Tokenism: The Voting Rights Act and the Theory of Black Electoral Success." *Michigan Law Review* 89 (March):1077.

———. 1991b. "No Two Seats: The Elusive Quest for Political Equality." *Virginia Law Review* 77.8 (November).

———. 1994. *The Tyranny of the Majority*. New York: The Free Press.

Gurr, Ted Robert. 1993. *Minorities at Risk: A Global View of Ethnopolitical Conflicts*. Washington D.C.: U.S. Institute of Peace Press.

Gutierrez, Gustavo. 1973. *A Theology of Liberation*. Maryknoll, N.Y.: Orbis Books.

Habermas, Jürgen. 1971. *Knowledge and Human Interests*. Boston: Beacon Press.

Halperin, Morton H., David J. Scheffer, & Patricia L. Small. 1992. *Self-Determination in the New World Order*. Washington D.C.: Carnegie Endowment for International Peace.

Hannum, Hurst. 1989. "The Limits of Sovereignty and Majority Rule: Minorities, Indigenous Peoples, and the Right to Autonomy." In *New Directions in Human Rights*, ed. Lutz, Hannum, & Burke. Philadelphia: University of Pennsylvania Press.

Harvey, David. 1989. *The Condition of Postmodernity*. Oxford: Basil Blackwell.

Havel, Vaclav. 1992. *Summer Meditations*. New York: Alfred A. Knopf.

Henkin, Louis. 1979. *How Nations Behave*, 2nd ed. New York: Columbia University Press.

———, ed. 1981. *The International Bill of Rights*. New York: Columbia University Press.

———. 1990. *The Age of Rights*. New York: Columbia University Press.

Henkin, Louis, Richard Pugh, Oscar Schachter, & Hans Smit. 1987. *International Law: Cases and Materials*. St. Paul: West Publishing Co.

Higgins, Rosalyn. 1994. *Problems and Process: International Law and How We Use It*. Oxford: Clarendon Press.

Hitler, Adolf. 1971. *Mein Kampf*. Boston: Houghton Mifflin Company.

Hobsbawm, Eric. 1982. "Gramsci and Marxist Political Theory." In *Approaches to Gramsci*, ed. Anne Showstack Sassoon. London: Writers and Readers Publisher Cooperative.

———. 1990. *Nations and Nationalism since 1780*. Cambridge: Cambridge University Press.

Hochschild, Jennifer L. 1996. *Facing Up to the American Dream: Race, Class, and the Soul of the Nation*. Princeton: Princeton University Press.

Howard, Rhoda E. 1985. "Law and Economic Rights in Commonwealth Africa." *California Western International Law Journal* 15.

———. 1989. "Human Rights, Development and Foreign Policy." In *Human Rights and Development*, ed. David Forsythe. New York: St. Martin's Press.

———. 1990. "Monitoring Human Rights: Problems of Consistency." *Ethics and International Affairs*, vol. 4. New York: Carnegie Council on Ethics and International Affairs.

———. 1992. "Dignity, Community, and Human Rights." In *Human Rights in Cross-Cultural Perspectives*, ed. Abdullahi An-Naᶜim. Philadelphia: University of Pennsylvia Press.

Hunter, Nan D. 1991. "Sexual Dissent and the Family." *The Nation* 253.11.

Hutcheon, Linda. 1989. *The Politics of Postmodernism*. London: Routledge.

International Commission of Jurists. 1981. *Development, Human Rights and the Rule of Law.* Oxford: Pergamon Press.

International Labor Organization. 1966. *Conventions and Recommendations.* Geneva: International Labor Organization.

IMF Assessment Project. 1992. *IMF Conditionality, 1980–91.* Arlington, Va.: Alexis de Tocqueville Institution.

Jacobson, Jodi L. 1993. "Closing the Gender Gap in Development." In *State of the World 1993.* New York: W. W. Norton & Company.

Janis, Mark. 1993. *An Introduction to International Law.* Boston: Little, Brown and Company.

Johansen, Robert. 1980. *The National Interest and the Human Interest.* Princeton: Princeton University Press.

Jones, Dorothy. 1992. "The Declaratory Tradition in Modern International Law." In *Traditions of International Ethics*, ed. Terry Nardin & David R. Mapel. Cambridge: Cambridge University Press.

Jordan, Barbara. 1992. "Civil Rights: Is It Still a Good Idea?" Remarks upon receiving the Annual International and National Freedom Award from the National Civil Rights Museum. Memphis, Tennessee. September.

Kain, Philip J. 1988. *Marx and Ethics.* Oxford: Clarendon Press.

Kamenka, Eugene. 1988. "Human Rights, Peoples' Rights." In *The Rights of Peoples*, ed. James Crawford. Oxford: Clarendon Press.

Kargarlitsky, Boris. 1990. *The Dialectic of Change.* London: Verso Press.

Kartashkin, Vladimir. 1989. *Human Rights: What We Argue About.* Moscow: Progress Publishers.

Kennedy, Paul. 1993. *Preparing for the Twenty-First Century.* New York: Random House.

Keohane, Robert. 1984. *After Hegemony: Cooperation and Discord in World Politics.* Princeton: Princeton University Press.

Keohane, Robert & Joseph Nye, eds. 1971. *Transnational Relations and World Politics.* Cambridge, Mass.: Harvard University Press.

———. 1977. *Power and Interdependence.* Boston: Little Brown.

———. 1987. "Power and Interdependence Revisited." *International Organization* 41.4.

Kershaw, Ian. 1995. "The Extinction of Human Rights in Nazi Germany." In *Historical Change and Human Rights, The Oxford Amnesty Lectures 1994*, ed. Olwen Hufton. New York: Basic Books.

Kim, Samuel S. 1984. *The Quest for a Just World Order*. Boulder: Westview Press.

Kly, Y. N. 1985. *International Law and the Black Minority in the United States*. Atlanta: Clarity Press.

Kothari, Rajni. 1989. *Rethinking Development*. New York: New Horizons Press.

Kothari, Rajni & Harsh Sethi. 1989. *Rethinking Human Rights*. New York: New Horizons Press.

Kratochwil, Friedrich V. 1989. *Rules, Norms, and Decisions: On the Conditions of Practical and Legal Reasoning in International Relations and Domestic Affairs*. Cambridge: Cambridge University Press.

Kubalkova, V. & A. A. Cruickshank. 1989. *Thinking about Soviet "New Thinking"*. Berkeley: University of California Press.

Kymlicka, Will. 1989. *Liberalism, Community, and Culture*. Oxford: Clarendon Press.

Laclau, Ernesto & Chantal Mouffe. 1985. *Hegemony and Socialist Strategy*. London: Verso Press.

Laski, Harold J. 1962. *An Introduction to Politics*. New York: Barnes & Noble.

Leary, Virginia A. 1992a. "Postliberal Strands in Western Human Rights Theory: Personalist-Communitarian Perspectives." In *Human Rights in Cross Cultural Perspectives*, ed. Abdullahi An-Na ͨim. Philadelphia: University of Philadelphia Press.

———. 1992b. "Lessons from the Experience of the International Labour Organisation." In *The United Nations and Human Rights: A Critical Appraisal*, ed. Philip Alston. Oxford: Clarendon Press.

Lenin, V. I. [1914] 1968. *National Liberation, Socialism and Imperialism*. New York: International Publishers.

———. [1914] 1970. "The Right of Nations to Self-Determination." *Lenin: Selected Works*. Moscow: Progress Publishers.

Levi, Werner. 1991. *Contermporary International Law*. Boulder: Westview Press.

Levine, Andrew. 1984. *Arguing for Socialism*. Boston: Routledge and Kegan Paul.

Linklater, Andrew. 1990. *Beyond Realism and Marxism*. London: Macmillan Press.

Lockwood, Jr., Bert, R. Collins Owens, III, & Grace Severyn, "Litigating State Constitutional Rights to Happiness and Safety: A Strategy for Ensuring the Provision of Basic Needs to the Poor," *William and Mary Bill of Rights Journal* 2.1 (Spring 1993).

Lukacs, Georg. 1968. *History and Class Consciousness*. Cambridge, Mass.: MIT Press.

Lukes, Steven. 1985. *Marxism and Morality*. Oxford: Oxford University Press.

————. 1990. "Reflections on the Revolutions of 1989." *Ethics and International Affairs*, vol. 4. New York: Carnegie Council on Ethics and International Affairs.

Luxemburg, Rosa. 1970. "The Russian Revolution." *Rosa Luxemburg Speaks*, ed. Mary-Alice Waters. New York: Pathfinder Press.

M'Baye, Keba. 1972. "Le Droit au developpement comme un droit de l'homme." *Human Rights Journal* 5.

————. 1981. "Chairman's Opening Remarks." In *Development, Human Rights and the Rule of Law*, ed. International Commission of Jurists. Oxford: Pergamon Press.

M'Baye, Keba & Birame Ndiaye. 1982. "The Organization of African Unity (OAU)." In *The International Dimensions of Human Rights*, ed. Karel Vasak. Westport: Greenwood Press.

McCarthy, Thomas. 1978. *The Critical Theory of Jürgen Habermas*. Cambridge, Mass.: The MIT Press.

McCullough, David. 1992. *Truman*. New York: Simon & Schuster.

McDonald, Michael. 1992. "Should Communities Have Rights? Reflections on Liberal Individualism." In *Human Rights in Cross-Cultural Perspectives*, ed. Abdullahi An-Na ͨim. Philadelphia: University of Pennsylvania Press.

McDougal, M., H. Lasswell, & L. Chen. 1980. *Human Rights and World Public Order*. New Haven: Yale University Press.

McKean, Warwick. 1983. *Equality and Discrimination under International Law*. Oxford: Claredon Press.

McKenzie, Nancy F. 1990. "Women, Law, and Social Change." *Monthly Review* 42.1.

MacKinnon, Catharine A. 1993. "Crimes of War, Crimes of Peace." In *On Human Rights: The Oxford Amnesty Lectures 1993*, ed. Stephen Shute & Susan Hurley. New York: Basic Books.

McLellan, David. 1971. *The Thought of Karl Marx*. London: Macmillan Press.

McNall, Scott G., Rhonda R. Levine, & Rick Fantasia, eds. 1991. *Bringing Class Back In*. Boulder: Westview Press.

Macpherson, C. B. 1962. *The Political Theory of Possessive Individualism*. Oxford: Oxford University Press.

————. 1967. "Natural Rights in Hobbes and Locke." In *Political Theory and the Rights of Man*, ed. D. D. Raphael. Bloomington: Indiana University Press.

————. 1973. *Democratic Theory: Essays in Retrieval*. Oxford: Clarendon Press.

————. 1977. *The Life and Times of Liberal Democracy*. Oxford: Oxford University Press.

————. 1987. *The Rise and Fall of Economic Justice.* Oxford: Oxford University Press.

Magdoff, Harry. 1991. "Are There Lessons To Be Learned?" *Monthly Review.* New York: Monthly Review Press 42.9.

Magnusson, Warren. 1990. "The Reification of Political Community." In *Contending Sovereignties: Redefining Political Community,* ed. R. B. J. Walker & Saul Mendlovitz. Boulder: Lynne Rienner Publishers.

Makinson, David. 1988. "Rights of Peoples: A Logician's Point of View." In *The Rights of Peoples,* ed. James Crawford. Oxford: Clarendon Press.

Mapel, David R. & Terry Nardin. 1992. "Convergence and Divergence in International Ethics." In *Traditions of International Ethics,* ed. Mapel & Nardin. Cambridge: Cambridge University Press.

Marable, Manning. 1992a. "Clarence Thomas and the Crisis of Black Political Culture." In *Race-ing Justice, En-gendering Power,* ed. Toni Morrison. New York: Pantheon Books.

————. 1992b. *The Crisis of Color and Democracy.* Monroe, Maine: Common Courage Press.

Marcum, John A. 1989. "Africa: A Continent Adrift." *Foreign Affairs* 68.1.

Marcuse, Herbert. 1958. "Preface." In *Marxism and Freedom* by Raya Dunayevskaya. New York: Columbia University Press.

Marie, Jean-Bernard. 1986. "Relations between Peoples' Rights and Human Rights: Semantic and Methodological Distinctions." *Human Rights Law Journal* 7.2–4.

Marks, Stephen P. 1982. "Principles and Norms of Human Rights Applicable in Emergency Situations: Underdevelopment, Catastrophes, and Armed Conflict." In *The International Dimensions of Human Rights,* ed. Karel Vasak. Westport: Greenwood Press.

Marx, Karl. [1891] 1966a. *Critique of the Gotha Program.* New York: International Publishers.

————. [1932] 1966b. *Economic and Philosophical Manuscripts.* Translated by T. B. Bottomore. New York: Continuum.

————. [1971] 1975. "Draft of an Article on Friedrich List's Book: Das Nationale System der politischen Okonomie." *Collected Works,* vol. 4. New York: International Publishers.

————. [1844] 1987. "On the Jewish Question." In *Nonsense upon Stilts* by Jeremy Waldron. New York: Methuen.

Marx, Karl & Frederick Engels. [1848] 1967. *The Communist Manifesto.* New York: Penguin Books.

————. [1932] 1970. *The German Ideology*. New York: International Publishers.

Matarasso, Leo. 1989. "Relations between Rights of Peoples and Human Rights." UNESCO. SHS-89/CONF. 602/5.

Mazrui, Ali. 1984. "Africa Entrapped: Between the Protestant Ethic and the Legacy of Westphalia." In *The Expansion of International Society*, ed. Hedley Bull & Adam Watson. Oxford: Clarendon Press.

Medvedev, Roy. 1989. *Let History Judge: The Origins and Consequences of Stalinism*. New York: Columbia University Press.

Mendlovitz, Saul H. & R. B. J. Walker. 1990. *Contending Sovereignties: Redefining Political Community*. Boulder: Lynne Rienner Publishers.

Mestdagh, Karel de Vey. 1981a. "The Rights to Development: From Evolving Principle to 'Legal Right': In Search of Substance." In *Development, Human Rights and the Rule of Law*, ed. International Commission of Jurists. Oxford: Pergamon Press.

————. 1981b. "The Right to Development." *Netherlands International Law Review* 28: 30.

Migdal, Joel S. 1988. *Strong Societies and Weak States*. Princeton: Princeton University Press.

Miliband, Ralph. 1973. "Polantzas and the Capitalist State." *New Left Review* 82: 83–92.

————. 1977. *Marxism and Politics*. London: Oxford University Press.

————. 1989. *Divided Societies: Class Struggle in Contemporary Capitalism*. Oxford: Clarendon Press.

Mill, John Stuart. 1975. *On Liberty*. New York: Norton Press.

Miller, James. 1993. *The Passion of Michel Foucault*. New York: Simon & Schuster.

Miller, Lyn. 1985. *Global Order*. Boulder: Westview Press.

Milne, A. J. M. 1986. *Human Rights and Human Diversity*. Albany: SUNY Press.

Minkowitz, Donna. 1991. "Murder as Usual: The Julio Rivera Gay-Bashing Case." *The Village Voice* 36.44 (29 October).

Moderne, Franck. 1990. "Human Rights and Postcolonial Constitutions in Sub-Saharan Africa." In *Constitutionalism and Rights*, ed. Louis Henkin & Albert J. Rosenthal. New York: Columbia University Press.

Nanda, Ved P. 1984. "Development as an Emerging Human Right under International Law." *Denver Journal of International Law and Policy* 13.2–3.

————. 1985a. "Development and Human Rights: The Role of International Law and Organizations." In *Human Rights and Third World Development*, ed. Shepherd & Nanda. Westport: Greenwood Press.

————. 1985b. "The Right to Development under International Law—Challenges Ahead." *California Western International Law Journal* 15.

Nardin, Terry. 1983. *Law, Morality, and the Relations of States*. Princeton: Princeton University Press.

Nettheim, Garth. 1988. " 'Peoples' and 'Populations': Indigenous Peoples and the Rights of Peoples." In *The Rights of Peoples*, ed. James Crawford. Oxford: Clarendon Press.

Nickel, James W. 1987. *Making Sense of Human Rights: Philosophical Reflections on the Universal Declaration of Human Rights*. Berkeley: University of California Press.

Nielsen, Kai. 1992. "Global Justice, Capitalism and the Third World." In *International Justice and the Third World*, ed. Robin Attfield & Barry Wilkins. New York: Routledge, Chapman and Hall.

Ollman, Bertell. 1971. *Alienation*. New York: Cambridge University Press.

————. 1990. "Introduction." In *The United States Constitution*, ed. Bertell Ollman & Jonathan Birnbaum. New York: New York University Press.

————. 1993. *Dialectical Investigations*. New York: Routledge.

Organization for Economic Co-Operation and Development (OECD). 1992. *Development Co-operation, 1992 Report*. Paris: OECD.

————. 1994. *Development Co-operation, 1993 Report*. Paris: OECD.

Partsch, Karl Josef. 1982. "Fundamental Principles of Human Rights: Self-Determination, Equality and Non-Discrimination." In *The International Dimensions of Human Rights*, ed. Karel Vasak. Westport: Greenwood Press.

Permanent Peoples' Tribunal. 1980. *Verdict: Permanent Peoples' Tribunal on the Filipino People and the Bangsa Moro People*. Rome: General Secretariat.

————. 1988. *Verdict: Permanent Peoples' Tribunal on the Policies of the International Monetary Fund and World Bank*. Rome: General Secretariat.

Peterson, V. Spike. 1992. "Security and Sovereign States: What Is at Stake in Taking Feminism Seriously?" In *Gendered States: Feminist (Re)Visions of International Relations Theory*, ed. V. Spike Peterson. Boulder: Lynn Rienner Publishers.

Phillips, Kevin. 1990. *The Politics of Rich and Poor: Wealth and the American Electorate in the Reagan Aftermath*. New York: Random House.

Pillsbury, George. 1994. "Voting Block." *The Nation*, 259.13 (24 October).

Pollis, Adamantia. 1982. "Liberal, Socialist, and Third World Perspectives of Human Rights." In *Toward a Human Rights Framework*, ed. Adamantia Pollis & Peter Schwab. New York: Praeger.

Popol Vuh: Antiguas Leyendas del Quiche. 1951. Edited and introduced by Ermilo Abreu Gomez. Excerpts translated by Ann Wright. Mexico: Mexico Espasa-Calpe Mexicana.

Prott, Lyndel V. 1988. "Cultural Rights as Peoples' Rights in International Law." In *The Rights of Peoples*, ed. James Crawford. Oxford: Clarendon Press.

Ramphal, Shridath S. 1981. "Key-Note Address." In *Development, Human Rights and the Rule of Law*, ed. International Commission of Jurists. Oxford: Pergamon Press.

Raphael, D. D. 1990. *Problems of Political Philosophy*. Atlantic Highlands: Humanities Press International.

Rawls, John. 1971. *A Theory of Justice*. Cambridge, Mass.: Harvard University Press.

Ray, James Lee. 1995. *Global Politics*, 6th ed. Boston: Houghton Mifflin Company.

Renteln, Alison Dundes. 1990. *International Human Rights: Universalism versus Relativism*. Newbury Park, Calif.: Sage Publications.

Reutlinger, Schlomo, et al. 1986. *Poverty and Hunger—Issues and Options for Food Security in Developing Countries*. Washington D.C.: World Bank.

Rich, Adrienne. 1979. *On Lies, Secrets and Silence: Selected Prose, 1966–1978*. New York: W. W. Norton.

Rich, Bruce. 1994. *Mortgaging the Earth: The World Bank, Environmental Impoverishment, and the Crisis of Development*. Boston: Beacon Press.

Rich, Roland. 1983. "The Right to Development as an Emerging Human Right." *Virginia Journal of International Law* 23.2.

———. 1988. "The Right to Development: A Right of Peoples?" In *The Rights of Peoples*, ed. James Crawford. Oxford: Clarendon Press.

Rodman, Kenneth A. 1989. "Nonstate Actors and U.S. Economic Statecraft toward South Africa." Paper presented to the Annual Conference of the International Studies Association, London.

———. 1994. "Public and Private Sanctions against South Africa." *Political Science Quarterly* 109.2 (Summer).

Rosenau, James N. 1990. *Turbulence in World Politics*. Princeton: Princeton University Press.

———. 1992a. "Governance, Order, and Change in World Politics" and "Citizenship in a Changing Global Order." In *Governance without Government: Order and*

Change in World Politics, ed. James N. Rosenau & Ernst-Otto Czempiel. Cambridge: Cambridge University Press.

————. 1992b. *The United Nations in a Turbulent World*. Boulder: Lynne Rienner Publishers.

Rousseau, Jean-Jacques. [1762] 1973. *The Social Contract and Discourses*. London: Dent and Sons.

Sabine, George H. & Thomas L. Thorson. 1973. *A History of Political Theory*, 4th ed. Hinsdale, Ill.: Dryden Press.

Sartre, Jean-Paul. 1963. "Preface." In *The Wretched of the Earth* by Frantz Fanon. New York: Grove Press.

Schachter, Oscar. 1976. "The Evolving International Law of Development." *California Journal of Transnational Law* 15.1.

Schaeffer, Robert. 1990. *Warpaths: The Politics of Partition*. New York: Hill and Wang.

Scheingold, Stuart A. 1974. *The Politics of Rights*. New Haven: Yale University Press.

Schelling, T. C. 1992. "Retinking the Dimensions of National Security: The Global Dimension." In *Rethinking America's Security: Beyond Cold War to New World Order*, ed. G. Allison & G. F. Treverton. New York: W. W. Norton.

Scoble, Harry M. 1984. "Human Rights Non-Governmental Organizations in Black Africa: Their Problems and Prospects in the Wake of the Banjul Charter." In *Human Rights and Development in Africa*, ed. Claude E. Welch, Jr. & Ronald I. Meltz. Albany: SUNY Press.

Seidman, Ann. 1991. "Man-Made Starvation in Africa." In *Religion and Economic Justice* ed. Michael Zweig. Philadelphia: Temple University Press.

Sen, Amartya. 1984. "The Right Not to be Hungry." In *The Right to Food*, ed. P. Alston & K. Tomasevski. Utrecht: Martinus Nijhoff Publishers.

————. 1990. "More Than 100 Million Women Are Missing." *The New York Review of Books*, 37.20 (20 December).

Senese, Salvatore. 1986. "The Law for the Rights of Peoples: A Difficult Search for the Construction of a New Universality." *Cahiers* 7 (November).

————. 1989. "Eternal and Internal Self-Determination." *Social Justice* 16.1.

Shapiro, Michael. 1989. "Textualizing Global Politics." In *International/Intertextual Relations*, ed. James Der Derian & Michael J. Shapiro. Lexington: Lexington Books.

————. 1989. "Representing World Politics: The Sport/War Intertext." In *International/Intertextual Relations*, ed. James Der Derian & Michael J. Shapiro. Lexington: Lexington Books.

Shepherd, George Jr. 1985a. "The Denial of the Right to Food: Development and Intervention in Africa." *California Western International Law Journal* 3.

———. 1985b. "The Power System and Basic Human Rights: From Tribute to Self-Reliance." In *Human Rights and Third World Development*, ed. Shepherd & Nanda. Westport: Greenwood Press.

———. 1990. "The African Right to Development: World Policy and the Debt Crisis." *Africa Today* 37.4.

Shivji, Issa. 1989. *The Concept of Human Rights in Africa*. London: Codesria Book Series.

Shue, Henry. 1980. *Basic Rights: Subsistence, Affluence and US Foreign Policy*. Princeton: Princeton University Press.

———. 1981. "Exporting Hazards." In *Boundaries*, ed. Brown & Shue. Toronto: Rowman and Littlefield.

———. 1984. "The Interdependence of Duties." In *The Right to Food* ed. P. Alston & K. Tomasevski. Utrecht: Martinus Nijhoff.

Siegel, Richard. 1994. *Employment and Human Rights: The International Dimension*. Philadelphia: University of Pennsylvania Press.

Sieghart, Paul. 1983. *The International Law of Human Rights*. Oxford: Clarendon Press.

———. 1985. *The Lawful Rights of Mankind*. Oxford: Oxford University Press.

Sigler, Jay A. 1983. *Minority Rights*. Westport: Greenwood Press.

Singer, Daniel. 1988. *Is Socialism Doomed?* New York: Oxford University Press.

Skogly, Sigrun I. 1993. "Structural Adjustment and Development: Human Rights—An Agenda for Change?" *Human Rights Quarterly* 15.4.

Slomanson, William R. 1995. *Fundamental Perspectives on International Law*, 2nd ed. St. Paul: West Publishing Co.

Smiley, Marion. 1992. *Moral Responsibility and the Boundaries of Community*. Chicago: University of Chicago Press.

Smith, Michael J. 1986. *Realist Thought from Weber to Kissinger*. Baton Rouge: Louisiana State University Press.

Soroos, Marvin S. 1986. *Beyond Sovereignty: The Challenge of Global Policy*. Columbia: University of South Carolina Press.

Stairs, Kevin & Peter Taylor. 1992. "Non-Governmental Organizations and the Legal Protection of the Oceans: A Case Study." In *The International Politics of the Environment*, ed. Andrew Hurrell & Benedict Kingsbury. Oxford: Clarendon Press.

Stavenhagen, Rodolfo. 1989. "Ethnic Conflicts and Their Impact on International Society." Paper prepared for a Colloquium at the University of Lausanne.

Steinberg, Marc W. 1991. "Talkin' Class: Discourse, Ideology, and Their Role in Class Conflict." In *Bringing Class Back In*, ed. McNall, Levine, & Fantasia. Boulder: Westview Press.

Stewart, Frances. 1989. "Basic Needs Strategies, Human Rights, and the Right to Development." *Human Rights Quarterly* 11.3.

Sullivan, Donna J. 1994. "Women's Human Rights and the 1993 World Conference on Human Rights." *The American Journal of International Law* 88.1 (January).

Szabo, Imre. 1982. "Historical Foundations of Human Rights and Subsequent Developments." In *The International Dimensions of Human Rights*, ed. Karel Vasak. Westport: Greenwood Press.

Szporluk, Roman. 1988. *Communism and Nationalism*. New York: Oxford University Press.

Tay, Alice Erh-Soon. 1978. "Marxism, Socialism and Human Rights." In *Human Rights*, ed. Eugene Kamenka & Alice Erh-Soon Tay. London: Edward Arnold.

Thelwell, Michael. 1992. "False, Fleeting, Perjured Clarence: Yale's Brightest and Blackest Go to Washington." In *Race-ing Justice, En-gendering Power*, ed. Toni Morrison. New York: Pantheon Books.

Tickner, J. Ann. 1992. *Gender in International Relations*. New York: Columbia University Press.

Triggs, Gillian. 1988. "The Rights of 'Peoples' and Individual Rights: Conflict or Harmony?" In *The Rights of Peoples*, ed. James Crawford. Oxford: Clarendon Press.

United Nations Children's Fund (UNICEF). 1994. *The State of the World's Children 1994*. New York: Oxford University Press.

———. 1995. *The State of the World's Children 1995*. New York: Oxford University Press.

United Nations Development Programme (UNDP). 1993. *Human Development Report 1993*. New York: Oxford University Press.

———. 1994. *Human Development Report 1994*. New York: Oxford University Press.

United Nations Secretary General. 1979. *Report of the Secretary General: The International Dimensions of the Right to Development as a Human Right* . . . E/CN.4/ 1334 (Jan.).

van Boven, Theodoor C. 1982a. "Distinguishing Criteria of Human Rights." In *The International Dimensions of Human Rights*. ed. Karel Vasak. Westport: Greenwood Press.

———. 1982b. *People Matter: Views on International Human Rights Policy.* Amsterdam: Meulenhoff.

———. 1986. "The Relations Between Peoples' Rights and Human Rights in the African Charter." *Human Rights Law Journal* 7.2–4.

———. 1989. "Human Rights and Development: The UN Experience." In *Human Rights and Development: International Views,* ed. David P. Forsythe. New York: St. Martin's Press.

Vasak, Karel. 1982. "Human Rights as a Legal Reality." In *The International Dimensions of Human Rights,* ed. Karel Vasak. Westport: Greenwood Press.

Vincent, R. J. 1984. "Racial Equality." In *The Expansion of International Society,* ed. Hedley Bull & Adam Watson. Oxford: Clarendon Press.

Waldron, Jeremy. 1987. *Nonsense Upon Stilts.* London: Methuen Press.

Walker, R. B. J. 1984. *Culture, Ideology, and World Order.* Boulder: Westview Press.

———. 1988. *One World, Many Worlds: Struggles for a Just World Order.* Boulder: Lynne Rienner Publishers.

———. 1989. "The Prince and the Pauper: Tradition, Modernity and Practice in the Theory of International Relation." In *International/Intertextual Relations,* ed. James Der Derian & Michael J. Shapiro. Lexington: Lexington Books.

———. 1990. "Sovereignty, Identity, Community: Reflections on the Horizons of Contemporary Political Practice." In *Contending Sovereignties: Redefining Political Community,* ed. R. B. J. Walker & Saul Mendlovitz. Boulder: Lynne Rienner Publishers.

———. 1993. *Inside/Outside: International Relations as Political Theory.* Cambridge: Cambridge University Press.

Wallerstein, Immanuel. 1974. *The Modern World-System I: Capitalist Agriculture and the Origins of the European World-Economy in the Sixteenth Century.* New York: Academic Press.

———. 1979. *The Capitalist World-Economy.* Cambridge: Cambridge University Press.

———. 1980. *The Modern World System II: Mercantilism and the consolidation of the European World-Economy, 1600–1750.* New York: Academic Press.

———. 1984. "The Future of the World-Economy: A World-Systems Perspective." In *The Global Agenda,* ed. C. W. Kegley, Jr. & E. R. Wittkopf. New York: Random House.

———. 1990. "Antisystemic Movements: History and Dilemmas." In *Transforming the Revolution,* ed. S. Amin, G. Arrighi, A. G. Frank, & I. Wallerstein. New York: Monthly Review Press.

————. 1991a. "The Construction of Peoplehood: Racism, Nationalism, Ethnicity." In *Race, Nation, Class: Ambiguous Identities*, ed. Etienne Balibar & Immanuel Wallerstein. London: Verso Press.

————. 1991b. *Geopolitics and Geoculture: Essays on the Changing World System.* Cambridge: Cambridge University Press.

————. 1992. "Liberalism and the Legitimation of Nation States: An Historical Interpretation." *Social Justice* 19.1.

Walton, John & Charles Ragin. 1990. "Global and National Sources of Political Protest: Third World Responses to the Debt Crisis." *American Sociological Review* 55 (December).

Wendt, Alexander E. 1987. "The Agent-Structure Problem in International Relations Theory." *International Organization* (World Peace Foundation and MIT) 41.3 (Summer).

West, Cornel. 1991. *The Ethical Dimension of Marxist Thought.* New York: Monthly Review Press.

————. 1992. "Black Leadership and the Pitfalls of Racial Reasoning." In *Race-ing Justice, En-gendering Power*, ed. Toni Morrison. New York: Pantheon Books.

————. 1993. *Race Matters.* Boston: Beacon Press.

Weston, Burns H. 1992. "Human Rights." In *Human Rights in the World Community*, ed. Richard P. Claude & Burns H. Weston. Philadelphia: University of Pennsylvania Press.

Weston, Burns H., Richard A. Falk, & Anthony D'Amato. 1990a. *Basic Documents in International Law and World Order,* 2nd ed. St. Paul: West Publishing Co.

————. 1990b. *International Law and World Order: A Problem-Oriented Coursebook.* St. Paul: West Publishing Co.

Wojnarowicz, David. 1991. *Close to the Knives.* New York: Vintage Books.

Wolff, Edward N. 1995. *Top Heavy: A Study of Increasing Inequality of Wealth in America.* New York: The Twentieth Century Fund Press.

Wood, Ellen Meiksins. 1986. *The Retreat from Class.* London: Verso Press.

World Bank. 1995. *Advancing Social Development: A World Bank Contribution to the Social Summit.* Washington D.C.: The World Bank.

Wronka, Joseph. 1992. *Human Rights and Social Policy in the 21st Century.* Lanham, Md.: University Press of America.

INDEX

247